PITTSBURGH THEOLOGICAL MONOGRAPHS

New Series

Dikran Y. Hadidian

General Editor

1

CLOUDED WITNESS

Initiation in the Church of England
in
The Mid-Victorian Period
1850-1875

FORTHCOMING PUBLICATIONS

Karl Barth's Free Theology of Culture. By Robert J. Palma. Preface by H. Martin Rumscheidt.

The Spirit within Structure; essays in honor of George Johnston on his Seventieth Birthday. Edited by E. J. Furcha.

The Mystical Sources of the German Romantic Philosophy. By Ernst Benz. Translated by Blair Reynolds and Eunice M. Paul.

For God and Clarity; New essays in honor of Austin Farrer. Edited by Jeffrey C. Eaton and Ann Loades.

The Church in History; Essays honoring the Sixty-fifth Birthday of Robert S. Paul. Edited by Horton Davies.

Social Concerns in Calvin's Geneva, 1535-1564. By William C. Innes.

The Christology of Karl Barth and its Political Implications. By Robert E. Hood.

Freedom or Order? The Eucharistic Liturgy in English Congregationalism, 1645-1974. By Bryan D. Spinks. Preface by Geoffrey C. Cuming.

The Defense of the Reformed Faith. By Ulrich Zwingli. Translated by E. J. Furcha.

In Search of True Religion: Reformation, Pastoral and Eucharistic Writings. By Ulrich Zwingli. Translated by Wayne Pipkin.

The Emergence of Contemporary Judaism. Vol. 3: **Reformation, Renaissance, and the Dawn of Contemporary Judaism.** By Phillip Sigal.

The Emergence of Contemporary Judaism. Vol. 4: **Judaism in Tension, 1750 to the Present.** By Phillip Sigal.

CLOUDED WITNESS

Initiation in the Church of England
in
The Mid-Victorian Period, 1850-1875

By

Peter J. Jagger

PICKWICK PUBLICATIONS

Allison Park, Pennsylvania

1982

Library of Congress Cataloging in Publication Data

Jagger, Peter John.
    Clouded witness.

    (Pittsburgh theological monographs. New series ; 1)
    Bibliography: p.
    Includes index.
    1. Initiation rites—Religious aspects—Church of England—History—19th
century. 2. Church of England—Liturgy—History—19th century. 3. England—
Church history—19th century. I. Title. II. Series. BX5148.J33 1982
234'.161'0942   82-22465
ISBN 0-915138-51-4

To Catherine and Mark

CONTENTS

FOREWORD

In the writing of Church History there is room for both the comprehensive and the specialized inquiry. It is highly necessary that strictly limited areas of time or space should be investigated to a depth impossible in a general survey. Mr. Jagger has chosen an untilled field, the theology and practice of baptism and confirmation in the mid-Victorian Church of England. This was the period of the Gorham Case, of the growth of ritualism, of Newman, Maurice, and Kingsley. The limitation of the study to twenty-five years has enabled Mr. Jagger to explore and make available a rich variety of sources which show the rank and file of the Church of England clergy engaged in controversy as well as the theological giants. It is a story of fascinating detail which points up the great issues at stake.

Thus we read of baptism being sought to ensure Christian burial in consecrated ground and of the confusion between baptism and registration of birth. Bishop Wilberforce's confirmation candidates doubled in twenty years, while the number of communicants remained much the same; and Bishop Fraser of Manchester confirmed 71,000 candidates in seven years. Many of the problems of those years are with us still, though confirmations are not now usually disorderly, and indiscriminate baptism is no longer universal. The Church was not so very different in 1950-1975!

Mr. Jagger has already placed us in his debt by editing two collections of baptismal liturgies (one still awaiting publication), and he has the necessary expertise to handle the mass of detail which he has investigated, and produced an interesting and convincing picture of his chosen period.

Dr. Geoffrey Cuming
Formerly a lecturer at King's College, London and Ripon College, Cuddesdon.

INTRODUCTION

The mid-Victorian period, 1850-1875, to which this study is confined, was of supreme importance in the history of the English people and of the Established Church. Ecclesiastically two important events mark the beginning of the period: in 1850 the Gorham Judgement was pronounced and in 1851 a never-to-be-repeated religious Census was carried out.

The Industrial Revolution, population increase and movement, urbanization, bad and overcrowded living conditions, excessive working hours, child labour, new leisure pursuits: all these factors contributed towards the unprecedented situation faced by the Church during this period. The church was ill-equipped to meet the situation and her failure to cope with the new society had grave and far-reaching consequences, marking a turning point for the worse in the religious life of England. Some Churchmen seemed unaware of the seriousness of the new situation, but at the same time many Episcopal Charges show how some of the bishops were alive to the desperate conditions of the slums and the numerous social problems of the new industrial society. Many believed that if the resources of the Church were directed to the slums, Christianity and social reform would transform the lives of the heathen masses. In common with political leaders of the time, many Churchmen failed to see that the unprecedented situation demanded a bold, radical and adventurous transformation of the old structures, and put their trust in a mere increase in the number of clergy and church buildings, which the Religious Census seemed to suggest was the root of the problem.

The Census revealed that of the 34,467 church buildings, 14,077 or 41%, belonged to the Church of England and contained 5,317,915 seats, 52% of the total available. Non-Anglican churches numbered 20,390 or 59%, with 4,894,648 sittings, or 48% of the total. The report also showed that working class areas were most in need of additional accommodation and confirmed the observation that Church attendance was much weaker in towns than in rural areas. It was clear that it could no longer be assumed that the English people were largely Christian, or members of the Established Church, or indeed of any Church.

1

While the facts revealed by the Census brought darkness and despondence to many bishops and clergy, there was no shortage of ideas, suggestions and experiments in methods of evangelism, and most of these had a direct bearing on the subject of Christian Initiation.

The Sacraments of initiation are, for the Church of England, of the very essence of the Christian life. Without baptism there can be no membership in the visible Church, or assurance of eternal salvation. Thus the masses must not be allowed to neglect their own or their children's baptism. Without Confirmation there can be no active participation in the second dominical Sacrament--Holy Communion. Thus the baptized masses must be made to realize the need for Confirmation and to this end must be instructed in the faith and brought into active communicant membership. This ideal was never fulfilled, and the Church's failure must partly be attributed to her own internal conflicts, which sapped a great deal of energy which could otherwise have been spent on what many regarded as her primary task, the evangelization of the alienated millions. There were three main groups within the Church: Evangelicals, High Church and Broad Church, with further divisions within each. The differences between them caused much heated controversy and bitterness, and distracted the attention of many of the most able churchmen, who were preoccupied in defending or denying various points of theology, philosophy and ritual, which left them little time to contribute their valuable thought and leadership to bringing the unchurched masses into the fold. At the same time the less tolerant partisans would willingly have solved all the disputes by unchurching their opponents.

The pamphlet war associated with the name of George Cornelius Gorham provides a significant illustration of party conflict in the Victorian Church. What at first seemed a local matter of episcopal discipline became an issue of national debate, having far-reaching repercussions and lasting effects. This protracted and complicated controversy stimulated a considerable number of books and pamphlets. [1]

Gorham's views on baptism had been suspect since 1811 when they nearly prevented his ordination. In 1848 Bishop Henry Phillpotts refused to institute him to the living of Brampford Speke, near Exeter, until he had undergone an examination into his doctrinal soundness. The examination ranged over 149 questions, went on for eight days and took 52 hours. The point at issue was that of baptismal regeneration, by no means a new controversy in the Church of England--the Gorham Case simply brought the subject to the surface as never before. Following the examination Bishop Phillpotts declined to institute Gorham, who appealed to the Court of Arches, which found his views contrary to the doctrine of the Church of England and upheld the Bishop's decision. Gorham, convinced that his views were compatible with the official doctrines of the Church of England then appealed to the Judicial Committee of the Privy Council. The final Judgement was given on 8th March, 1850: "The Court was unanimous in holding that Gorham's doctrine was not contrary or repugnant to the declared doctrines of the Church of England, and that therefore the Judgement of Sir H. Jenner Fust in the Arches Court of Canterbury ought to be reversed." Phillpotts objected to this reversal and was adamant in his refusal to institute Gorham, who was eventually instituted on the authority of the Archbishop of Canterbury, but without Phillpotts' consent.

The Gorham case constitutes the only large-scale doctrinal clash on baptism in the history of the Church of England. Broadly speaking Gorham's doctrinal position was Calvinistic, but different from that of most Evangelicals. He believed that infants were not worthy recipients of baptism and that an act of 'prevenient grace' was required to make them worthy, otherwise no spiritual grace was conferred in the Sacrament. Confusion in the use of the word 'regeneration' was the cause of much unnecessary controversy. Sometimes it was used to mean justification (a new status), and sometimes to mean sanctification (a new nature). Gorham's use of the word was neither clear nor consistent. He was firmly convinced that justification was by faith and not by baptism. Phillpotts, and most High Churchmen, believed that both justification and the beginning of sanctification were conferred at baptism.

Members of the High Church party were united in their opposition to the decision of the Privy Council. The Reverend William Goode, a leading Evangelical and spokesman for the party during the Gorham controversy, was scathing in his attack against the High Churchmen, saying that if they found the Judgement unacceptable then they ought to quit the Church of England. Instead of bringing an end to the controversy, the Judgement simply worsened the situation. Each party insisted that its views were the correct interpretation and so attack led to counter-attack, pamphlet was answered by pamphlet, sermon by sermon, letter by letter. Some advocated tolerance, but their cries were often unheard and unheeded.

If the Church of England doctrine of baptism had not lacked clarity and precision, and had been concisely and unquestionably stated, much of the Gorham controversy could have been avoided. There were those within the Church who commended this lack of doctrinal exactness, which gave the Church of England its comprehensiveness; such Churchmen saw no need for a dogmatic statement. But there were others who both wanted and demanded a dogmatic pronouncement on the subject. Many others were satisfied with the existing formularies, seeing them as both sufficient and clear and believing their own interpretation to be the correct one. Some were convinced that the decision of the Judicial Court altered the doctrinal position of the Church of England and was a threat to her catholicity; others were equally convinced that the decision did not alter any doctrine.

Undoubtedly a victory for the Evangelical party, the Gorham Judgement created problems for many High Churchmen and also brought a number of issues to the fore in the Church's life. When the Privy Council issued its Judgement the whole complex question of the relationship between the Established Church and the State and the move for Disestablishment emerged once again. Even Dissenters and Roman Catholics were not slow to use the controversy to support their own call for Disestablishment. The disgruntled High Churchmen called for a revival of Convocation, feeling that if pronouncements on doctrine had to be made they should come from a properly constituted Church body and not from a secular Court, which had neither the ability to pronounce on such matters nor the assurance of divine guidance. The cause had many supporters and there is little doubt that the Gorham Judgement did influence the ultimate revival of the Convocations, Canterbury in 1852 and York in 1861.

The controversy was also responsible for the introduction of the Diocesan Synod. On February 28th, 1850, Bishop Phillpotts wrote to Dr. Pusey thanking him for his suggestion of a diocesan synod and continued: "If the Judgement be to the effect of regarding baptism as an open question, or anything like it, I shall be greatly inclined to act on the suggestion." In a Pastoral Letter Phillpotts informed his clergy that he was to hold a Synod in order to make a declaration on the baptismal issue. Gradually the more progressive bishops realized the value of such synods and introduced them, receiving support from the High Churchmen and opposition from the Evangelicals. Some churchmen believed that neither Convocations nor diocesan synods were sufficient to meet the crisis of the times, and called for a General Synod, a meeting of the 'collective episcopate'; this eventually led to the birth of the Lambeth Conference. Yet another body which came into being as a result of the pressures of this turbulent period was the Church Congress, which emerged in 1861.

A serious result of the Gorham Judgement was the increased number of Anglican secessions to Rome, although in the main Pusey's influence still held the Tractarians together within the Church of England, otherwise the secessions would have been even more numerous.

There is no doubt that the controversy concerning the baptismal regeneration of infants tore the Church asunder at a critical period in her history, and some would argue that too much time and effort was spent on it. However, as will be seen, what the Church believes about Baptism, Confirmation and Holy Communion is of the utmost importance in her evangelistic work and building up of 'the faithful'.

The Religious Census indicated to the Established Church both the size of the dissenting body and that of the unchurched masses--indicating the enormous task she had to face. Contrary to popular opinion the Church was not blind to what was happening; even though she was unsuccessful and unable to stem the tide, she did respond to the demands of the new society with vigour and experimentation. In the midst of all this arose one of the most controversial ecclesiastical issues of the 19th century. Together, these various factors provide the life setting against which this subject must be examined, for it is only in this context that it is possible to begin to understand and appreciate the importance of Christian Initiation in the life of the Church of England during the mid-Victorian period.

NOTE

1. The most recent major work on the subject of the Gorham Judgement was written by J. C. S. Nias, **Gorham and the Bishop of Exeter** (1951). Nias lists ten pages of pamphlets and books consulted by him during his research into the subject and thus provides an invaluable bibliography on the Gorham issue. However, a number of important sources have not been listed by him, and the aftermath of the Judgement was much deeper than he seems to indicate.

BAPTISM

Introduction

Canons, Articles, Rites and Rubrics, all provide information appertaining to baptism in the Church of England. These
sources contain the Church's theology of baptism, her liturgical
directions concerning its administration and the pastoral implications of the rite. But, as the Gorham controversy revealed,
these formularies were open to a variety of interpretation and
each party was convinced that theirs was the right one. For
mid-Victorian churchmen it was here that the trouble began,
not in the lack of official statements, but in a dogmatic declaration on the meaning of these formularies.

Some felt that the Judgement of the Judicial Committee
confirmed that, in the Church of England, what one believed
about baptism was a matter of personal interpretation. This
satisfied the Broad Churchmen and at least some of the Evangelicals. High Churchmen were very dissatisfied, however, believing
that the Judicial Committee had neither the right nor the ability
to make a doctrinal pronouncement. Their call for a National
Synod which, they believed, could make an official statement
on the subject, was influenced by their conviction that such
a synod would reverse the Judgement of the Judicial Committee
and make a pronouncement favorable to their own position.

While the theology of baptism had many facets, for
mid-Victorian churchmen that of baptismal regeneration was
paramount, demanding most of their attention and causing the
greatest controversies. The actual meaning of baptismal regeneration was the crux of the Gorham controversy.

I. THE THEOLOGICAL SITUATION

A. The conflict between the High Church and Evangelical Parties over Baptismal Regeneration and Conversion

George Sandby, vicar of Flixton, Suffolk, wrote in 1851: "Both parties vindicate their differences of opinion by an appeal to our Articles and Liturgy, both professing to find support therein for their opposite views. Which party therefore is wrong, and which right--and who is to decide the controversy?" [1] There were those who felt that a meeting of the episcopate ought to be convened and that the 'corporate episcopate' should give an official interpretation of the controversial formularies. This suggestion never materialized and even if it had, evidence suggests that there would have been little possibility of the bishops coming to a common agreement on this particular subject; members of the bench were as much divided on this issue as the parochial clergy and the laity.

Bishop Henry Phillpotts was a central figure in the mid-Victorian baptismal controversy, which shook the Church of England to its very foundations. Whatever his opponents said about him, it had to be admitted that Phillpotts was consistent in his belief that the Church of England held and taught baptismal regeneration. His Charge of 1845 contains a precise statement of his baptismal theology: "Baptism is not merely the seal of a new covenant, but also God's method of giving to us a new nature, wherein we are born of the Spirit, and are thus really, though mystically, made one with Christ, and, through Christ, with the Father". [2] For Phillpotts, baptismal regeneration implied the giving of a new nature and this he urged his clergy to preach to their people.

Connop Thirlwall, Bishop of St. David's, was a brilliant scholar and though considered a leader of the Broad Church he was not intolerant about other schools of thought. He took part in all the ecclesiastical discussions of the day in a liberal and unbiased spirit, thus it is not surprising that in his Charge of 1851 he touched upon the Gorham controversy and in doing so brought out an important point: "The whole controversy confessedly turns on the condition of regeneration in infant baptism, it was not clear that the disputants were agreed as

to the meaning of the term regeneration. But I believe I may
go much further and say that it is evident, from their language,
that they did not understand it in the same sense". [3] Thirlwall
was not the only one to realize that there was some inconsistency
in the use of the term 'regeneration' and thus a need for clarifica-
tion in language and terminology. There were many occasions
when members of the opposing parties did not use the term
in the same sense. If they had been more precise and consistent
there would, no doubt, have been far less controversy and bitterness. Some, however, were both clear and consistent in their
use and understanding of the term 'regeneration' and were reasonably clear as to what their opponents meant by the term.

A sermon preached by Bishop John Kaye suggests that
the word 'opponent' is too mild a description: "Baptismal regeneration forms a subject of angry controversy...it divides the members of our communion into two parties, one which scarcely
allows the name of Christian to those who do not hold it...I
am myself convinced that there is much exaggeration in the
language of both parties". [4]

Such deep division, conflict and bitter controversy
were provoked through attempts to interpret and express the
meaning of a theological term--'baptismal regeneration'. But
such disparity of interpretation, and the accompanying conflict,
was nothing new in the Church of England. The Gorham case
simply focussed attention, to a greater extent than ever before,
onto a subject which had been a matter of controversy for some
considerable time.

There seems little doubt from the formularies of the
Church of England that officially she does hold and teach baptismal regeneration, but there were those who denied even this.
For others the controversial issue centered upon the question:
Who are right recipients for baptismal regeneration and in what
sense can the newly baptized be described as 'regenerate'? How
the parish priest answered these questions ultimately affected
his pastoral work. Thus it is important to understand what the
opposing parties believed concerning the nature of baptismal
regeneration.

The High Church Party

J. B. Mozley, who was appointed Regius Professor
of Divinity at Oxford in 1871, was an avowed Tractarian and
one of the ablest theological minds in the later Tractarian Movement. In the 1856 edition of his book **The Primitive Doctrine
of Baptismal Regeneration** he states: "The regeneration of

adults cannot be ascertained with certainty", but, "in the case of infants we can assert...infants...are certainly regenerate after baptism and if they die as infants are certainly saved". [5] Later Mozley was to state that some of his former views on the subject of baptism and baptismal regeneration had been mistaken. This change caused some misgivings among not a few of his fellow High Churchmen. [6] Most High Churchmen of the period were confident in their assertion that through baptism infants were regenerate, in the sense that they received a new nature, which included the forgiveness of sin and incorporation into Christ.

When the Reverend Dr. John Morris, Rector of Elstree, preaching on 'Regeneration in Baptism' expressed surprise that anyone could doubt that baptismal regeneration, which implied new birth, was not the clear teaching of the Baptismal Office, Catechism and Confirmation, he was simply expressing the convictions of the majority of High Churchmen. [7] Unfortunately Evangelicals also vindicated their very different views by an appeal to the Church's Articles and Liturgy. Both parties also claimed scriptural support for their position. High Churchmen went one step further and found considerable evidence for their doctrinal stance in the teaching of the early Fathers.

In teaching baptismal regeneration many High Churchmen were dependent upon what Dr. Pusey had said and written on the subject. But Pusey, in turn, was also dependent upon what others had written not only in Scripture and Patristic works, but also in more recent writings. Dr. Richard Mant, Chaplain to the Archbishop of Canterbury, who had given the Bampton Lecture in 1812, later produced two tracts based upon his lecture. To these he gave the title Two Tracts: Intended to convey Correct Notions of Regeneration and Conversion according to the Sense of Holy Scripture and the Church of England. Among the authorities quoted by Mant was the work of Daniel Waterland (1683-1740). Waterland was an Anglican theologian of considerable learning, widely read in the Fathers and in the writings of Continental and Roman Catholic theologians. What Waterland wrote on baptismal regeneration had a considerable influence upon the High Church party's views on this subject.

In his Bampton Lecture, An Appeal to the Gospel, Mant had put forward the idea of baptism as the vehicle of justification, a view which was to be more fully developed by John Henry Newman and fully supported by Pusey.

Strictly speaking, John Henry Newman is outside the scope of this work in that he had seceded from the Church of England and was received into the Roman Catholic Church on October 9th, 1845. However, he did have a profound effect upon the views and teaching of the early Tractarians.

In his Apologia Newman publicly acknowledged the influence which Dr. Edward Hawkins, Provost of Oriel College, Oxford, had had upon his theological development, saying of him "He was the first who taught me to weigh my words, and to be cautious in my statements...as to doctrine, he was the means of great additions to my belief...he gave me the Treatise on Apostolic Preaching by Sumner, afterwards Archbishop of Canterbury, from which I was led to give up my remaining Calvinism and to receive the doctrine of baptismal regeneration". [8] During his Anglican period Newman began to work out the theory of baptism as the means of justification. His Lectures on Justification, first published in 1838, underwent little change when they were republished after his secession. These lectures provide a clear picture of Newman's understanding of justification and of baptism as the vehicle of justification. Here he states: "Justification renews, therefore, I say it may fitly be called renewal". He goes on to state: "It is a parallel mode of speaking to say that justification consists in renewal, or that renewal constitutes justification". He argues that because of the essential union between justification and renewal, they are practically interchangeable terms. He can even argue that justification is a "sort of sacrament" and baptism being the sacrament of renewal shows how the two are closely linked--"God's justification does not merely work some change or renewal in us; but it really makes us just...I observe, then, we become inwardly just or righteous in God's sight, upon our regeneration". [9]

He goes on to say that in justifying us God takes away what is past by bringing in what is new: "Such is justification as manifested in us continually all through our lives; but is it not plain that in its beginning it will consist of scarcely anything but pardon? because all that we have hitherto done is sinful in its nature, and has to be pardoned; but to be renewed is a work of time, whereas as time goes on, and we become more holy, it will consist more in renewal, if not less in pardon, and at least there is no original sin, as when it was first granted, to be forgiven. It takes us then at Baptism out of original sin, and leads us all through life towards the purity of Angels. Naturally, then, when the word is used to denote the beginning of a justified state, it only, or chiefly, means acceptance; when the continuance, chiefly sanctification". [10] Newman's writing and preaching leave us in no doubt that for him baptism, regeneration and justification were very much bound together and were part of a sacramental process.

When Pusey's tracts on baptism were vehemently attacked, Newman's pen and acute mind came to the aid of his friend. He wrote an article in full support of what Pusey had written on the subject and, in so doing, indicated the close affinity which existed in their views about baptism. [11] But Newman not only wrote about baptism, he also preached a number of important sermons on the subject, which provide further details clarifying his position. He was utterly convinced that baptismal regeneration was the teaching of Scripture. In a sermon entitled Regenerating Baptism, he preached on the text "By one Spirit are we all baptised into one body". Here he put before the congregation his own firm conviction on the subject: "As there is One Holy Ghost, so there is one only visible Body of Christians which Almighty God 'knows by name', and one Baptism which admits man into it. This is implied in the text, which is nearly parallel to St. Paul's words to the Ephesians: 'There is one Body, and one Spirit, one Baptism'. But more than this is taught us in it; not only that the Holy Ghost is in the Church, and that Baptism admits into it, but that the Holy Ghost admits by means of Baptism, that the Holy Ghost baptises; in other words, that each individual member receives the gift of the Holy Ghost as a preliminary step, a condition, or means of his being incorporated into the Church; or, in our Saviour's words, that no one can enter, except he be regenerated in order to enter it". [12]

To those who refuse to accept what he believes as the scriptural view of baptism, Newman puts the question: "The ordinary and intelligible reason for the Baptism of infants, is the securing to them the remission of sins, and the gift of the Holy Ghost--Regeneration: but if this sacred privilege is not given to them in Baptism, why, it may be asked, should Baptism be administered to them at all?" [13] Baptism is the only means of entering His Kingdom: "By this new birth the Divine Shechinah is set up within him, pervading soul and body, separating him really, not only in name, from those who are not Christians". [14] For both Newman and Pusey post-baptismal sin was a solemn and important issue. Both felt that the neglect of this doctrine was a grave error. Newman wrote: "There will be no good...anywhere till the doctrine of post-baptismal sin is recognised". All that Newman had to say on the subject of baptism, in sermons, lectures and writings, provides a good example of the strong line which the early Tractarians took on the issue and indeed continued to take after Newman's 'unfortunate departure' from the Church of his birth.

Like Newman, John Keble also believed baptismal regeneration to be a doctrine essential to the life and well-being of the Church. Following the Gorham Judgement, Keble wrote to his parishioners: "So we were left in doubt whether little children regularly baptised were really made members of Christ or no: the clergy need not teach it, and we need not believe it".[15] He was convinced that to reject baptismal regeneration was to place the work of the Church, parents and teachers in jeopardy: "How can they do their proper work with the souls of these little ones if they do not ground it upon the grace of baptismal regeneration?" [16] During the Gorham controversy Keble and Pusey were continually corresponding on the issue, but it was Pusey who took the leading role.

The scholarly and reasonable Dr. Pusey was one whose views on baptism, as on many other subjects, were both sought and respected, at least by those belonging to the High Church party. He shared Newman's conviction regarding the close link between baptism, regeneration and justification. In one sermon he stated that the sacraments are "The channels whereby...He conveys these exceeding Gifts to us. ...All which we have, we have in Him, by being made members of Him. And members of Him we are made and preserved through His Sacraments. The one engrafteth us into, the other maketh us, what in It is given to the faithful, the Body of Christ". [17]

For Pusey baptism was a new birth, an entrance into a new world, the communication of a new nature. In baptism sin is pardoned as the recipient is washed and made clean. His views on the subject were reached only after a great deal of research and thought. In a letter to Newman, on February 24th 1834, he shared his thoughts about a possible tract on baptism, one which would, in non-technical terms, bring out the true doctrine of baptism in its warmth and life, whereas the Low Church thought it essentially cold.

Three of the Tracts for the Times, numbers 67, 68, 69, were written by Pusey on the subject of baptism. These tracts were subsequently enlarged and formed an elaborate and exhaustive treatise on baptism. It was Pusey's work in this field which established him as one of the leaders of the Oxford Movement. His object in writing on the subject was stated in the Preface to the composite work: "The immediate object was to aid in removing the perplexities of different individuals, who were harassed by the conflicting opinions, which in these last times, have existed on the subject of Holy Baptism". He goes on to say: "I wished to recall men, from their abstract way of looking upon the question as a subject of theological controversy, to their Saviour's feet". Unfortunately, while many shared Pusey's views on baptism and appreciated his treatise on the subject, it had the reverse effect to what he had hoped. Instead of bringing calm to troubled waters it stirred up more conflict and opposition from those who differed from him, who questioned both the method of his approach, especially his wide use of patristic material and the conclusions he drew from the evidence.

A very different work, written by E. H. Hoare, **Baptism**

According to Scripture (1850), set out to examine every passage of Scripture relating to baptism. Reviewing Hoare's book, The Record of February 21st 1850 stated: "It forms a complete counterpart to Dr. Pusey's work which might have been justly entitled 'Baptism according to Tradition'. What the Fathers and other men may have said on the subject can have no weight, but as far as it agrees with the Scripture". Of Hoare's book The Record commented that it examined the many passages of Scripture "with great fairness and judgement". A letter to The Record from a clergyman expressed the opinion: "If the prejudice of the Tractarians allowed them carefully to read that treatise (Hoare's book) they could not fail to see that they have nothing in Scripture to support their views".

Whatever Pusey's opponents felt about his views, for him baptismal regeneration gave meaning, purpose and depth to the Christian life. He wrote: "Baptismal regeneration, as connected with the Incarnation of our Blessed Lord, gives a depth to our Christian existence, an actualness to our union with Christ, a reality to our sonship to God, an interest in the presence of our Lord's glorified Body at God's right hand, a joyousness amid the subduing of the flesh, an overwhelmingness to the dignity conferred on human nature, a solemnity to the communion of saints who are the fullness of Him Who filleth all in all, a substantiality to the indwelling of Christ, that to those who retain this truth the school who abandoned it must needs appear to have sold its birthright. But it is one thing to hold baptismal regeneration, and another to hold merely that there is no regeneration subsequent to baptism. A mere negative view must always be a cold one". [18]

In **Scriptural Views of Holy Baptism** Pusey defines regeneration "to be, that act whereby God takes us out of our relation to Adam, and makes us actual members of His Son...This is our new birth, an actual birth of God, of water and the Spirit... herein then also are we justified, or both accounted and made righteous, since we are made members of Him Who is alone Righteous; freed from past sin, whether original or actual; having a new principal of life imparted to us, since having been made members of Christ we have a portion in His Life...we have also the hope of resurrection and of immortality, because we have been made partakers of His resurrection". [19]

One who shared Pusey's high view on baptismal regeneration was Robert Isaac Wilberforce. Like Pusey, he wrote and said much on the subject of baptism. In his book **The Doctrine of Holy Baptism** (1849) Wilberforce develops the theory that: "Sacraments are the extension of the Incarnation, through their agency the Son of God effects that great work, which He took our nature to discharge...Hence is a true belief in Baptismal grace as intimately allied in theory to the doctrine of Atonement and of Mediation, as history shows that they have been practically connected". [20] He was adamant in his conviction that God bestows the grace of regeneration through baptism and that He bestows it on all baptized infants. He said: "Regeneration...is Christ's act, whereby He bestows that new nature, which is gained by union with Him...The peculiar purpose of sacraments is, to join us to that renewed nature of the second Adam, which is the fountain of all renewal both for our bodies and our souls". [21] His theological understanding of baptism, as a sharing in what Christ has achieved, was developed more fully in a sermon, The Sacramental System, which he preached before the University of Oxford in 1850: "In Baptism...we partake of that hallowed nature, which entered into the line of humanity in the New Head of our race, that from Him it might be communicated to all His brethren. Thus does the recreation, which began in Him, extend to His members...And into us also there is a new life infused by supernatural process". [22]

Another who felt that belief in baptismal regeneration was crucial to other doctrines was Henry Parry Liddon. Writing to the Reverend A. M. Christopher he said: "If baptismal regeneration is not the doctrine of the Church of England the language of the Baptismal Service is very misleading for plain people". It was this firm conviction which prompted him to write of the Gorham Judgement: "It seems to me that the natural sense of this language will outlive the subtleties upon which the Gorham Decision was based; and that if the Church of England had desired to leave the matter an open question, or to deny the revealed doctrine of Baptismal Grace, she would have done better to omit from her Formularies passages which, to ordinary apprehensions, seem to affirm the doctrine more explicitly than does the corresponding language of the Church of Rome...If unhappily, I did not believe in baptismal regeneration, I should lose my faith in more than one revealed truth besides". [23]

Bishop Ashurst Turner Gilbert of Chichester, a strong opponent of the Oxford Movement, expressed an opinion very similar to that of Liddon concerning the fundamental importance of the doctrine. In his Charge of 1847 he said: "The denial of baptismal regeneration is never unaccompanied with other errors", and "Our Church holds and intends that her Ministers should hold the doctrine of baptismal regeneration". [24] On July 2nd 1850, Archdeacon Henry Edward Manning wrote to Bishop Gilbert arguing that to dispute the doctrine of baptismal regeneration was heresy and that this heresy had now received the sanction of law. He wrote: "I do not see how the Church of England can permit two contrary doctrines on baptism to be propounded to her people, without abdicating the divine authority to teach as sent from God. It is no question of more or less, better or worse, but whether we are in or out of the faith and Church which our Lord founded by His Apostles". [25]

Samuel Wilberforce was also an avowed advocate of the doctrine. To one of his clergy he wrote of his belief that baptized infants were regenerate, and went on to say: "Now the question for us at the moment is not, are these doctrines true, but are they the doctrines of the Church of England? If they are, you cannot as an honest man, eat the bread offered for her ministers and teach otherwise". He continued: "I shall point out, to those in danger of the opposite errors of the Church of Rome, that as honest men they cannot minister in the Church of England holding the doctrine of the Church of Rome". [26] His own brother, Robert Isaac, was among those who applied this stricture and found themselves wanting, and seceded to Rome. Addressing candidates for ordination, Wilberforce was dogmatic in what he expected of them. "The Church of England", he said, "holds baptismal regeneration, and all seeking ordination must hold and agree to teach the doctrine". [27]

Baptismal regeneration became the watchword of the Tractarians. High Churchmen not only believed and taught the doctrine in its fullest sense, but they were also emphatic in declaring that this was the clear teaching of the Church of England. They were sincerely convinced that it was the duty of every honest clergyman both to believe and teach the doctrine. In practice the situation was far from their ideal; their opponents not only took the opposite view, but also tried to explain away what High Churchmen believed was the plain and obvious meaning of the Baptismal Service and the formularies of the Church.

For High Churchmen there was only 'One Baptism', and what they believed about baptism applied equally to both infants and adults. They believed that through baptism the stain of original sin was washed away and that this was the result of the inward working of the Holy Spirit. Because all men are sinners baptism is necessary for salvation, for all men. Through baptism man is made a partaker of the divine nature and en-grafted into Christ. He is made a member of the visible Church and, as such, endowed with all the gifts and graces necessary for salvation and needful for the Christian life. Through baptism man receives a new nature, and thus a moral change takes place-- it is an actual birth from above. For them, all this was contained and summed up in the term "Baptismal regeneration".

The Evangelical Party

During the early part of the nineteenth century not

all Evangelicals rejected outright the doctrine of baptismal regeneration. At least some of them believed that regeneration was the teaching of both Church and Scripture, but their understanding of the doctrine was far from that of the later High Church party. [28] Charles Simeon deeply revered the two dominical Sacraments, regarding them as real means of grace, but denied that they had any saving effect. Simeon never wrote a single treatise on baptism, so what he believed and taught on the subject has to be culled from various sources. These beliefs can be said to represent the views of some Evangelicals of his day, and of a later period, although for other members of the party they caused some uneasiness. [29] Simeon's sermon The Baptism of the Spirit gives some insight into his position: "Baptism", he says, "is necessary for all who embrace the faith of Christ; and it is replete with blessing to all who receive it aright. Even the outward ministry of it gives us a title to the blessing of the Christian covenant...But if we receive it not aright we are still like Simon Magus...in the gall of bitterness and the bond of iniquity. To receive any saving benefit...we must have not only the sign but the thing signified, i.e. baptism with the Holy Ghost and fire, death to sin and new birth to righteousness."

Baptism was admission into the New Covenant and into the Ark, the Church of Christ, but for Simeon there was a distinction between the visible and the invisible Church. Baptism was something objective, in a Covenant sense, and therefore must be unconditional. But baptism and regeneration should not be confused. Simeon believed that in the early Church the two terms were virtually synonymous, because: "None but the truly regenerate persons would submit to the rite". Regeneration was absolutely necessary for salvation, whereas baptism could be dispensed with "under some circumstances". [30] It is interesting to note that this close association between regeneration, baptism and salvation, and the qualification that God is not bound by His Sacraments, was a position adopted by one of the chief opponents of the Evangelicals, Bishop Henry Phillpotts. Unlike Simeon, Phillpotts believed that baptism was necessary for salvation, and regeneration always accompanied baptism—but even so he says God is not bound by His Sacraments. "We may", said Phillpotts, "perceive the great necessity of this Sacrament, where it may be had". Without it, where it may be had: "We cannot enter into the Kingdom of God. Whether, where Baptism may not be had, God is ever pleased to give regeneration, as Scripture is silent, so likewise is the church". [31]

Simeon had no time for a doctrine of baptism which "tends to lull men asleep in their evil ways, to make them think that they do not need a new nature..." He saw the chief source of error as the failure to distinguish between a change of state and a change of <u>nature</u>. Baptism, for him, brought about a change of state, entitling us to the blessings of the <u>new</u> covenant. It is not a change of nature, although this may be communicated at the time the ordinance is administered. He was fully convinced that the Prayer Book Reformers in using the word 'regeneration' did not mean conversion or a change in our nature. "They use it", he said, "for the beginning of that process by which we are changed, and not the change as if effected at once". He seemed happy with the term 'baptismal regeneration' so long as it was not identified with conversion. He was equally happy with the Prayer Book services of baptism and their references to regeneration. The language of the Prayer Book service in this matter was, he felt, no stronger than that of St. Paul on the same subject. [32]

It is impossible to say how many Evangelicals held a 'high doctrine of baptism'; that they existed cannot be denied and they included William Wilberforce [33] and the famous Evangelical preacher Henry Melvill, [34] but unfortunately, unlike the High Church party, little about them and their teaching has been preserved.

While the Evangelical Party did not disregard the Sacraments, their piety and understanding of the Christian Faith were not centered upon them. They saw both baptism and the Lord's Supper as no more than symbolic and commemorative acts, enjoined by scripture. Their approach to the Sacraments largely explains the meagreness of the information available. There were some Evangelicals who completely rejected baptismal regeneration; this branch of the party was far less tolerant than those already mentioned. They denied that any divine grace was conveyed by baptism. Regeneration was, for them, the result of conversion and was in no sense tied up with baptism. Conversion was uppermost, and what they believed about baptism had to fit their views on conversion. Because of their somewhat Calvinistic theology, and their rejection of baptismal regeneration, many of these 'extreme' Evangelicals curtailed and mutilated the Baptismal Service so as to bring it near to their own notions of regeneration. Bishop Blomfield expressed strong disapproval of these mutilators. He said that their treatment of the service was a clear admission that the language of the Prayer Book taught baptismal regeneration in such a plain way that it could not be escaped and had to be omitted by those who found it unacceptable.

In 1848 the evangelical paper The Record made a continuous and fervent attack on the Prayer Book doctrine of baptismal regeneration; its avowed aim was to obtain an official alteration of the rite. Every opportunity was taken to achieve a position more favorable and acceptable to the Evangelicals.

Evangelicals who held, or were favorable towards, the doctrine of baptismal regeneration were forced to abandon their position during the Gorham controversy. Such a change was to be expected when the term became the rallying cry of the High Church party. When baptismal regeneration became one of the chief points of contention between the parties, the Evangelicals began to call it a "soul-destroying error". With such widespread antagonism and indifference there was little possibility that any member of the Evangelical Party would express, at least openly, any toleration or understanding, let alone a qualified acceptance of baptismal regeneration.

Gorham's views were not really representative of the Evangelical party as a whole, but the fact that the High Church party gathered under the flag of baptismal regeneration pressurized the majority of the Evangelicals to rally under the opposing flag--that of the Reverend G. C. Gorham. He was able to defend his own views and position and, in doing so, demonstrated a firm and confident grasp of the subject. The chief Evangelical advocate of his views on baptism was, however, his champion William Goode. [35] During this controversy Evangelicals realized that the conflict was a fight for existence and that they must present their own case as fully and carefully as possible. As their chief exponent and leading pamphleteer Goode put forward a moderately low view of baptism. They were willing to allow the doctrine of baptismal regeneration, but insisted upon the conditions of faith and repentance, albeit not always denying that infants may receive the grace of the Sacraments. [36] Goode attempted to show that the Church of England does not affirm that all children, duly brought to baptism, are recipients of grace. In January 1864 Archdeacon Dodgson, a Canon of Ripon Cathedral, preached two sermons in the Cathedral, supporting the doctrine of baptismal regeneration. Goode, at the time Dean of Ripon, charged him with preaching a doctrine contrary to that of the Church of England. The Dean brought the case before the Bishop, and the correspondence and pamphlets which followed give a good example of the nature and content of mid-Victorian debates on this subject. [37]

All this public controversy seemed tragic to many churchmen, including Charles James Blomfield, Bishop of London, who referred to the issue in his Charge of November 1850, saying that to remain silent "May serve to increase, or perpetuate the unhappy divisions which cripple the energies, and impair the usefulness of our Church, and enable our adversaries to assail us with weapons of our own forging". There were many churchmen who, like Blomfield, realized that the complex and protracted controversy which surrounded the name of G. C. Gorham was having a devastating effect upon the whole life of the Church of England. Looking back on the Gorham controversy many have wondered why it was pursued with such vigor and earnestness by leading churchmen, who could have given the time consumed by the controversy to the evangelization of the alienated millions.

The fact is that it was not a controversy merely about theological words and doctrinal statements. Thoughtful churchmen needed no reminding that what the Church believed about baptism had a fundamental effect upon the whole of her pastoral and evangelistic work. An article in The English Churchman of January 1850 concluded: "The question of baptismal regeneration is in a large sense a practical one; the question is, How are you to treat, and in what state are you to suppose, the visible members of the Church of Christ, whom you have to instruct as children, and whom you have to exhort as adults?" Were all the baptized to be treated as having received a new nature and thus in no real need of conversion? Or was the rite of baptism to be seen as little more than a sign of a new relationship with God in Christ, which had to be sealed by a true conversion which involves a transformation of man's nature, both moral and spiritual? If baptism always involved the giving of a new nature, whatever the age or condition of the recipient, then there was no need for a conversion. It was felt that such a position would imply that the baptized masses, who made up the urban communities, said to be living in heathen darkness, were, after all, Christians and members of the Church. Surely to accept such a theological interpretation of baptism would stultify any evangelistic enterprise among the teeming populations of the new industrial areas.

Thus the controversy was not a mere quibble over the theological definition of a term which had often been used rather vaguely and in different ways. It was a crucial debate concerning the meaning and importance of a Sacrament which lay at the very foundation of the Church's life. As such it was not simply a doctrinal matter, but one which inevitably influenced the whole of the Church's pastoral and evangelistic work.

Both Evangelicals and High Churchmen had to face up to the question of the spiritual condition of the millions of baptized persons who had lapsed from the Church. Were they to be treated as members of Christ and His Church? Had they through their own deliberate neglect broken the covenant relationship with God created through baptism? Could they be blamed for neglecting and falling away from a Church which had in fact neglected them? Or was their position simply that, through neglect, they had fallen from grace but were, nevertheless, still members of Christ and His Church and as such only needed leading back into the fold of the Church? Could it be that the way of life of these baptized heathen masses was a living proof that baptism without conversion was of no avail? The heart of the mid-Victorian conflict between the two parties was the meaning of baptismal regeneration and its relation to conversion.

Baptismal Regeneration and Conversion

During the early part of the nineteenth century the alternative terms 'baptismal regeneration' and 'conversion' denoted the alternatives of 'High Church' and 'Evangelicals', of 'objective' and 'subjective' religion. Evangelicals preached the need for conversion and the amendment of life, and in doing this contradicted what the High Church party believed and taught about the objective side of baptism, expressed in its understanding of baptismal regeneration. On the other hand, what High Churchmen believed about baptismal regeneration limited the place and application of conversion in their preaching. This clear division between the two concepts is illustrated in the life of John Henry Newman, who saw his acceptance of the doctrine of baptismal regeneration as indicating his defection from Evangelicalism.

But while these two concepts became the 'watchwords' of the opposing parties, part of the problem was due to confusion. Theological terms were often used in different senses; language often lacked clarity and precision. This was certainly true among the ranks of the Evangelicals because many supposed that baptismal regeneration denied the need for any spiritual change in those who had been baptized. Perhaps the root of the problem was the failure to distinguish between a 'change of nature' and a 'change of state'. Certainly Archibald Campbell Tait felt that this was the heart of the matter. He wrote: "In Article XXVII you will find an exposition which may help you to a right understanding of the word 'Regeneration' which has caused to some minds so much difficulty. This difficulty has very frequently arisen from the mistaken idea that 'conversion' and 'regeneration' are to be used as interchangeable terms. A further question is frequently raised, namely whether the change wrought by Holy Baptism is an actual change of condition, or merely a change of relation towards God, and upon this point the Church of England has, as I think, pronounced no authoritative decision. It is certain that every person baptised has a right thence forward to speak of God in a special sense as his Father". [38]

During the mid-Victorian period confusion and controversy on this subject went beyond the bounds of the Church of England. Charles Haddon Spurgeon preached a sermon in June 1864 on the subject of baptismal regeneration in which he openly attacked the Church of England's teaching. The Church of England, he said, was the only Protestant Church in England which taught baptismal regeneration: "I find that the great error which we have to contend with throughout England (and it is growing more and more) is...the doctrine of baptismal regeneration. We will confront this dogma with the assertion that Baptism without Faith Saves No One". [39] What Spurgeon had to say did not go un-noticed in the Church of England where he, or at least some of his views, had both supporters and opponents. Two sermons were preached in Regent's Park Chapel by W. Landels. The first, preached in August 1864, bore the title <u>Baptismal Regeneration: Remarks on the Controversy between the Rev. C. H. Spurgeon and certain Evangelical Clergymen of the Church of England</u>. Both sermons supported Spurgeon and attacked the Church of England's doctrine of baptismal regeneration. [40] A counter-attack came from Walter G. Abbott, Curate of St. Paul's Walworth, who, in a sermon of which 17,000 copies were said to have been distributed, strongly attacked Spurgeon's sermon on baptismal regeneration. It was a new facet to the controversy and like so many other mid-Victorian debates prompted numerous publications.

In a series of letters on baptismal regeneration Charles Crosthwaite charged Spurgeon with mistaking regeneration for conversion, and then accusing the Church of England of teaching that every infant is converted in baptism. Crosthwaite said that Spurgeon gave his own interpretation to the term 'baptismal regeneration' and not that of the Church. Crosthwaite himself believed that regeneration always accompanied infant baptism. For him regeneration meant that God adopts our children. [41] And this, he said, was what the Church meant by the term. Correspondence following this statement made it clear that many were unwilling to accept such a simple explanation of regeneration which, it was felt, implied far more than adoption.

What then did the opposing parties believe and teach concerning the relationship between regeneration and conversion?

For George Howard Wilkinson, a prominent 'Catholic Evangelical', regeneration involved conversion: We are 'regenerate' in order that we may be converted. This conversion he saw as the beginning of growth in the Christian life and not the end. Baptism and conversion were both essential for the Christian life and were very much the two poles of his preaching. [42]

Reviewing a sermon preached by the notable Evangelical Gerard Noel, <u>The Christian Observer</u> offers a good account of what many Evangelicals of the period believed about the relation between conversion and baptism: "We think, that Mr. Noel stands perfectly clear of the fatal error of confounding

Baptismal with <u>Converting</u> grace, and urges on every baptised person, as well as on every other man, the imperative duty of deep and anxious enquiry whether he has really, by personal faith and repentance, laid hold of the promise of the covenant of grace and is not only baptised externally by water, but really with the Holy Ghost and with fire". [43]

Frederick Meyrick (1827-1906), a non-residentiary Canon of Lincoln, an ardent evangelical controversialist, wrote a useful pamphlet <u>Baptism; Regeneration; Conversion</u>. For him, regeneration in baptism, rightly understood, is the doctrine of the Church of England, but it is not conversion. It is, he says a "change of federal relation and of spiritual condition but not of moral disposition". Drawing evidence from Anglican Formularies, Scripture and the Fathers, he concludes: "Inaccurate use of the word regeneration has included Conversion, but strictly speaking regeneration is the starting point of Sanctification". Of conversion he writes: "It is a change of disposition wrought by the renewing power of the Holy Ghost". He sees regeneration and conversion as supplementing one another. "We may or may not", he says, "be conscious of the moment at which Conversion begins. It is best when the beginning of Conversion is so early that we are unconscious of its commencement". [44] While his separation of regeneration and conversion would please many Evangelicals, his conviction that the ideal situation is an "unconscious Conversion" would be most unsatisfactory to many members of his party, for most of whom conversion was the result of a conscious act of mature faith and something of which the recipient ought to be fully aware.

By contrast many High Churchmen insisted that baptism brought about not only a change in status, but also a moral change. However, William Walsham How, a leader among the moderate High Churchmen, was unwilling to say that any moral change occurred in and through baptism: "I am myself a little shy of insisting upon the new birth into the covenanted family of God, the seal of the new relationship, the admission into the new status of privilege, the bestowal of gifts and promises. No doubt grace is given...But I dare not assert that this latter grace produces at the moment of Baptism an actual moral inherent change". [45]

For many High Churchmen the real problem was the multitudes who, having been baptized and declared regenerate, had fallen from grace. Robert Isaac Wilberforce found no difficulty in holding a thorough-going doctrine of baptismal regeneration and, at the same time, preaching the need for conversion. In his Charge of 1845 he stated: "To preach conversion may be deemed in some way inconsistent with that assertion of the doctrine of baptismal regeneration...But in truth, the two principles present not the slightest inconsistency...Why should this prevent us from telling men who live in sin that they need conversion? The grace which has been given to them in Baptism will not save them unless they use it...Why not imitate then our ancient worthies in calling the Baptised sinner to conversion?" [46] Three years later he returned to the same theme, telling his clergy: "Regeneration in baptism does not supersede the need of converting the careless; but neither is conversion unconnected with the regenerating union with Christ, which in baptism He had previously bestowed". [47]

Whatever the Evangelicals said about their High Church opponents regarding baptismal regeneration, they could not honestly say that a high doctrine of baptism excluded missionary activity. Nor could they say that it led to a neglect of the baptized masses, with the consolation that because they were baptized, all was well. For these were the very people whom Robert Isaac Wilberforce described as: "Baptised sinners in need of conversion". For many of the High Church party baptism was a real incentive to their evanglistic work, which for them was twofold: To call the lapsed baptized sinner to repentance and conversion, and to lead the unbaptized to baptism and into the fellowship of Christ's Church. God, through baptism, had already begun His great work in the lives of most of these people--they had been baptized, but had failed to use their baptism. They had been set upon the road to sanctification, but had failed to get beyond the starting point. In practice a High Church doctrine of baptismal regeneration was anything but a deterrent to evangelism; to not a few High churchmen it was a greater incentive to work in the new, over-populated, industrial areas in an all-out attempt to convert the masses. The records of many High Church slum priests bear witness to this fact.

NOTES

1. George Sandby, To the Laity: A Practical Address upon recent and coming events within the Church (1851) 14.

2. H. Phillpotts, A Charge 1845 30.

3. C. Thirlwall, A Charge 1851 32-33.

4. See John Kaye, A Sermon on Baptismal Regeneration (1850).

5. J. B. Mozley, **The Primitive Doctrine of Baptismal Regeneration** (1856) 129-30.

6. See J. B. Mozley, **A Review of the Baptismal Controversy** (2nd ed. 1863). For High Church reaction see L. E. Elliott-Binns, **English Thought 1860-1900: The Theological Aspect** (1956) 269.

7. John Morris, <u>Regeneration in Baptism: A Sermon</u> (1846) 18-20.

8. John Henry Newman, **Apologia Pro Vita Sua: Being a History of Religious Opinion** (1890, first published 1865) 8-9.

9. John Henry Newman, **Lectures on the Doctrine of Justification** (1st ed. 1838, 3rd ed. 1874) 86-8.

10. <u>Ibid.</u>, 102.

11. John Henry Newman, **The Via Media of the Anglican Church: Illustrated Lectures, Letters and Tracts written between 1830-1841** (2 Vols. 1901) Vol. II 'Letter addressed to a Magazine on behalf of Dr. Pusey's Tracts on Holy Baptism and of Other Tracts for the Times' 1837. 145-94.

12. John Henry Newman, **Parochial and Plain Sermons** (1st ed. 1836, New ed. 8 Vols. 1891) Vol. III, Sermon XIX "Regenerating Baptism", 271.

13. <u>Ibid.</u>, 273.

14. <u>Ibid.</u>, Sermon XVIII "The Gift of the Spirit", 266-7.

15. John Keble, **Occasional Papers and Reviews** (1877) "A Pastoral Letter to the Parishioners of Hursley" 239.

16. <u>Ibid.</u>, 249.

17. E. B. Pusey, **Sermons during the Season from Advent to Whitsuntide** (1848) 220.

18. **Tracts for the Times** No. 67, 4th ed. 12-13.

19. E. B. Pusey, **Scriptural View of Holy Baptism** (4th ed. 1836) 23-24.

20. Robert Isaac Wilberforce, **The Doctrine of Holy Baptism: with remarks on the Rev. W. Goode's "Effects of Infant Baptism"** (1849) 9.

21. R. I. Wilberforce, A Charge 1848 5-6.

22. R. I. Wilberforce, The Sacramental System: A Sermon preached at St. Mary's Church, before the University of Oxford, on Sunday, March 10th, 1850 (1850) 15-16, 18.

23. John Octavius Johnston, **Life and Letters of Henry Parry Liddon** (1904) 234.

24. A. T. Gilbert, A Charge 1847 20-1.

25. See Francis Warre Cornish, **The English Church in the Nineteenth Century** (1910) Part I, 329.

26. R. K. Pugh ed., **The Letter-books of Samuel Wilberforce 1843-68** (1970) 84-5. A number of other letters also record what Samuel Wilberforce believed about the doctrines of baptismal regeneration, e.g.: 85-6, 241-2.

27. Samuel Wilberforce, **Addresses to the Candidates for Ordination on the questions in the Ordination Service** (1867) 72.

28. See R. W. Church, **The Oxford Movement: Twelve Years 1833-1845** (lst ed. 1891, 3rd ed. 1909) 262-3. L. E. Elliott-Binns, **The Early Evangelicals, A Religious and Social Study** (1953) 392-4. Horton Davies, **Worship and Theology in England, III: From Watts and Wesley to Maurice 1690-1850** (1961) 226-7.

29. See Arthur Pollard and Michael Hennell, **Charles Simeon 1759-1836** (1959) 106.

30. See Ibid., 106-7, 109, 111-12.

31. W. Simcox Bricknell, **The Judgement of the Bishops upon Tractarian Theology** (1845) 374.

32. Pollard and Hennell, op. cit., 108-10.

33. See A. R. Ashwell and R. G. Wilberforce, **Life of the Right Reverend Samuel Wilberforce...**(3 Vols. 1880-82) Vol. I, 46.

34. See Elliott-Binns, **Early Evangelicals** 394. See also George Body, **The Life of Temptation** (1872) 1-4, and **The Wilderness Way** (1886) 174.

35. William Goode, A Letter to the Bishop of Exeter (1850).

36. See G. R. Balleine, **A History of the Evangelical Party in the Church of England** (1951) 225-7. J. C. S. Nias, **Gorham and the Bishop of Exeter** (1951) 151-3.

37. William Goode, A Reply to Archdeacon Dodgson's Statement, prefixed to his sermons on the Sacraments; with remarks on the sermons (1864). Archdeacon Dodgson, The Sacraments of the Gospel: Two Sermons, preached in Ripon Cathedral on January 3 and January 17, 1864. With a full account of the proceedings of Dr. Goode, Dean of Ripon, respecting them; and the whole correspondence relative thereto, which has passed between him and the author (2nd ed. 1864).

38. Randall Thomas Davidson and William Benham, **Life of Archibald Campbell Tait: Archbishop of Canterbury** (2 Vols. 1891) Vol. II, 567-8.

39. C. H. Spurgeon, Baptismal Regeneration: A Sermon, delivered...June 5th, 1864. The Book of Common Prayer weighed in the balance of the Sanctuary: A Sermon, delivered...September 15th, 1864.

40. W. Landels, Baptismal Regeneration...A Sermon preached...August 28, 1864. Baptism Rightly Received: A Sermon delivered...September 11th, 1864.

41. See Charles Crosthwaite, **Baptismal Regeneration, as bearing upon Justification by Faith Only; ...A series of Letters** (1865).

42. See Arthur James Mason, **Memoir of George Howard Wilkinson...** (2 Vols. 1909) Vol. I, 127-8, 355-6. G. H. Wilkinson, Sermon, **The Invisible Glory: in Sermons** (1908) 298-9.

43. The Christian Observer, October 1853, 704.

44. See Frederick Meyrick, Baptism; Regeneration; Conversion (n.d.).

45. Frederick Douglas How, **Bishop Walsham How: A Memoir** (1899) 476.

46. Robert Isaac Wilberforce, A Charge 1845 12-13.

47. R. I. Wilberforce, A Charge 1848 6. See also C. J. Blomfield, A Charge 1850 32.

B. The Broad Churchmen

There were some churchmen whose views on baptism, as on numerous other theological points, did not fit into either of the two main parties associated with the mid-Victorian baptismal controversy. Some of these men belonged to what was commonly called the Broad Church, sometimes known as 'Liberal Anglicanism'. The Broad Churchmen were not a party in the sense of the Evangelical and High Church parties, but rather a set of individuals, many of whom disagreed with each other. They were men of a restless critical attitude of mind, often drawn together by the hostility they provoked rather than by their common ideas. Because of this group's rather nebulous nature, opinions differ about who actually belonged to it. [1] Along with a critical attitude there often went a desire to re-state certain Catholic doctrines, but at the same time many of them were extremely loyal to the Book of Common Prayer and in this they were united with both Evangelicals and Tractarians. However, in spite of all they had in common, the individuality of each of these men must never be forgotten. The term 'Broad Churchmen' is vague and is often used as an 'umbrella' term to cover a group of men with very different theological ideas and approaches.

For the purpose of this work it is convenient to examine together the views on initiation held and taught by some of these very independent churchmen and so they are grouped here under the heading Broad Churchmen, without any intention of categorically placing them in that school.

Of these independent minds, Frederick Denison Maurice had the most to say on the subject of baptism; it was a recurring theme in many of his published works and ultimately it was his views on this subject which caused him to part company with both the Evangelicals and the High Churchmen.

In August 1836 Maurice began, with some difficulty, to write a series of letters on baptism. His object was to show that in the position of each of the parties, of which he listed three--Evangelicals, High Church and Educational--there was a great truth asserted. While he agreed with and defended what each of the parties said, at the same time he felt that each party was wrong when it began to deny the truth held by the others. Eventually Maurice gave up this project and began to write a series of letters on Quakerism. [2] In his second letter to a Quaker, Maurice set out to examine, along the lines of his previous project, the subject of baptism. This letter makes up a valuable part of his magnum opus, **The Kingdom of Christ,** the first edition of which covered three volumes and over 1,000 pages. [3]

Here his independent spirit of critical enquiry becomes clear as he sets out his baptismal theology; much of his later writing on baptism is an amplification of what he wrote here. He sent a copy of what he had written to his mother and in the accompanying letter he expressed his personal feelings on the subject: "I have written what I thought was most likely to bring people back to simple and trustful views, but in doing this, I have been forced to go into many wearisome arguments and oppose many people whom I would willingly agree with and support. [4]

What he wrote caused anger to both Pusey and the Tractarians in general. For Maurice this was regrettable, for the ideas of the Oxford group had attracted him, and of their views on baptism he had said: "Here I dreamed for a while that I should have a real point of union". But this was not to be, and instead they parted company. It was the publication of Pusey's Tracts on Baptism which shattered this dream and prompted the remark: "Instead of affording me the least warrant for the kind of teaching which appeared to me alone Scriptural and practical, it made such teaching utterly impossible". [5] Maurice declared it was "A tract which drove me more vehemently back on what I took to be the teaching of our own Catechism--that by Baptism we claim the position which Christ had claimed for all mankind. At the same time this conviction put me in direct opposition to the Evangelicals". [6] But, commented his biographer, "Pusey's Tract represented everything that he did not think and did not believe, till at last he...made up his mind that it represented the parting point between him and the Oxford school." [7] What Maurice found so unacceptable about Pusey's teaching was the view that: "The baptised child was holy for a moment after its baptism, in committing sin it lost its purity. That could only be recovered by acts of repentance and a system of ascetical discipline...I saw that I must be hopelessly and for ever estranged from this doctrine and from those who taught it, unless I abandoned all my hopes for myself and for the world". [8]

During his lifetime Maurice wrote a considerable number of books, but of his second letter to a Quaker, he wrote: "Nothing I have written had so important an effect on my life". For Maurice the work of Christ was of cosmic significance and on this conviction he built his theology of baptism. Baptism, for him, declared the actual relation in which men stood to God.

They were his children, but it was not baptism which made them such. Baptism brought about no change in the baptized. For every human being was, by right, a son of God from the moment of his birth. He saw baptism as simply the means by which the child is set within the circle of light which had been always shining for all mankind and was gradually to lead it into the fulness of truth. [9]

Maurice heartily approved of what the compilers of the Articles and Catechism said about baptism, that it is a "regeneration" and a new birth, a grafting into the Church, an adoption as sons of God: "I believe that they felt they were never bearing a stronger witness to those truths which the Romanist opinions had hidden from the faith of man--for the finished salvation in Christ--for the justification of men by His Resurrection--than when they were using this language". The declaration by the Prayer Book Reformers: "The Baptism of young children is in any wise to be retained in the Church as most agreeable with the institution of Christ", is seen by Maurice as a comfort to all Christian parents. [10] Throughout his teaching, the baptism of infants is taken as normal. He believed that in a Christian family men were bound to claim for their children the rights and privileges of churchmanship.

Maurice believed that at baptism infants received the Holy Spirit and were made members of the Church. But what he actually meant when he asserted that the Holy Spirit was given in baptism was not expressed in conventional theological terms: "Tell those who have thought that the gift of the Spirit is not really connected with this divine adoption and fellowship, that there is a mighty difference between the hope of sudden and casual visitations, and the belief of a power abiding with you by night and day, of whose presence sin may make you unconscious, to whose presence repentance may restore you, but of which it is a sin to doubt whether He is with you of truth". [11] He states in **The Kingdom of Christ**: "We suppose every Christian infant to be taken under the guardianship and education of God's Holy Spirit. In the faith of this truth the well instructed parent brings up his child".

Baptism is seen by Maurice as the sacrament of "constant union"--the witness, the pledge, to every man and every child who receives it that he is a son of God--adopted by Him, admitted as a member of Christ and inheritor of the Kingdom of Heaven. And so in **The Kingdom of Christ** he writes (of infants) that in baptism, the "sacrament of constant union", there is the "strongest and plainest assertion that the baptised child is regenerate; that it is a child of God...taken into covenant with God, that it is really and truly a spiritual creature, redeemed by Christ, and adopted into union with Himself". While rejecting the High Church interpretation of baptismal regeneration, for him the law and principle of baptism is "based on the death of the old carnal nature, and the rising up of a new man in us".

The chief emphasis of his baptismal theology is the relationship which baptism creates--which emphasizes its corporate nature. On the one hand it creates a unity with Christ and a sharing in His nature and a covenant relationship with God; at the same time it unites the baptized with the whole people of God and mankind: "Thou belongest to the head of thy race, thou art a member of His Body...thou hast the nature of the Divine Son, thou art united to Him in whom is life, and from whom the life of thee and of all creatures comes". [12] In a very real way it was a high theology of baptism--but not in the usual sense.

His rejection of the Tractarian theological interpretation of baptismal regeneration caused misgiving among its supporters and aroused their hostility and angry opposition. At the same time his unconventional approach and exposition caused confusion among the Evangelicals. Whatever the reactions of others, Maurice cannot be charged with treating the subject lightly. His understanding of the meaning and implications of baptism was not developed along traditional lines, nor did he use traditional theological terminology to express it. Nevertheless, what he said was sound and worthy of careful consideration. His theological approach and understanding of the sacraments of initiation, as on so many theological matters, was so independent that it is impossible to fit him into any party.

One last quotation shows how Maurice was willing to work out not only the theological implications of his position, but also the practical ones: "We are baptised into the Name of Father, and of Son, and of Holy Ghost. The Spirit with whom we are taken into covenant accompanies us through all our pilgrimage. If we accept the teaching of our Baptism Service and of our Catechism, we must ascribe to Him all the good thoughts of the child, its perceptions of the unrealised world in which it is dwelling, its intuitions of a spiritual world with which it has to do, its power of receiving and returning affection, its capacity of understanding and of making itself understood. To the same source we must trace the awakening of conscience in the boy, his acknowledgement of a law against which his inclinations are struggling, his sense of powers which are to wrestle with the earth and to subdue it, his faculties of learning, his craving for fellowship".[13]

Maurice undoubtedly had a strong influence on the baptismal theology of Charles Kingsley, whose views on the subject were expressed in a number of sermons preached to a variety of congregations. In one he said: "Your heavenly Father...sent His Son into the world to die for you; when you were but an infant He called you to be baptised into His Church, and receive your share of His Spirit". [14] For Kingsley, the gift of God's Spirit was by no means confined to infants or to the Sacraments. The Spirit is given to men in every circumstance of life, in the hour of need man "shall be baptised with the Holy Spirit and with fire". [15]

Life was seen by Kingsley as a continual battle between the spirit and the flesh, but God gives his Spirit to those who are joined to Christ through baptism: "At your baptism God gave you the right to call Him your loving Father, to call His Son your Saviour, His Spirit your Sanctifier". [16]

Kingsley's teaching that Christ is within every man and every child expresses something of his understanding of the Incarnation and the redemptive work of Christ. Christ took upon Himself human nature and redeemed it and in so doing He declared all men to be children of God. Baptism is a recognition of man's sonship. [17] The baptized are members of God's family, children of God and sharers in the Covenant. Nevertheless, says Kingsley, they must be converted, they must turn to God with their whole heart and will, they must make their choice between God and sin. But even if a man gives way to the power of sin he does not lose his baptismal status, for the grace of God remains within him, struggling to lead him out of sin into good, out of darkness into light. [18]

Many of the implications of Kingsley's baptismal theology are outlined in a sermon of simple language addressed in 1851 to a congregation of working men. In this sermon, The Message of the Church to Labouring Men, Kingsley speaks of the Sacrament as a sign--"and what a sign"--baptism is the witness of a blessing not meant merely for the high born--it is free to all, even the poorest and the most degraded: it is his birthright, simply because he is a human being. Baptism, says Kingsley, works no miracles; it proclaims a miracle which has been from all eternity. It proclaims that we are members of Christ, children of God, citizens of a spiritual kingdom. For Kingsley this kingdom was a kingdom of love, justice, self-sacrifice, feedom, equality. "These spiritual laws, says Baptism, are the true ground and constitution of all human society, and not rank, force, wealth, expediency, or any outward material ground whatever, not they, but the kingdom of God". [19] He sees baptism as a sign of washing or purification: It testifies of the right of each, because the will of God for each is, that they be pure. It is this baptismal sign, says Kingsley, which declares the dignity of man, and his rights as a human being and a child of God.

Such was the baptismal theology which prompted Kingsley, the socialist and reformer, to speak out boldly: "How dare you, in the face of that Baptismal sign of the sprinkled water, keep God's children exposed to filth, brutality and temptation, which festers in your courts and alleys, making cleanliness impossible--drunkenness all but excusable--prostitution all but natural--self-respect and decency unknown?...In that font is a witness for education and for sanitary reform, which will conquer with the might of an archangel when every other argument has failed to prove that the masses are after all not mere machines and hands to be used up in the production of a wealth of which they never taste, when their numbers are, as far as possible, kept down by economical and prudent rulers, to the market demand for members of Christ, children of God and inheritors of the kingdom of Heaven". [20]

Unfortunately, Kingsley's theological understanding and deep convictions concerning the social implications of baptism were not shared by the majority of his clerical brethren in the mid-Victorian period. One can only speculate upon how much more evangelistic work would have been carried out by the Established Church among the alienated urban masses, if more of her clergymen had shared Kingsley's insights and convictions concerning the wider implications of baptism.

What for Charles Kingsley was a 'sign' was, for Thomas Arnold, a 'seal', and a seal which can be broken. As the Israelites through disobedience and sin broke the seal of circumcision so, said Arnold, it is with baptism: "The seal of baptism has proved no surer mark than the seal of circumcision; again have the people whom He brought out of Egypt corrupted themselves". Because the seal can be broken it carries no guarantee on which the baptized can take comfort. "We have", said Arnold, "the Christian's sure seal; not that outward seal of baptism, which is too often broken, but the seal of God's Spirit, that as Christ was, so are we in this world". While, strictly speaking, Thomas Arnold is outside the mid-Victorian period, his influence as a Broad Churchman is seen in others. One who was taught by Arnold, and influenced by both Maurice and Kingsley, was the New Testament scholar F. J. A. Hort, for whom an important issue was the question as to when the Holy Spirit is given. He asked: "Is the Holy Spirit given only in baptism (I mean of course not till baptism), or given before but increased in baptism, or...is it given to every human creature, and is baptism only its seal and assurance? This is a point on which I should much like to have a long talk with Maurice". [21] F. D. Maurice's baptismal theology, based upon the cosmic significance of the work of Christ, would have left Hort in no doubt concerning his beliefs and position on this rather complex question.

Another influential churchman who comes under the Broad Church 'umbrella' is Frederick Temple, whose ideas have much in common with his Rugby predecessor, Thomas Arnold. Speaking about baptism and confirmation, he expressed the opinion that the theology of initiation is connected with the fundamental principles of human nature: "The grace of God's spirit is given for different purposes at different times of life; but the gift cannot avail unless it is used by the recipient. If it is not 'stirred up' by the active co-operation of the will and the energies, it will be dormant and useless in the soul. Hence the number of baptised and confirmed persons who are as though they had never received the gift at all". [22]

Temple described baptism as "the bestowal of a germ of spiritual vitality which, if cultivated, will grow with a child's growth like his natural faculties, and enable the higher but feebler impulses of his humanity to triumph over those lower selfish ones, which are unhappily the stronger". [23] Temple's correspondence connected with the Gorham controversy gives us an insight into his position on some of the points at issue. On the whole he could agree with the baptismal service, but would have welcomed some changes in expression. He felt that the words "To regenerate him <u>with</u> Thy Holy Spirit" were likely to mislead people. The language of Scripture, which speaks of baptism in highly exalted terms in that it implies a moral and spiritual change, was generally related to adults; it was, said Temple, absurd to apply the same theological meaning to baptism now. He felt that this is just what the High Church party did. [24]

When Temple attempts to explain more fully the meaning of regeneration when related to infant baptism, the Broad Church approach to theology, and baptism in particular, becomes apparent. In the process of regeneration he sees two powers at work-- "natural conscience and the grace of God". How much of the process can be attributed to each of these powers no one can tell. [25] At baptism the infant is "positively promised" that it will receive grace; by which Temple means the gift of the Holy Spirit. But this gift will "certainly come at the time when it is best for him that it should come; but may be rejected then by himself".

Frederick Temple's Broad Church position is seen in his attitude to the Gorham Judgement. Unlike the two opposing parties who would exclude from the Church all those who held a baptismal theology contrary to their own, Temple would exclude neither. He would, he said, include both in the Church, even if this meant having two contrary doctrines put forward authoritatively. Such a situation would have been inconceivable to High Churchmen.

Another Broad Churchman, Connop Thirlwall, speaking on the Gorham Judgement and the controversial term 'baptismal regeneration', said that the most approved descriptions of baptismal regeneration did not include "at least as an essential element, an inward change of moral nature. These descriptions point not to a change of habit or disposition, but to a new state, relation or capacity, which is by no means invariably attended with any perceptible moral effects". [26] Thirlwall did not believe that baptism conferred any moral change. Well aware of the disputable point about when the Holy Spirit is given, he told his clergy: "It appears to me that we may very well believe this gift to be really received, and yet need not adopt the theory of an infused virtue, or a mysterious earnest of the Holy Spirit, or of an initial and seminal grace". These theories, he felt, were based upon the assumption that the gift cannot be really bestowed unless it takes immediate effect. He believed that the gift of the Holy Spirit is given according to the capacity of the recipient, not immediately, but dispensed by God according to His good pleasure under the conditions of the baptismal covenant. For Thirlwall the idea of a covenant is essential to the nature of baptism. He agreed with Gorham that "in all cases alike the benefit to be realised by the recipient, when he has come to years of discretion, depends on his acknowledgement and fulfillment of the contract". [27]

The Judgement, which provoked Bishop Thirlwall to speak to his clergy on the subject of baptismal regeneration, also inspired the "Germanised preacher of dangerous fascination", Frederick W. Robertson, to preach two sermons on baptism to his congregation at Trinity Chapel, Brighton. The first of these was preached on March 10th, 1850, two days after the Gorham Judgement was given. "Men of equal spirituality", said Robertson, "are ready to sacrifice all to assert, and to deny, the doctrine of baptismal regeneration. And the truth, I believe, will be found, not in some middle, moderate, timid doctrine, which skilfully avoids extremes, but in a truth larger than either of these opposite views, which is the basis of both, and which really is that for which each party tenaciously clings to its own view as to a matter of life and death". [28]

He rejects the idea that the gift of God's Spirit must await the administration of the rite of baptism. Baptism does not create man a child of God, but proclaims him to be such. He vehemently rejects the belief that: "The Spirit of God is given--the germ is implanted; but it may be crushed--injured--destroyed". He mocks those who yearn for their baptismal purity which they believe they have lost through venial sin after baptism. [29]

What he calls 'modern Calvinism' believes that baptismal regeneration in the case of infants means a change of state-- "though what is meant by a change of state were hard to say". They believe, says Robertson, "The real benefit of baptism, however, only belongs to the elect...This view maintains that you are not God's child until you become such consciously. Not until evidence of a regenerate life is given--not until signs of a converted soul are shown". For them it is faith that makes a man a child of God: "The Romanist says Baptism, the Calvinist says Faith, makes that true, which was not true before. It is not a fact that God is that person's Father, till in the one case Baptism, in the other Faith, have made him such".

The doctrine of the Bible and the church as Robertson understood it, is then set forth: "Christ...proclaimed God the Father--man the Son: revealed that the Son of Man is also the Son of God. Man--as man, God's child. He came to redeem the world from the ignorance of the relationship which had left them in heart aliens and unregenerate. Human nature, there- fore, became viewed in Christ, a holy thing and divine. The Revelation is a common humanity, sanctified in God. The appear- ance of the Son of God is the sanctification of the human race.

Robertson then draws out the implications of his belief: "Man is God's child, and the sin of man consists in perpetually living as if it were false...To be a son of God is one thing: to know that you are and call Him Father, is another--and that is regeneration...Baptism is a visible witness to the world of that which the world is for ever forgetting. A common humanity united in God. Baptism authoritatively reveals and pledges to the individual that which is true of the race. Baptism takes the child and addresses it by name...you are a child of God... Observe, then, baptism does not create a child of God. It authori- tatively declares him so. It does not make the fact: it only reveals it. If baptism made it fact then and there for the first time, baptism would be magic". [30]

The following Sunday he preached his second sermon on the subject, dealing with two objections to his understanding of the Sacrament: (i) The apparent denial of original sin and (ii) The apparent result that baptism is nothing.

His view on baptism does not, he says, belittle it: "I should rather say baptism is everything. Baptism saves us...Bap- tism proclaims separately, personally, by name, to you--God created you--God redeemed you. Baptism is your warrant, you are His child. And now, because you are His child, live as a child of God: be redeemed from the life of evil which is false to your nature into the Life of Light and Goodness, which is the Truth of your Being". [31]

Robertson's views on baptism were certainly somewhat 'unorthodox', but they had much in common with those of other Broad Churchmen and men of independent minds who were seeking to re-state traditional Catholic doctrines. Among such independent minds we may include the seven authors who contributed toward the book **Essays and Reviews** (1860) which at first attracted very little attention, but when it was denounced for its liberalism by Bishop Samuel Wilberforce it became the object of hostile condemnation from many quarters. A meeting of bishops at Fulham in 1861 condemned it. The Lower House of Convocation proposed synodical condemnation, which was pronounced in 1864. [32] The book contains only a few rather fleeting references to baptism, but these provide an example of the Broad Church conviction of the necessity of free inquiry in religious matters. [33]

The restless inquiring spirit of the Broad Churchmen and the views they expressed, and the changes they sought to introduce, were unacceptable to the majority of their fellow churchmen. True, many of the old conflicts were no longer matters of great controversy but, as in the case of baptism, most of the problems and underlying differences still remained. However, if nothing else, the Broad Churchmen encouraged a spirit of inquiry which demanded that old ideas be re-examined and, if found wanting, reformed and re-stated. Unfortunately, even when churchmen agreed that change was needed this was slow to take place.

The Colenso Controversy of the 1860's provided the Broad Churchmen with a banner under which they could gather. It was suggested that a subscription list, opened on behalf of Colenso, enabled the 'liberal clergymen' to make more than a gesture regarding their position. Bishop John William Colenso was much influenced by his friend F. D. Maurice, to whom he dedicated a book of sermons. His somewhat advanced and liberal views stirred up the wrath and opposition of his fellow bishops. Thirlwall, who had spoken to his clergy about Colenso, [34] was the only English bishop who refused to sign a declaration calling for his resignation. The controversy which prompted such grave and widespread opposition, and resulted in a practically unanimous censure from his episcopal brethren, began as a result of his work on the Pentateuch. The publication of his book **The Pentateuch and Book of Joshua Critically Examined** (1863) sparked off an immediate and widespread controversy which inspired numerous publications and a lengthy Convocation debate. [35]

Colenso's work in the field of biblical criticism had a direct effect upon his baptismal theology and practice. In Part II of his work on the Pentateuch he asked if the bishops and clergy really accepted "the truth of the Scripture account of the Deluge". He pointed out that the prayers in the Baptismal Office, which made reference to this story, assume its reality and historical truthfulness. He refused to accept a rationalization of its inclusion in the Baptismal Office, being of the opinion that the Book of Common Prayer bound the clergy "to express unfeigned belief in the story of the Deluge, as it is told in these chapters of Genesis". Some clergy were able to satisfy their conscience, in using this Office with the view that the Deluge 'is a legendary narrative'; Colenso refused to accept such an approach. For those who, like himself, felt that they could not conscientiously use the prayer he says: "I see no remedy...but to omit such words; to disobey the law of the Church on this point, and take the consequences of the act--should any over-zealous brother clerk or layman drag them before a Court or enforce a penalty". [36]

Drawing his Preface to **The Pentateuch** to a close, Colenso writes that there are clergy who have come "to doubt and to disbelieve some portions of the Church system...and who do not feel it to be a light thing, Sunday after Sunday, to stand at the Sacred Font and use at each Baptism, in the holy Presence of God and in the face of a Christian congregation, such words..or those other words in the same service...'and didst also lead the children of Israel Thy people, through the Red Sea, figuring thereby Thy Holy Baptism'; with similar references in other services to different parts of the Mosaic story, which cannot be regarded as historically true". Bishop Colenso appealed to the English laity, in defence of their religious liberty, to work for Parliamentary action to change the situation of the clergy of the National Church: "To give room for the free utterance of God's truth in the Congregations, instead of worn-out formulae of a bygone age".

Archibald Campbell Tait, who had a great deal to say on the Colenso issue, drew up a declaration, addressed to Colenso, which on the 9th February 1863 was signed by forty-one bishops. [37] This declaration objected to what Colenso had written about the Baptismal Office in the Preface to his book on the Pentateuch. Presumably other members of the episcopate had no strong objections to the use of Old Testament typology in the baptismal service.

Long before the publication of his work on the Pentateuch Colenso had felt that the baptismal service was open to question and speculation. As vicar of Forncett, Norfolk (1846-1853) he agreed with complaints made by Dissenters against the administration of baptism in the Church of England. His ideas of infant baptism have a ring of Maurice about them: "Thank God, we do not believe them (infants) to be then only first taken under the love of God in Christ, though formally taken into the Christian Covenant and admitted to all its hopes and promises". The record of his ten-week journey in Natal tells of numerous baptisms administered by Colenso which seem to have caused him no problems, and one assumes that he used the Prayer Book rite. [38] He did, however, strongly oppose, in the missionary situation, the discipline of enforced separations, in the case of polygamous marriages, before the candidates were baptized. [39] Some years later he wrote his book **St. Paul's Epistle to the Romans: newly translated, and explained from a missionary point of view** (1861); in this work he minimizes the necessity for conversion and makes baptism irrelevant. It was his liberal views on baptism which enabled him to take his strong line on the subjects of polygamy and baptism. The first move to charge him with heresy was prompted by what he wrote in this book, and only later was interest fixed on his book on the Pentateuch.

What Colenso believed about baptism is well summed up in one of his Natal sermons. In this he speaks of the baptism of infants as a "beautiful symbol of our faith that they are already in fact--yes, from their very birth hour--the children of God. And in this way infant baptism in our Church is a protest for which we may be thankful, against all exclusiveness, against all appropriation of the love of God by any. The Church declares by it that no merit, not even faith, is needful to make the human soul the object of the love and care of the Father of spirits". [40]

The position of the Broad Churchmen cannot be described as a via media, in the sense of a middle easy way which avoided ultimate commitment. They were, on the whole, men of deep conviction, who refused to accept the traditional lines of theological thought. To baptism, as with other doctrinal issues, they applied an independent open-mindedness which, in a number of cases, led to convictions which demanded personal sacrifice. F. D. Maurice's views on baptism led to his break with the High Church party and misunderstanding from many quarters. For Charles Kingsley, baptism had deep social implications which he sought to apply at personal cost. Bishop Thirlwall stood out against his episcopal brethren in support of Colenso, while Colenso himself refused to retract his views, even when all were set against him. There is no doubt that what these independent churchmen had to say on the subject of baptism did make a valuable contribution to this part of the Church's teaching and practice during the mid-Victorian period. As with the approach and spirit of the other parties, that of the Broad and independent churchmen has had far-reaching and lasting effects.

NOTES

1. See M. A. Crowther, **Church Embattled: Religious Controversy in Mid-Victorian England** (1970) 29-39; also Owen Chadwick, **The Victorian Church,** Part I (1966) 544-5.

2. See Frederick Maurice, **The Life of Frederick Denison Maurice: Chiefly told in his own letters** (2 Vols. 1884) Vol. I, 202-12.

3. Frederick Denison Maurice, **The Kingdom of Christ, or Hints on the Principles, Ordinances and Constitutions of the Catholic Church in Letters to a Member of the Society of Friends** (3 Vols. 1837). See also Peter J. Jagger, "Baptism into the Kingdom of Christ: In the teaching of F. D. Maurice", **Faith and Unity,** Vol. XVI, No. 3, July 1972, 52-5.

4. Maurice, **The Life of Frederick Denison Maurice,** Vol. I, 219-20.

5. Ibid., 221, 236-7.

6. Ibid., 182.

7. Ibid., 186, see also 204, 221, 236-8.

8. Ibid., 237.

9. Ibid., 156, 214, 269.

10. Frederick Denison Maurice, **The Faith of the Liturgy and the Doctrines of the Thirty-nine Articles. Two Sermons.** (Cambridge 1860) 59-60.

11. Maurice, **The Life of Frederick Denison Maurice,** Vol. I, 331-2.

12. Frederick Denison Maurice, **Sermons Preached in Lincoln's Inn Chapel** (6 Vols. 1891) Vol. I, 81.

13. Maurice, **Faith of the Liturgy,** 19-20.

14. Charles Kingsley, **The Good News of God: Sermons** (1st ed. 1863, reprinted eleven times between 1866 and 1890) Sermon XXX, True Prudence 243.

15. See Ibid., Sermon XIV Heroes and Heroines 118-19. Sermon X, The Race of Life 79-80.

16. Charles Kingsley, **Twenty-five Village Sermons** (7th ed. 1866), Sermon VI, The Spirit and the Flesh 61-3.

17. Ibid., Sermon IX, Hell on Earth 90. See also **The Good News of God**, Sermon XXIII, Human Nature 188-9.

18. See Charles Kingsley, **Twenty-five Village Sermons**, Sermon XIV, Our Father in Heaven 132-4; see also 168, 192, 204, 225.

19. Charles Kingsley, The Message of the Church to Labouring Men: A Sermon Preached...June 22nd, 1851 (1851) 21.

20. Ibid., 23.

21. Arthur Fenton Hort, **Life and Letters of Fenton John Anthony Hort** (2 Vols. 1896) Vol. I, 76.

22. E. G. Sanford ed. **Memoirs of Archbishop Temple** (2 Vols. 1906) Vol. II, 47-8.

23. Ibid., 48.

24. See Ibid., 499, 501.

25. Ibid., 502.

26. See C. Thirlwall, A Charge,1851 33-4.

27. Ibid., 40.

28. Frederick W. Robertson, **Sermons Preached at Trinity Chapel, Brighton: Second Series** (6th ed. 1859). Sermon IV, Baptism 50-1.

29. Ibid., 55-7.

30. Ibid., 62-3.

31. Ibid., Sermon V, Baptism 81-2.

32. See C. Thirlwall, A Charge, 1866 42-5; J. Sinclair, On Free Thought: A Charge, 1865 16-19.

33. See **Essays and Reviews** (1st ed. 1860; copyright

ed. Leipzig 1862) 77, 312-14, 319-20, 362.

34. C. Thirlwall, A Charge, 1863 88-90.

35. See: Anonymous (A Barrister), **History against Colenso: Examination of the Witnesses** (Dublin 1863); William Irons, My Word Shall not Pass Away: A Sermon preached in St. Paul's Cathedral January 3rd 1864 (1864); A. McCaul, **Some Notes on the First Chapter of Genesis with reference to statements in "Essays and Reviews"** (2nd ed. 1861); James Thomas O'Brien, A Charge, 1863; E. B. Pusey, Case as to the Legal Force of the Judgement of the Privy Council... (1864); **Chronicle of Convocations,** 1862, 1010-51, 1091-1113; 1863, 1094; 1865, 2377-96; 1866, 482-95; 1868 passim.

36. John William Colenso, **The Pentateuch and Book of Joshua Critically Examined. Part II** (1863) xxii-iv.

37. There is some debate about who was responsible for the drawing up of this declaration. Tait was claimed as responsible--see R. T. Davidson, **Life of Archibald Campbell Tait...**(1891) Vol. I, 342-3; R. G. Wilberforce claimed it for his father--see **Life of Bishop Wilberforce,** Vol. III, 120. See also The Guardian 4 March 1863, 202; and A. M. G. Stephenson, **The First Lambeth Conference 1867** 134; Tait, Vol. I has a whole section on Colenso, 326-64. The Colenso Controversy had some influence upon the calling of the First Lambeth Conference, although Stephenson feels that this has been over-rated, see 120-49, 267-94.

38. See John William Colenso, **Ten Weeks in Natal: A Journal of a First Tour of Visitation among the Colonists and Zulu Kafirs of Natal** (1855) 32, 75, 166.

39. Ibid., 139-41.

40. See George W. Cox, **The Life of John William Colenso D.D. Bishop of Natal** (2 Vols. 1888) Vol. II, 90.

C. The Subject of Baptism

Article XXVII 'Of Baptism' states: "The Baptism of young children is in any wise to be retained in the Church, as most agreeable with the institution of Christ". What this Article lays down as the proper subject for baptism was accepted and believed, without question, by the majority of mid-Victorian clergy and laity in the Church of England. But while infant baptism was the generally accepted norm, there were some who questioned this and who freely voiced their disapproval and doubts.

Infant Baptism

An examination of every relevant passage of New Testament Scripture, in an attempt to discover the true meaning of baptism, led E. H. Hoare, in 1850, to conclude that baptism with water is the means appointed by Christ "as the door of entrance into His Visible Church...or Kingdom of God on earth". He saw faith as the means appointed by God by which men were admitted into Covenant with Him: "It was the command of the Lord Jesus Christ that baptism, which is now the token of the Covenant, should be administered only to believers...true believers only are acknowledged by Christ as rightful members of His Church. Yet as Abraham's children were admitted to circumcision together with himself, it is hence inferred that the children of believers in Christ should be baptised as well as their parents: no prohibition of their admission to the Ordinance having been given. This conclusion is confirmed by Christ's kind reception of the children that were brought to him". [1] Numerous churchmen of this period approached the subject in a way similar to that of Hoare and came to the same or similar conclusions, which they then put forward as a rationale in support of the practice of infant baptism. But while Hoare saw infant baptism as acceptable--at least not prohibited--he did not advocate a general baptism, or that infant baptism should be administered on the grounds of Christian charity, to anyone who applied for it, a practice advocated by Mandell Creighton. [2] Hoare found infant baptism agreeable to Scripture only in the case of the children of believing parents. M. F. Sadler wrote of baptism as the 'Sacrament of Responsibility'; he too accepted the validity of infant baptism, but agreed with Hoare that it should be administered only to the children of Christian or believing parents--this, he believed, was the apostolic practice. [3]

A letter to the Editor of The Record at the time of the Gorham controversy claimed to represent the Evangelical position on the matter. The Evangelical view, says the writer, is that infant baptism rests entirely on the covenant which God made with Abraham, which was a covenant of grace including the Church of God. This covenant was made to believers and their children. The blessings of the faithful are conferred on their infants as such, and as plainly distinguished from children of unbelievers. He is quite confident that the baptism of infants should be confined to the children of believing parents. [4]

This view found support in a sermon by Bishop George Moberly in Salisbury Cathedral, in which he stated that the normal case of baptism implied in the First Epistle of Peter, from which his text was taken, was Adult Baptism. He raised the question: If the normal case were adult baptism, what is the true view to be taken in regard to those who are baptised as infants?" He accepted the same position as that put forward by Hoare and Sadler, that those born of Christian parents have "a right to claim baptism, as one born within the family of God...He has a birthright of being put into the same condition and advantage as his parents enjoy, and so he is brought to the font, and there receives the washing water". [5] Throughout this revealing sermon Moberly confined his support to the children of believing parents and in this conviction there is a real link between this moderate High Church bishop and his more evangelical brethren.

With but a few exceptions, the High Churchmen were united in their belief that infants were proper subjects for baptism. For them, baptism was the only means of entering the visible Church, it was essential for salvation and offered the only assurance of life beyond the grave. To neglect this Sacrament, or to deny it to infants in general, was to deny a birthright in what Christ had obtained for them by His Incarnation, sacrificial death and resurrection. For High Churchmen there could be no denying baptism to children in general, nor confining it to the children of believing parents; they saw the practice as agreeable to the mind of Christ and in accordance both with Scripture and the Fathers. For them there was no lack of warrant to support such a practice; evidence in support of their position was both clear and plentiful. Pusey's views on the subject were High and adamant and both convincing and unquestionable to his fellow Tractarians. [6]

Maurice had no doubt about the theological correctness of administering baptism to infants; indeed his acceptance of this practice lies at the foundation of much of what he has to say on the subject of baptism. Infant baptism is a declaration of man's entire and utter dependence upon God. For Maurice the practice did not rest upon the accumulation of sufficient scriptural evidence, it was a practice which declared and demonstrated a fundamental theological principle, the supremacy of God and the dependence of man upon the grace of God and divine initiative. [7]

The liberal views of the Broad Churchmen find a clear expression in the writing of A. P. Stanley, who saw infant baptism as "a recognition of the good there is in every human soul".

There were, however, those who realized that the acceptance and practice of infant baptism did raise a number of difficult problems and indeed this issue lay at the heart of the controversy over baptismal regeneration. John Gibson, who wrote a valuable book, **The Nature and Effect of Baptism**, was one who accepted infant baptism as agreeable to the mind of Christ and the tenor of Scripture, but at the same time he was very much aware of some of the difficulties which accompanied the practice. Although insisting that repentance and belief are essential in adult baptism, he did not feel that these were essential requirements in the case of infants. Even though they lack faith and repentance, and are unconscious recipients of the Sacrament, "Whatever spiritual grace the Lord has for their souls in baptism, that in baptism He can and does bestow". [8] Some felt that faith and repentance were also essential in the case of infants, but this requirement could only be met by vicarious faith. [9]

For some churchmen it was the inability of children to offer the necessary conscious faith and repentance that made them unsuitable candidates, while for Cornelius Gorham it was the fact that they were born in original sin. An answer to this dilemma was found by Gorham in the doctrine of 'Prevenient Grace'. To recipients of prevenient grace before baptism, baptism bestows regeneration, justification and adoption as sons of God. His opponents were quick to point out that all Gorham was doing was substituting an act of prevenient grace for the Sacrament of baptism. He was making baptism no more than the outward seal of what had already been given. Edward Badeley, a barrister involved in the Gorham case, commenting on Gorham's use of the term 'prevenient grace' said that the use of such a phrase was unknown to the primitive Catholic Church. The Record of 21st February 1850 published a letter which dealt with the subject of prevenient grace, in which the writer said that the Bishop of Exeter and his advocates wrongly repudiated the phrase and doctrine of 'prevenient grace'. The object of the letter was to prove that those who rejected this doctrine were in error. The correspondent concluded: "I have shown that both the words and the important truth they uphold were sanctioned in all places, at all times, and by all". What some objected to was not the use of the term 'prevenient grace' and the doctrine which lay behind it, but the way it was used by Gorham as a substitute for baptism. Pusey heartily disagreed with Gorham's understanding of this doctrine which, he felt, left everyone in a state of uncertainty. "No one", said Pusey, "knows whether they have this act of prevenient grace and no one knows what state they are in, even following their baptism". What many wanted to deny was the theory that an act of prevenient grace was necessary for the efficacy of infant baptism.

Sufficient has been said to show that, while the majority of mid-Victorian churchmen accepted infant baptism as the norm, not all churchmen were willing to allow the belief and practice to go unchallenged, or at least unqualified.

Adult Baptism

At least some churchmen of this period felt that while in the New Testament adult baptism was the norm, the children of believers were now also suitable candidates. The majority saw no contradiction between the contemporary practice of infant baptism and the teaching of the New Testament on this subject. There were a few, however, who felt the need for certain theological modifications when stating what was conferred in the case of infant baptism. Only a minority strongly objected to infant baptism—believing that adult baptism was more in line with the New Testament theology of baptism and ought to replace the present practice. But perhaps this was to be expected in a Church where the practice of infant baptism had been firmly entrenched for centuries. As with clergy of other denominations, those of the Church of England who found infant baptism unacceptable had only the Baptist Church to turn to. In view of these facts it is not surprising that at this period little was said on the subject and even less done.

Adult baptism was on the increase, but this was largely due to the general neglect of infant baptism, resulting from the sociological situation of the time, rather than from any theological objection to infant baptism. MacKonochie, who was anything but an advocate of the Baptist position, recorded how at St. Alban's he witnessed a growing number of adult baptisms; of the 295 administered in 1863 many were adults. This increasing number of adult baptisms was due to evangelistic activity rather than the influence and advocacy of adult baptismal theology. Nevertheless, in many parishes, adult baptisms were a rare occurrence, and adult baptism by immersion was something of a novelty. [10]

Edward Bickersteth's useful **Treatise on Baptism** includes a chapter on adult baptism. The New Testament subjects of baptism were, he wrote, "chiefly those of grown-up persons", but he was willing to accept that the baptism of a household would include younger persons. He made no attempt to suggest that adults were the proper subjects for baptism--but he did set out, in considerable detail, the "Warrant for Infant Baptism". [11]

One of those in favor of adult baptism was Philip Gell. He pointed out: "The alternative, however, still remains. Parents have right over their children either to seek baptism for them while they are infants, or to defer it till they can judge and make profession for themselves." [12]

In the new society of the mid-Victorian period, with its population movement and mass urbanization, many did defer the baptism of their infants, but not on any theological grounds; it was pure neglect. Charles Richard Sumner's Visitation Charge of 1862 tells of an open-air service, directed to reach the masses, at which notice was given that baptism would be administered on a particular day; this notice resulted in the baptism of 516 children. [13] The open-air service responsible for these baptisms may not have been a common feature in the Church's life at this period (although it was a form of evangelistic outreach used increasingly), but the situation it brings to light, of a general neglect of baptism among the masses, was all too common at this time.

NOTES

1. E. H. Hoare, **Baptism According to Scripture** (1850) 78-9.

2. Louisa Creighton, **Life and Letters of Mandell Creighton** (2 Vols. 1913) Vol. II, 67.

3. M. F. Sadler, **The Sacrament of Responsibility or Testimony of Scripture to the Teaching of the Church on Holy**

Baptism with special reference to the case of infants and answers to objections (new ed. 1870) lxiii–iv.

4. The Record, January 17th 1850.

5. George Moberly, Infant Baptism and Confirmation: Two Sermons Preached in Salisbury Cathedral (1876) 17.

6. E. B. Pusey, Parochial Sermons (1876) Vol. III, 20–2. See also Tracts for the Times Nos. 67, 68, 69.

7. Frederick Denison Maurice, The Church a Family: Twelve Sermons on the Occasional Services of the Prayer Book (1850) 47.

8. John Gibson, The Testimony of the Sacred Scriptures, The Church of the First Five Centuries and The Reformed Church of England to the Nature and Effects of Holy Baptism (1854), see 25–59.

9. But see Maurice, The Church A Family 46–7; Moberly, Infant Baptism and Confirmation 19–21.

10. Church Times, April 23rd 1875.

11. See E. Bickersteth, A Treatise on Baptism; Designed as a Help to Due Improvement of that Holy Sacrament, as administered in the Church of England (2nd ed. 1844) 105–35.

12. Philip Gell, Thoughts on the Liturgy; The Difficulties of an honest conscientious use of the Book of Common Prayer (1860) 41.

13. C. R. Sumner, A Charge, 1862 7.

D. The Ecumenical Significance of Baptism

The mid-Victorian baptismal controversy had a divisive effect upon the whole life of the Established Church. Conflict and controversy between Evangelicals and High Churchmen led to charges of heresy, demands for resignations and to numerous secessions. Even Broad Churchmen found their supposedly tolerant views on the subject resulting in further opposition and division.

There were many other issues relating to baptism which, during this period, were causes of division, not only in the Church of England. There was controversy over lay baptism, the registration of births, baptism and burial, and the language of the Baptismal Office in the Book of Common Prayer, to name but some. And yet, in spite of the endless controversies which surrounded this subject, there were those who saw baptism as a sacrament of union, uniting men with God, and with Christ the Head of the Church; uniting men with one another, uniting Christians across the barriers of schism and denominational differences. These voices were neither loud nor numerous and their impact was slight, but they were there and what they had to say did not always fall upon deaf ears.

Chief among the exponents of baptism as the sacrament of unity was the prophetic F. D. Maurice. While his book **The Kingdom of Christ** was written before the mid-Victorian period, Maurice lived through it (at least to 1872) and remained firm in the convictions he expressed in this work. For him baptism was above all else the means of entering the Kingdom of Christ. Very much aware of the theological differences between the various parties in the Church of England, he set out to show that each party held and expressed some valid truth, some facet of baptismal theology which was essential to an understanding of the whole. What each party taught was vital, but their error and weakness was the fact that they emphasized only a part of the truth, and their enthusiam to teach what they felt to be vital led them to deny other facets which were equally true and important. Maurice believed that the whole truth, a sound baptismal theology, could only be achieved by the fusing together of these many and varied views. [1]

Maurice saw the nature and function of baptism as providing an ordinance of divine institution, ordered by God as the means of entering the Kingdom of His Son, the Kingdom of Christ, marking a completely new relationship between God and man. The new relationship created through baptism was seen as one of union--a union with God in Christ, and between men. Maurice himself expressed his sacramental theology thus: "In the idea of sacrament is necessarily implied, that all the virtue and life of the creature consists in its union with a Being above itself. It is dead to itself; it lives in him". [2] His study of the Sacrament of Baptism led him to the conclusion that: "Baptism is a Sacrament, grounded upon the atonement made for mankind by Christ...", a belief also expressed by Robert Wilberforce. [3] Baptism is the first of the signs indicating the true state of mankind as a fellowship of Christ bound together in the Holy Spirit. "God", wrote Maurice, "has appointed this water, as the witness and seal of the universal fellowship established between man and man...". It brings men into a new relationship, out of separation, into union with God and man. [4] Too much emphasis upon what baptism does for the individual, as in the teaching of the High Church party, was seen by Maurice as a threat to the corporate nature of the Church. [5]

But baptism is not only the sacrament of constant union with God, it is also the sacrament of constant union with the whole people of God: "Baptism asserts for each man that he is taken into union with a Divine Person...But this assertion rests upon another, that there is a society for mankind which is constituted and held together in that Person...further it affirms that this unity among men rests upon a yet more aweful and perfect unity, upon that which is expressed in the Name of the Father, the Son and the Holy Ghost".

Constant union with God, membership in the Kingdom of Christ, constant union with the whole people of God, and membership of the human race, all find their place in Maurice's understanding of baptism as the sacrament of unity. Here is an exposition of the ecumenical significance of the Sacrament which defies and goes beyond conventional theological language and understanding. His insight into the ecumenical significance of baptism was, as in many other things, beyond the grasp and comprehension of many of his fellow churchmen.

In 1864 an ardent defender of the High Church position, Richard F. Littledale, wrote a reply to a Pastoral written by the Roman Catholic Bishop of Birmingham, William Ullathorne. In this reply he puts baptism forward as the sacrament of unity, saying that it admits us "into fellowship with the Church and into corporate union with the Church's Divine Head". By baptism we are made members of the Church Catholic. [6] He asks the question: "Is not the Church's unity broken so long as all baptised persons do not evidently belong to the same visible fold?" In spite of the schism in the Church, he feels that there must be some invisible unity underlying this outward division and this unity is grounded in baptism. [7] Can the corporate advantages of baptism be forfeited by non-Catholics? At what point do non-Catholics cease to be members of that Church Universal into which they were admitted at the font? These were but some of the questions on which he demanded an answer from the over-dogmatic Roman Catholics of his day. While his approach is on the negative side, in that he raises questions rather than gives theological answers, there is underlying what he says the conviction that through baptism we are made members of the Universal Catholic Church, and that in and through this Sacrament there is an indissoluble unity between the baptized members of the divided Church.

Another High Churchman who shared his conviction was William Allen Whitworth (1840-1905), a writer on both doctrinal and mathematical subjects, co-editor of The Messenger of Mathematics till 1880, and later Prebendary of St. Paul's. In an address to a branch meeting of the English Church Union Whitworth stated: "All the baptised are members of Christ, and baptised into the one Body. This One Baptism constitutes a real sacramental unity which cannot be broken--it creates something deeper than the cracks and fissures of schism--so that, after all, our unhappy divisions do not make the Church other than one". [8]

Mandell Crieghton and others spoke and wrote on the same lines and what all had to say on the ecumenical significance of baptism shows that at least some mid-Victorian Churchmen were not unaware of this important implication of the Sacrament.

If baptism was to have any ecumenical significance or value, its validity when administered by others must be unimpeachable. To meet the test of validity a number of conditions must be fulfilled. [9] During this period there were those who felt that it was of practical importance that baptisms duly administered by those outside the Church of England may, and ought to, be accepted by her ministers and people, without scruples, as truly valid. Such a charitable view was in fact no more than a recognition of the decision reached by the Court of Arches in the case of Martin and Escott, in 1841, that: "The law of the Church is beyond all doubt that a child baptised by a layman is validly baptised". [10] The only essentials were seen as the proper use of matter (water) and the proper words (the invocation of the three Persons of the Trinity). With this Judgement the official position of the Church of England was declared to be that she recognized and accepted the validity of lay baptism. But a Court decision did not satisfy everyone and some clergy of the Church of England persisted in looking upon all lay baptism and baptisms administered by Non-conformists (which they looked upon as lay baptisms) as invalid. And so, in spite of the official pronouncement in the case of Martin and Escott, lay baptism continued to be a vexed issue and a subject of controversy, not only within the Church of England, but between churchmen and those of other denominations. Bitter controversy on this issue both blinded men to the ecumenical significance of baptism and overshadowed and stultified what others were saying in this connection.

With the increase of population there was an increase of Dissenters and this, as the Religious Census of 1851 indicated, was not to be taken lightly. One result of this increase was the fact that baptisms by Dissenters were more numerous than ever before. For many churchmen this constituted a very real problem. How were such baptisms to be treated? Writing towards the end of the nineteenth century, Warwick Elwin expressed the feelings of many churchmen, especially those belonging to the High Church party, for whom the decision of 1841 was unacceptable. He regarded baptism by Dissenters as lay, unauthorized, heretical and schismatical. Such baptisms were grossly irregular and their validity uncertain. The only sufficient answer to such a dilemma was the conditional baptism of those baptized by Dissenters. [11]

Tractarians of the period included the Methodists with the Dissenters and charged them with heresy and unchurched them--they too were to receive conditional baptism.

Scottish Presbyterians, English Dissenters and Methodists who sought membership in the Church of England were treated by many churchmen as unbaptized, or their previous baptism being in such doubt as to require conditional baptism. But even Roman Catholics were not allowed to escape. The Guardian of 1852 reported the case of nine persons, eight from one family, converts from the Roman Catholic Church, who on being received into the Church of England were all baptized by the incumbent. This action was very much questioned by The Guardian. [12]

Within the Church of England there were those who saw the heart of the problem as being the confusion between validity and regularity. Lay and Dissentient baptisms could be seen as irregular and yet, at the same time, recognized as valid. Frederick Tymons, in a paper on 'The administration of Holy Baptism', argued that the bishop alone had a right to baptize--but under him the priest had the power to baptize--while the deacon, if no priest is present, may baptize. He discussed the question of lay baptism which he saw as valid, regular and lawful in cases of necessity. But he added: "Even in usurped, non-necessary administration of baptism, we must not confound validity with regularity". [13]

A very different approach was taken by Robert Isaac Wilberforce who, in his book **Church Courts and Church Discipline,** wrote of the disputed question of lay baptism, the validity of which may be readily admitted, by those who totally deny its efficiency. He observed that while there were those who accepted the validity of heretical and schismatical baptism, it was generally agreed that this did not admit them into the Church's communion until some subsequent act did away with their participation in schism and heresy. For many mid-Victorian churchmen this subsequent act was baptism based upon the complete rejection of the previous baptismal act. The alternative, seen by some as more charitable, was conditional baptism. [14] Other High Churchmen, however, saw the subsequent act as Confirmation.

One of them was George Moberly, consecrated Bishop of Salisbury in 1869, and another the moderate Edward Harold Browne, Bishop of Ely and later Bishop of Winchester who, had he been younger, might well have succeeded Tait as Archbishop of Canterbury; addressing the clergy and churchwardens at his Primary Visitation of 1865 he had some important things to say on the subject of lay baptism. The question had been put to him, privately, whether those baptized by a Dissenting minister, on seeking confirmation, ought to be first baptized. His public answer to the question was: "A Clergyman has no right to instil doubts as to the validity of his baptism into the minds of anyone who has been baptised with water in the name of the Holy Trinity". Iteration of baptism was not admissible. "Confirmation is the only legitimate means of supplying whatever may be defective in dissenting or lay baptism". [15] William Howley, Archbishop of Canterbury until 1848, accepted for Confirmation a Unitarian baptized in the name of God but not the threefold name, believing that the defects would be supplied at Confirmation. [16]

While men like Bishops Howley, Moberly and Browne were willing to accept the validity of lay and non-Anglican baptisms, seeing Confirmation as supplying anything which might be defective, some of their episcopal colleagues were unwilling to accept either their views or their solution. Prohibition of lay baptism was put forward for consideration at the first Lambeth Conference by Bishop William Mercer Green of Mississippi. He wrote to Archbishop Longley on August 5th 1867, expressing his approval of the projected Lambeth Conference and intimating his wish "that some general desire may be expressed by the Bishops for the more decided disapproval of Lay Baptism, and for its ultimate repudiation by the Church". [17] Green's feelings were shared by others but, at the time, the issue was not felt to be of sufficient magnitude to warrant a Lambeth pronouncement.

Thus the validity of lay and Non-conformist baptisms remained an open and vexed question. Instead of baptism being a sacrament of unity, it was all too often a cause of hostility, indifference and division, and thus for many, both within and without the Church of England, anything but an ecumenical sacrament.

NOTES

1. See Peter J. Jagger, "Baptism into the Kingdom of Christ: In the teaching of F. D. Maurice", **Faith and Unity** Vol. XVI, No. 3, July 1972, 52-5. This article shows how Maurice dealt with the situation which existed in the Church of England at that period and the synthesis he put forward.

2. Maurice, **Kingdom of Christ** Vol. I, 94.

3. Ibid., 115. See also Robert Isaac Wilberforce, **The Doctrine of Holy Baptism** 8-9.

4. Maurice, **Kingdom of Christ** Vol. I, 153-4. See also Davies, **Watts to Maurice** 307-8.

5. Maurice, **Kingdom of Christ** Vol. I, 96.

6. Richard Frederick Littledale, **Unity and the Rescript. A Reply to Bishop Ullathorne's Pastoral against the A.P.U.C.** (1864) 13. See also John Hungerford Pollen, **Narrative of Five Years at St. Saviour's Leeds** (Oxford 1851) 175-6.

7. Littledale, op. cit., 14.

8. William Allen Whitworth, Schism: An Address delivered at a Branch Meeting of the English Church Union (1889) 5.

9. See Peter J. Jagger, "Christian Unity and Valid Baptism", Theology Vol. LXXIV, No. 615, September 1971, 404-13.

10. See Walter George Frank Phillimore, **The Ecclesiastical Law of the Church of England** (2 Vols. 2nd ed. 1895) Vol. I, 491-501. Warwick Elwin, **The Minister of Baptism** (1889). Wil-

liam Maskell, **Holy Baptism: A Dissertation** (1848). William Maskell, A First Letter on the Present Position of the High Church Party in the Church of England... (1850) 48-9.

11. Elwin, op. cit., see 306-7, 319-23.

12. The Guardian, May 24th 1852, 194.

13. See Frederick Tymons, Notes on the Administration of Holy Baptism: A Paper... (Dublin n.d., c. 1867).

14. Robert Isaac Wilberforce, **Church Courts and Church Discipline** (1843) 112-14.

15. E. H. Browne, A Charge 1865 14-15.

16. See Edward Bellasis, Memorials of Mr. Serjeant Bellasis 1800-1873 (1895) 54-5. High Churchmen felt that in this case there was need for unconditional baptism as Unitarian baptism in the name of God was invalid.

17. MS. **Lambeth Papers: Archbishop Longley,** Vol. 6, Letter 286.

II. THE PASTORAL SITUATION

Introduction

During the nineteenth century baptism raised a number of pastoral issues affecting in various ways and degrees much of the life of the Church of England. Some of these issues were to the fore of the Church's life in the mid-Victorian period, but this does not imply that they were confined solely to this era.

The new urban society created numerous problems for the Established Church in her administration of baptism. A new phenomenon of the time was the growing neglect of the Sacrament. Rural life and close contact with the local parish priest had always encouraged parents to see that their children were baptized, and this as soon as possible. The threat of infant mortality, coupled with the Church's teaching that parents could be sure of the eternal salvation of their baptized infant who died prematurely, had been, and in many cases still were a stimulus to action. But for the majority living in the new urban areas, the teaching of the Church and her theological niceties were neither close nor very relevant. More relevant was the problem of obtaining Christian burial for a child who died unbaptized. For a short time the Registration Act caused a neglect of baptism, but this was the result of confusion rather than of objections to the Sacrament. A major difficulty was that of procuring sponsors who fulfilled the requirements of the Church, or even people who were willing to fulfil the office of sponsorship. Insufficient churches and the inaccessibility of existing churches, plus the inadequate number of clergy to meet the needs of the vastly increased population all made their contribution towards the growing neglect and indifference of the masses with regard to baptism.

Moreover, while the new society raised a number of unprecedented problems for the Church of England, her own internal conflicts and difficulties hampered many of her attempts to deal with the new situation in which she found herself. Many churchmen felt that the conflict surrounding the Gorham Judgement did considerable damage in the field of baptism, causing uncertainty and neglect among the laity, and confusion and hostility among the clergy.

In considering the pastoral problems it will be seen how at least some of these were very much bound up with underlying theological principles, for example in the case of sponsors and burial. In a few cases, pressure from outside the Established Church brought the issue into a wider area of conflict; for example, education in church schools, which included the teaching of the Catechism and baptismal instruction, and also the problems connected with burial. Churchmen were divided in their attitudes towards these issues; some opposed the reform which was being demanded by outsiders, while others were willing to try to rectify those aspects of the Church's organization and teaching which were hindering her work and effectiveness.

A. The Neglect of Baptism

Confirmation figures are a prominent feature in many Episcopal Charges of this period; they were often compared and analysed, criticized and praised. Here, it was felt, was evidence of the Church's evangelistic success or failure. The Victorian concern for, and interest in, facts and figures is seen in the many tables attached to Episcopal Charges relating to increased church buildings, building funds, schools and scholars, Sunday schools and attendance, missionary giving and Confirmation returns, but this concern did not generally embrace baptism. While aware of the growing neglect of baptism, there was little attempt to introduce baptismal returns in order to analyse the problem; in fact, figures relating to baptism are found in very few publications of the period. While bishops used their Charges to bring important issues before their clergy, the decline and neglect of baptism, and the pastoral problems connected with this Sacrament were rarely mentioned.

Unlike confirmation figures, those relating to baptism were in fact not easily obtainable by the bishops, or indeed by the ecclesiastical authorities in general. An Act of 1812 directed that churchwardens should send copies of their registers, annually, to the registrar of the diocese. The efficiency of church wardens in this matter eludes analysis because registrars did not generally keep copies of returns for extensive periods; this also means that national figures are unobtainable, and it is impossible to establish a full or accurate assessment of the position. From the available evidence no more than a very general picture of the situation, as it existed in this period, can be built up.

There were some churchmen who were opposed to the idea of making parochial returns. Indeed, when it was suggested at the Canterbury Convocation of 1859 that the bishop's annual questions might be extended to include questions relating to the number of baptisms, persons confirmed, congregations and communicants, there was very strong disapproval and opposition to the suggestion. Some felt that such statistics were unnecessary and would not add to the Church's efficiency, and if made public they could be wrongly used and could do a great deal of harm to the Church. [1] No doubt Non-conformist use of the 1851 Religious Census caused many churchmen to feel uneasy about such suggestions. A few churchmen, however, were interested in baptismal figures and the extent to which the Sacrament was being neglected. An article in the Church Times of 23rd May 1863 tells of a Lenten Mission in which the visitation of 1,200 houses revealed that, of their occupants, nearly 400 were unbaptized. The Bishop of London felt that this neglect of baptism was the fault of the Church. He suggested that careless and irregular administration of the Sacrament, the mutilation of the Office and the insignificant place often assigned to the font, were some of the main causes of this neglect. A more careful observance of what the Church directed concerning this Sacrament, plus careful and systematic teaching by the clergy, would he believed lead to a greater understanding and valuation of baptism. [2]

When William D. Maclagan, later Archbishop of York, was appointed to the living of Newington in 1869, he found that because of the non-residence of the former incumbent, baptism had been much neglected and a considerable number of children were unbaptized. One of his first and chief aims was to seek out all who had been so neglected. On his first Easter day in the parish he baptized fifty children in the afternoon and thirty adults in the evening. [3] With a parish population of 15,000 he found that to rectify such neglect was no easy task. Charles Fuge Lowder tells of how, on arriving at St. George's Mission, East London in 1856, he found a large number of children, of various ages, as well as numerous adults, unbaptized. Even after 2,500 baptisms, because of the influx of population and the ignorance and prejudice of many parents, much still remained to be done. [4] A letter to the Editor of The Guardian in 1850 suggested that the neglect of baptism was rampant in densely populated districts, where thousands were served by only a couple of clergymen. [5] Even John Keble in his small country curé was aware of the widening influence of this neglect and warned his village congregation about it. He told them never to neglect baptism as did many, especially in large towns: "Whatever becomes of you and wherever you go...never be at all slack nor encourage others to be slack about Holy Baptism". [6]

Henry Edward Manning, who left the Church of England and joined the Church of Rome because the Gorham Judgement destroyed his faith in Anglicanism, wrote to Pusey in 1864 saying he believed "that the number of those who have never been baptised to be very great in England, and to be increasing every year". He attributed this neglect to a number of factors: (i) the formal disbelief in baptismal regeneration in a number of Protestant ministers, (ii) the studied rejection, as a point of religious profession, of the practice of infant baptism, (iii) the sinful unbelief and neglect of parents in every class of the English people, who often leave whole families of children to grow up without baptism. He did, however, feel that there had been some improvement. He also admitted that during the last thirty years there had been a revival of care among Anglican clergy in the administration of baptism and of attention on the part of parents in bringing their children to baptism; but at the same time he felt that this reaction was by no means proportionate to increasing neglect. [7]

High Churchmen of the period occasionally charged Evangelicals with a neglect of this Sacrament. [8] Because of their high doctrine of baptism, Tractarians were zealous to baptize as many candidates as possible and to this end they sought out all who had not received this sacrament of new life. Evangelicals, on the other hand, with their emphasis upon conversion, did not share the fervor of their more Catholic brethren, although there were some exceptions to the rule, and not all Evangelicals were neglectful, as most High Churchmen inferred. Perhaps a more accurate picture of the situation was given in a Christian Observer of the period, where the writer admitted: "Individuals undoubtedly there have been and still are, who may be justly open to the charge...but we must not judge of the whole by a comparatively small part". He goes on to show how Evangelicals of the period did anything but neglect the sacrament of baptism. [9]

Honest churchmen of the period were willing to admit that the increasing neglect of baptism was, to some extent, the fault of the Church and that some internal reform and renewal would help to rectify what appeared to be an ever-worsening situation. Concern about it prompted members of the English Church Union to send a Petition to Convocation 'On the notorious neglect of Public Baptism in many parishes'. Reasons for this neglect were given as (i) failure to bring it to the notice of the public, (ii) the neglect of clergy to warn people to bring their children for public baptism, (iii) suppression of the Church's voice in respect of the fundamental doctrine of regeneration. [10] This petition indicates the conviction of at least one group that the neglect of baptism was largely due to the failures of the clergy.

Undoubtedly the Church of the mid-Victorian period must take some blame for this increasing neglect of baptism, but it was also largely due to factors beyond her control. The vastly increased population and the mushrooming of the new urban communities created problems which proved too much, not only for the Church, but for many others. In such a rapidly changing situation the Church cannot be altogether blamed for not having sufficient clergy to cope, or indeed for the lack of Church buildings in the right places. Nor can she take all the blame for the ignorance and neglect among the masses. Lowder tells of how, among the dockland population, there was a tremendous ignorance about baptism which kept many away from the Sacrament. He tells of how some seemed to think that it was something like vaccination and asked if it would hurt them. The growth of secularism, advocated through lectures and pamphleteers, helped to create resentment among the poor towards both Christianity and its official representatives, and persuaded at least some not to have their children baptized. [11]

The problem of obtaining sponsors deterred many from having their children baptized, workhouse chaplains for example found that this prevented their having inmates baptized in the parish church. To solve this problem Archbishop Tait stated in Convocation that workhouse chaplains could use the service of private baptism, obviating the need for sponsors and thus avoiding the neglect of baptism among the workhouse inmates. Such baptisms were to be registered as 'private' in the register of the parish church in which the workhouse was situated. [12]

An examination of the available evidence reveals how some churchmen during this period were not only acutely aware of the increasing neglect of baptism, but also deeply concerned about how the situation could be rectified. Some parish clergy took the matter into their own hands. Such a priest was the vicar of the parish of Christ Church, Luton, which had a population of 15,000. He wrote a pamphlet to his parishioners explaining what he thought were the reasons for this neglect and emphasizing the need for parents to seek baptism for their children. He outlined three classes of neglectors: (i) The Ignorant who confound baptism with Registration, supposing that when their children have been registered it is "as though they have been baptised". With this he connects the idea that parents bring their children to baptism to be given their name and not because they see baptism as entrance into the Church of Christ. (ii) The Negligent, those who know what baptism is all about and believe it is the right thing to be done, but who keep putting off the baptism of their children, and this continually, until in many cases whole families of children go unbaptized. Such a situation must have been very prevalent in the new urban areas. (iii) The Mistaken, the Baptists, who neglect infant baptism--to these could be added others like secularists. [13]

But such ignorance over the meaning and importance
of baptism was not confined to the lower classes. The biographer
A. W. Tilby, writing of Lord John Russell, says: "To him, as
perhaps to the majority of laymen, baptism was merely a formal
ceremony of initiation, a species of ecclesiastical birth certificate". [14] If such a highly educated man as Lord John Russell
could hold such an opinion, how can the ignorant working-class
parents be blamed for confusing Registration with baptism?

Registration

The general indifference and ignorance of the masses
living in the new industrial conurbations, coupled with the increasing alienation of this class from the Established Church, were
major factors in the growing neglect of baptism. Among government attempts to administer effectively the new society was
the Registration Act of 1837. This Act was one of the greatest
single factors which caused a considerable decrease in the number
of children baptized in the Church of England, as Bishop C.
T. Longley of Ripon recognized. When addressing his clergy
in 1841 he said that the neglect of baptism had "unhappily become more prevalent through the prejudicial influence of the
Registration Act".

Before this Act the only record and legal evidence
of births was in the baptismal registers of the parish churches.
This led some Dissenters to have their children baptized in the
parish church, purely for civil reasons, rather than in their own
chapel. The parish church registers were also the only legal
records of marriages and deaths. Dissenters listed this as one
of their grievances, in support of disestablishment. [15] Irregularities, negligence and inefficiency among the clergy of the Established Church were put forward in support of the call for a
civil registration, separate from that of the parish churches.

As early as 1834 Dissenters began to demand a general
registration of births, marriages and deaths, and the right to
baptize, marry and bury according to their own forms. To achieve
this they began to petition the House of Commons. [16] Strictly
speaking, the system of the Established Church providing legal
evidence of births was defective, in that parish registers recorded
baptisms and not births. In spite of growing opposition to the
system, the Government of the time felt they had no officials
whom they thought sufficiently competent to discharge this
duty, and they were unwilling, at that time, to incur the expense

of a separate staff to undertake the work. William Brougham, the Lord Chancellor's brother, brought the matter before Parliament in 1834, but the scheme was not accepted. In 1836 Lord John Russell brought in the Registration Bill, for which he had been fighting since 1834, and in 1837 the Registration Act was passed and came into force on the first of March in that year. [17]

Churchmen were deeply concerned about the separation between civil registration and baptism and many of them felt that baptism was a sufficient registration for members of the Established Church. Some clergy expressed this conviction in a variety of ways--vocally, by placards and through letters to their parishioners. At least some of the laity shared their priest's convictions, or accepted and obeyed what he said; some refused to provide the Registrar with the necessary information and paid the penalty of either a summons or even imprisonment. [18] Just before the implementation of the Act there was, at least in some places, an increase in the number of baptisms under the old law. On the Sunday before the Act, the collegiate church at Manchester, which was accustomed to baptize some sixty children each Sunday, baptized three hundred and sixty. [19]

At least some churchmen appreciated the feelings of those Dissenters who wanted a legal registration of births, marriages and deaths, without having to submit to religious rites to which they conscientiously objected. Many of them sincerely and strongly objected to compulsory conformity to the rites and ceremonies of the Established Church. Bishop John Kaye told his clergy that, if these things were a cause of hardship to Dissenters, they were hardships in the removal of which he would "most cordially co-operate". [20]

From its introduction, the new law requiring legal registration of every birth was the cause of much confusion; many people were uncertain whether or not it abolished the need for baptism. Certainly many of the unchurched masses believed this to be the implication, while most Dissenters no longer felt the need to take their children to the parish church for baptism. To combat the confusion created by the new Act, the S.P.C.K., in 1840, published a leaflet entitled Registration and Baptism. The leaflet, produced in the form of a letter from The Minister of the Parish to Christian Parents stated: "This letter is to caution you against a strange notion which sometimes prevails that the Registration of the birth does away with the necessity of Baptism". It went on to say that the duty of parents to bring their child "to be christened--that is, made a member of the Church of Christ by the holy Sacrament of Baptism--remains altogether unchanged". "Remember", says the letter, "that a child until it is baptised remains in a heathen state; is not a member of the Church of Christ". The letter ends with an earnest exhortation that the parents do not neglect the baptism of their infant, but present it at the font without delay. In spite of such attempts to clarify the situation, and remove the confusion caused by the Registration Act, it remained a cause of continual decline in the number of baptisms administered by the Church. Bishop Phillpotts, in his Charge of 1842, told his clergy of a situation inherited by one clergyman in a large populous mining parish: "He found a lamentable and growing deficiency in the parochial register of the baptised". To attribute the situation entirely to the Registration Act did not satisfy him. He set out to rectify the situation, preaching about it to his congregation, and talking to non-churchgoers in their homes; he also wrote tracts on the subject, which he distributed to those unable to hear him either at church or in their homes. His work in this field was met by opposition and abuse, anonymous letters and tracts. But, remarked Phillpotts, before the year was over, scores of children whose baptism had been suspended by Registration, were brought to the font. His congregation increased, his communicants increased threefold and confirmation candidates were more than fourfold. Phillpotts urged his clergy to follow the example of this zealous clergyman.

Letters published in religious newspapers of the period reveal a number of other problems created by the Registration Act; they also offered various solutions to eliminate the confusion which continued to prevail in spite of verbal and written exhortation, by bishops to their clergy and clergy to their people. A letter to The English Churchman objected to the practice of giving the Christian Name at Registration, thus prior to baptism. "The Act of Parliament does not", says the writer, "demand that the Christian name be given prior to baptism, it says the child's Christian name to be given, if any". There is no need to return to the Registrar to give the name after baptism. The child's Christian name will be registered by the Clergyman who baptises it and that will be sufficient for every purpose". Confusion on this issue was to continue for many years.

A letter to The Guardian suggested a possible means of removing the confusion: a notice from the Registrar, fixed on the church door, would help. Such a Notice might read: "Several persons having ignorantly supposed that to register their children's birth is the same as baptism, I am requested to give notice that my registration does not do away with the necessity for baptism, nor entitle any children whatsoever to the rite of Christian burial". ...Registrar. [21] While this suggestion was felt to be of some value, it was observed that the misinformed masses, who never entered a church, would never see such a notice.

Further correspondence on the subject continued to

appear in the pages of The Guardian. One correspondent expressed what he believed was the attitude of the masses: "The unfortunate system, which in their minds is designed to supercede the necessity and, as a matter of fact, in nine cases out of ten does practically discourage the administration of baptism to their children". This writer was reflecting on the situation as it was in 1851, fourteen years after the introduction of the Act.

A letter to the Church Review in 1865 tells how clergymen were finding that poor parishioners were being put to great inconvenience and cost by having to give notice of a birth to a distant Registrar. This same point was still being raised by the clergy ten years later. [22]

Whatever mid-Victorian churchmen felt on this subject the voice of Dissenters and Secularists eventually won the day. Civil Registration was established by Act of Parliament and the privileged position of the Established Church was weakened even further. The worst fears of some of the clergy had come to pass, in that registration did cause a considerable decline in the number of infants baptized in the Church. One more link between the Church and the unchurched urban masses had been severed. However, the change was not without its good effects: it did help to remove the tension and opposition of Dissenters. It did help to clarify the meaning and purpose of baptism, although the confusion of baptism as the giving of the Christian name with the true purpose of the Sacrament, as entrance into the Church of Christ, continued to create problems and misunderstanding. The decrease in the number of baptisms stimulated some of the clergy to greater evangelistic activity, forcing them to go out among their people to try to clarify a confused issue. In many ways what the Church lost by the introduction of the Registration Act was the vast number of meaningless and conventional baptisms, rather than the baptism of the children of the faithful. Nevertheless, it did weaken the Church, in that it gave the Dissenters more opportunity to increase their strength and position by baptizing the children of parents living in the overcrowded industrial areas. Further, Dissenting baptisms and the general neglect of baptism raised another controversial issue, that of the necessity of baptism for Christian burial.

NOTES

1. Chronicle of Convocation, February 1859, 85-6.

2. C. J. Blomfield, A Charge, 1850, 36-7.

3. F. D. How, **Archbishop Maclagan: Being a Memoir** (1911) 80-1.

4. C. F. Lowder, **Twenty-one Years in St. George's Mission: An account of its origin, progress and works of charity** (1877) 100.

5. The Guardian September 10th 1850, 643. This neglect in over-populated slum areas was rectified to some extent by the zealous work of numerous High Church priests. In the district of St. Alban the Martyr it is recorded how between 1884-1894 there were 8,237 baptisms, see **Father Pollock and His Brother: Mission Priests of St. Alban's Birmingham** (1911) 41.

6. John Keble, **Village Sermons on the Baptismal Service** (1869) 33.

7. Henry Edward Manning, **The Working of the Holy Spirit in the Church of England. A Letter to the Rev. E. B. Pusey** (1864) 9-12.

8. Anonymous, **Who are the Ritualists? A Warning** (n.d. c.1874) 4-5.

9. The Christian Observer February 1852, 85-6.

10. See G. Bayfield Roberts, **The History of the English Church Union** (1895) 20.

11. See Owen Chadwick, The Established Church under Attack in **The Victorian Crisis of Faith,** Anthony Symondson, ed. (1970) 93.

12. See correspondence on this subject in The Guardian, May 26th 1875, 672.

13. See T. J. Lee, **A Clergyman's Advice and Counsel to his Parishioners on the subject of Infant Baptism** (1864).

14. A Wyatt Tilby, **Lord John Russell: A Study in civil and religious liberty** (1930) 115-16.

15. Owen Chadwick, **The Victorian Church**, Part 1 (2nd ed. 1970) 80-1. But there is evidence that even before the Registration Act the children of at least some Methodists were being baptized outside the parish church. See Bernard C. Holland, **Baptism in Early Methodism** (1970) 104-16, 170-6.

16. William Law Mathieson, **English Church Reform, 1815-1840** (1923) 110-12.

17. See 6 & 7 Wm. IV c.85. **Hansard**, xxii, 400; xxiii, 950; xxvi, 1092; xxix, 12; xxxi, 368-70, 375-7; xxxiv, 1023, 1122.

18. British Magazine. 14, 1838, 326, 362.

19. British Magazine, 11, 1837, 475 cf. 10, 1836, 620.

20. J. Kaye, A Charge 1834, 91.

21. The Guardian, August 27th 1851.

22. Church Review, August 12th 1865, 752. The Guardian, January 13th 1875, 47.

B. Baptism and Christian Burial

Two separate issues were involved in the controversy which surrounded the subject of baptism and Christian burial. First, there was the question of those baptized by Dissenters and laymen: could the Established Church accept such baptisms as valid, giving the recipients the right to Christian burial according to the Prayer Book Service? Secondly, there was the problem of the widespread neglect of baptism: to neglect baptism was to forego the right to Christian burial.

The subject of lay baptism and the right of those who had received such baptism to Christian burial underwent an extensive and elaborate debate in the case of Kemp vs. Wickes. The Reverend John Wight Wickes, an Anglican clergyman, refused to bury an infant child of two of his parishioners who had been baptized by a Dissenting Minister. On December 11th 1809 Sir John Nicholl declared his Judgement in the case: that a child baptized by a Dissenter with water and the invocation to the Trinity, was baptized in the sense of the rubric to the Burial Service, and of the 68th Canon, and therefore that the burial of such a child was obligatory on the clergyman. It was pointed out that the promulgation of the Canon in 1603, before the legal existence of Dissenters, could have no possible reference to those who were later to bear such a title. It was felt that the Canon in question related to baptisms performed by lay people in cases of emergency. Nicholl's Judgement was followed by numerous publications, showing how many churchmen were unwilling to accept either the Judgement or the conclusions of the investigation. Refusing to accept the Judgement, some churchmen still refused Christian burial where valid baptism was in doubt.

The subject came to the fore in Church life once again when, in 1839, T. S. Escott, the vicar of Gedney, Lincolnshire, refused to bury Elizabeth Ann Cliff, a child baptized by a Wesleyan Minister. Escott argued that the minister was not in Holy Orders. Consequently the baptism was lay baptism and as such invalid; the child could not, therefore, be buried with the Prayer Book Service for Burial. On May 8th 1841, Sir Herbert Jenner-Fust delivered his Judgement on this case, known as Mastin vs. Escott; he confirmed the Judgement pronounced thirty years before in the case of Kemp vs. Wickes. Once again a variety of publications followed a Judgement which many found unacceptable. Another case was brought before Jenner-Fust in 1844, when action was taken against the Rev. W. H. Chapman for refusing the Church's Burial Service to an infant baptized by an Independent Minister. In this case, Tichmarsh vs. Chapman, Chapman pleaded that the baptism was heretical and schismatical and therefore void. The Judgement laid down that: "Both lay and heretical baptism are irregular and contrary to the order of the Church; but both are valid for the purpose of burial". The child was said to be sufficiently baptized to have a legal claim to burial. But in saying this Jenner Fust pointed out that the Court was not entering into any theological controversy: "To what extent the sufficiency goes, is not for this Court to determine, whether it does, or does not, confer spiritual grace, the Court gives no opinion". Some later writers on the cases of Kemp vs. Wickes, Mastin vs. Escott, Tichmarsh vs. Chapman, were at pains to show that all that these cases decided was that lay baptism is 'sufficient' to give a person, so baptized, the legal right to be buried in a churchyard; they were not making any pronouncement on the theological validity of lay baptism. Such an interpretation was usually given by High Churchmen, for whom lay baptism always included dissenting baptisms.

Contrary to expectation, these official Judgements did not bring an end to this controversy and some churchmen continued to refuse Christian burial where valid baptism was in doubt. Tractarians tended to be the most difficult and dogmatic on this issue, while other clergy of the Church of England believed this refusal to be both wrong and misinformed. The view was expressed by many that the formularies of the Church were never intended to exclude those who had been baptized with the correct form and matter, but not by a person in Holy Orders. The rubric of the Burial Office only forbade its use to those dying unbaptized.

The High Church Bishop Henry Phillpotts gave his own interpretation of the Judgement of Escott, which he expressed in his Charge of 1842: "It only decided...that a minister is bound to bury an infant, who has been baptised by a layman. It did not...decide that he is bound to bury an adult who, having been so baptised, had never sought to have the deficiencies of his baptism duly supplied". Bishop Edward Copleston of Llandaff, in the same year, expressed the view that the decision of the court on the matter of burial should be accepted, but he felt that such baptisms were still in need of completion, either by solemnly receiving the infant into the Church or by Confirmation. While he did not wish to bar those outside the pale of the Church of England from Christian burial, he did object to the minister of the parish being compelled to read the service of the Church over those who neither belonged to, nor wished to belong to, the Church of England. [1]

During the years which followed the Judgements of the 1840's there was a growing opposition to the indiscriminate use of the Order of the Burial of the Dead, which eventually led to the presentation of a Memorial to the Archbishops and Bishops. Members of both Evangelical and Tractarian parties signed the memorial which, on the surface, seemed to indicate a certain degree of unanimity in this matter. However, a letter to the Editor of The Record entitled "Memorial Respecting the Burial of the Dead' pointed out that Tractarians supported the Memorial because they did not recognize dissenting baptism. But, suggested the writer, Evangelicals supporting the Memorial "have not thoroughly considered what the Memorial asks". Correspondence which followed brought to light numerous cases where burial had been refused to those baptized by Dissenters. [2]

The issue remained a point of controversy throughout mid-Victorian times. Indeed, the correspondence columns of the Church Times in 1875, at the end of this period, show how the burial issue, especially in relation to Dissenters and those baptized by them, was still very much a live question [3]; even in 1885 a Barrister, Charles Henry Glascodine, in a paper to the Cardiff branch of the English Church Union, spoke scathingly of the very churchyards of the Church of England being thrown open to all. [4]

To later and more liberally-minded generations the controversy surrounding the burial of those baptized by Dissenters in the churchyards of the parish churches of England has little meaning or significance. But for those who lived through the period and the controversy, the issues were not at all simple. For many members of the Church of England, to allow such burials implied that the Church knew no difference between Dissenters, or those actively opposed to her, and her own most attached and dedicated members. Dissenters charged the Church with bigotry and a fear that she would desecrate her churchyards through the burial of Dissenters; this latter point seems to have been confined chiefly to the minds of Dissenters. Most churchmen were concerned about the question of who was and who was not a fit subject for burial in consecrated ground set aside for the burial of Christians, according to a service intended to commit such departed persons to God's eternal keeping. Legally the clergy of the Established Church were bound to bury all but the unbaptized and those who had committed suicide. [5]

Hard uncharitable words and bitter accusations were uttered by some Dissenters against the clergy of the Church of England, some of whom did deserve the attack. Heated controversy over the burial rights of those who had received either lay or Dissenter's baptism caused many churchmen, and Dissenters, to lose sight of a much graver problem, the neglect of baptism among the masses living in the sprawling slums of the new industrial areas. In these new communities were vast numbers of children of non-practising Christian parents, who, for various reasons, had not been baptized and were thus neither legally nor spiritually eligible for burial in consecrated ground, with the use of a Christian burial service. During a Canterbury Convocation debate on Prayer Book Revision, one speaker, Canon Potter, spoke of such burials as being rather like the burial of dogs, without any Christian service being read over them. It was the distressing nature of such burials, and the desire to have departed loved ones buried in a religious and devout manner, in consecrated ground, which acted as a goad to many parents to procure baptism for their infants at the earliest possible moment. Fear of children dying unbaptized prompted many to seek baptism within a few days of birth; indeed, in some cases within a few hours. This same sense of urgency was also one of the reasons behind the widespread practice of private baptisms. With the Church's firm refusal to give Christian burial to unbaptized infants, plus the ever-present threat of death, the hostility of Dissenters and the laity was understandable.

During the nineteenth century the infant mortality rate was very high, because of the appalling social conditions. Many mothers, forced by poverty to work long hours, neglected their babies and infants, either leaving them alone or farming them out to 'baby minders', who often fed them badly and un-hygienically. There was also the practice of keeping babies quiet by administering what were called 'infant preservatives' containing narcotics, such as Godfrey's Cordial, which often resulted in premature death. Those children who survived these hazards often succumbed to the long hours, excessive work and unhealthy, even dangerous, conditions in the mills and workshops which employed them. Such a social environment never allowed parents to ignore the threat of death which hung over themselves and their children.

In 1854 a letter to The Guardian stated that many of the poor only sought baptism "as an introduction to Christian burial". [6] and five years later J. C. Proby was writing to the Bishop of Winchester: "This last solemn rite is, I am firmly persuaded, in 999 cases out of 1,000, the one and only reason that induces parents to bring their children to be baptised". He was sure that if unbaptized infants were to be buried with the same service as the baptized, there would be very few baptized infants to be found among those of the poorer classes. [7] Powerful as it was, the ever-present threat of premature death, even combined with the Church's laws which denied Christian burial to the unbaptized, was not enough to prevent the majority of parents in the new large densely populated industrial areas from neglecting baptism and this led to many refusals of Christian burial to such children.

Failure to have children baptized was, in many cases, due to the indifference or the lack of concern of parents. There were also adults who, for various reasons, had not been baptized as infants, and as adults were reluctant to present themselves for baptism; in this category were many who were regular churchgoers. When death overtook such people, even though they had professed and practised the Christian Faith, they were not eligible for Christian burial. These, and other such hard cases, caused deep concern and distress for many clergymen. Eventually this concern led to the matter being debated in the Canterbury Convocations of 1873, at which there was a move to draw up a service to be used in such hard cases.

Those who opposed the suggestion still remained firmly convinced that no form of service should be provided for the unbaptized and, in the end, their opinion prevailed. And so, at the end of the mid-Victorian period, the issue continued to be one of controversy--a deeply felt pastoral problem for some, and a theological dilemma for others. One can only assume, for in the nature of the case no evidence is available, that the more liberally-minded and the more charitable, would from time to time turn a blind eye to the letter of ecclesiastical law and, using the Church's Burial Service, bury 'such hard cases', even though unbaptized. On the other hand, High Churchmen in their doctrinal rigor continued to apply the letter of the law and refused to carry out such burials using the Burial Service, however distressing to the bereaved. In doing this they were, in the case of the unbaptized, being loyal to the Prayer Book. This denial of Christian burial to the unbaptized and, in numerous cases, to those baptized by laymen and Dissenters, caused deep distress. Such churchmen, however right they may have been, helped to drive a deeper wedge between the Established Church and the people of the nation, for there is evidence that in some of these cases the mourners sought other ministers to officiate at the funeral.

NOTES

1. Bricknell, **Tractarian Theology** 321-2. Bricknell gathers together a considerable amount of evidence on this subject, see 281-322. See also C. S. Grueber, A Letter on the Proposed Alteration of the Order for the Burial of the Dead (1863).

2. The Record, January 23rd 1851; January 27th 1851; March 20th 1851.

3. See Church Times 1875, 429, 439, 604, 660. Also an article on 'The Burial Bill' Church Times, April 30th 1875, which expressed the dissatisfaction of some against the Bill.

4. Charles Henry Glascodine, **Establishment and Discipline** (1885) 13.

5. See Church Quarterly Review, Vol. II, April 1876-July 1876, which contains a valuable contemporary article on the subject 'The Burial Question', which traces the evolution of the controversy up to 1876.

6. The Guardian, August 9th 1854, 626.

7. J. C. Proby, A Letter to the Right Rev. The Lord Bishop of Winchester on the Revision and Re-arrangement of the Liturgy (Winchester, 1859) 7.

C. Baptismal Instruction

There were many facets to the baptismal problem faced by the Church of England during the period of this study. Ignorance concerning the true nature and purpose of baptism, further confused by the Registration Act, caused many parents to neglect the baptism of their children. There was also an increasing neglect of the Christian Faith and the organized church by the vast majority of the working-class, even among those who had been baptized in infancy. Unbaptized churchgoing adults who failed to rectify this omission plus those who, through population movement, had gradually drifted from the Church, all helped to create a new situation for the Church. Instruction and Christian education were seen by not a few churchmen, from all parties, as part of the answer to the complex problem, the growing neglect of baptism.

The Church of England, as the Church of the nation, had a sense of duty and responsibility in addition to an obligation to offer religious education to the people of the land, not only to children, but also to adults. It was thought that if parents were instructed in the Christian Faith they would not neglect the baptism of their children and would also realize their responsibility to train their children in the Faith and in morals. Such education needed to be extended to all classes of the community.

For at least some churchmen the issue of education was not unrelated to baptism. Archdeacon G. A. Denison believed baptism was an essential preliminary to education in any church school: "I cannot take one step in educating a child who has neither received or is not...in a definite course of preparation for Holy Baptism: and in the latter case I should not admit the child into the school until Holy Baptism has been received". [1] For Denison such views were by no means theoretical; in practice he refused to allow into his schools any child who had not been baptized and received into the Church, although he realized that others did not share this conviction. Some churchmen felt that it was right to admit unbaptized children into church schools, but not to teach them the Catechism. [2] Yet others felt that if such children were to be admitted into church schools, then they ought to be taught the Catechism.

Among the clergy there was concern over the need to educate parents in order that they might understand the meaning of baptism and realize the need to have their children baptized, and also understand the responsibility of the Church to provide a Christian education for her baptized children. Evidence of the actual instruction of parents immediately prior to the baptism of their children is sparse. John Keble's views on this matter, expressed in his sermons on the Baptismal Office, probably reflect the feelings and practice of at least some of his brother clergy. In these sermons he puts forward the plea that parents should give sufficient notice of a request for baptism to allow the Pastor to have "time to enquire about the persons intended to be sponsors and, if need be, to talk with them or with the parents, since...all who take part should at least be trying to be holy". [3]

Pre-baptismal instruction of children was thought to be necessary and was in fact practiced by members of all the ecclesiastical parties. For slum priests and Sisters the preparation of adults, young people and children was a priority in pastoral work. Where such preparation was carried out it was done with care and conviction, often resulting in many baptisms. William D. Maclagan, an avowed advocate of such preparation, committed a large part of this work to his parish workers. He tells of how baptismal instruction of children was given in their homes in the presence of their mothers. Such instruction sometimes resulted in unbaptized parents hearing, for the first time, the meaning of this Sacrament and being moved to offer themselves for baptism. [4]

The baptismal controversies of the period, especially that surrounding the Gorham Judgement, and the confusion they caused in the minds of both clergy and laity, did not help those who took baptismal instruction seriously. In view of such controversies, what were they to teach? If they taught the views of their party it was realized, at least by the educated laity, that other and often opposing views were both held and taught within the Church of England. Following the Gorham Judgement, Walter John Trower, Bishop of Glasgow, wrote in a Pastoral Letter to his clergy that the implications of the Judgement would make the priest's work as a teacher most difficult: "In educating children, and also in teaching our people, it makes a wide difference whether we address them as possessors of a gift and grace sufficient to incline their will and to strengthen their natural inability to please God; or whether we teach them that they must wait for such a gift, without which they cannot serve God acceptably". [5]

Once baptism had been administered, either to infants, children or adults, it was felt by many clergy that further grounding in the faith was required and this depended largely upon the help of others. Among attempts to meet this need was a book written by John Gibson, called **The Nature and Effects**

of Holy Baptism. Gibson hoped that it would be suitable for young persons of serious, thoughtful minds. He reminded parents of their responsibility to watch over their baptized infants, calling upon them to bring them up in the way of Christ. They were to speak to their children concerning the meaning of their baptism, encouraging them to prepare for confirmation. He considered it a great thing for parents to have a book, which they could put in the hands of an intelligent son or daughter, and say: "There is what the Primitive Church really did hold as to Baptism. There is what the Church of England really does teach". [6] His earnest piety was typical of many sincere people of the Victorian period, but a reader today will probably wonder if he was not over-optimistic, for his book contains 419 pages of far from easy reading, in a rather homiletic style.

Post-baptismal instruction, general religious instruction in day schools, and catechetical instruction in both church and school were, of course, very much bound up with preparation for confirmation and it is in this sphere that a considerable amount of evidence is available, giving a valuable insight into the ideas and practice of mid-Victorian churchmen.

Sin After Baptism

A subject not unrelated to post-baptismal instruction, and the Christian way of life expected of the baptized, is that of sin after baptism. It was, however, a problem chiefly for members of the High Church party. The perils of post-baptismal sin were the subject of much Tractarian teaching and writing; the faithful were admonished to avoid such sin because of its fearful consequences. The Tractarians taught that even the baptized can, through sin, lose the privilege of being children of God. The chief High Church exponent of the subject was Edward Bouverie Pusey and it was around him that controversy became most heated.

It was Dr. Pusey's high doctrine of baptism which brought him, and many others, face to face with the problem of post-baptismal sin. He saw it as deadly and believed there was no absolute renewal provided after that of baptism. [7] In one of his Parochial Sermons Pusey outlines the ideal development of one who, through holy baptism, has been made a child of God; he concludes: "This is the happy lot of those who, though more or less slowly, still steadfastly on the whole, grow on in their baptismal grace; with their falls, their giddiness and forgetfulness of childhood, yet never interposing any such grievous sin, as should check the influx of that life in them. Supported by prayer, strengthened by Confirmation, admitted into closer Communion in the Holy Eucharist". [8]

Dr. Pusey taught that in baptism a man becomes a new self, a changed man, a new creation, a member of Christ. Newly born and newly formed; after the image of Him who created him, he has nothing to do with his former way of life, his former sins. But the re-creation brought about through baptism can never take place again. Through the grace of God in baptism, sins are suddenly and painlessly blotted out. Following sin after baptism there can be no returning to the state of baptismal purity. Sin after baptism can be forgiven, but only upon deep contrition. Through the Sacrament of Absolution pardon is given, life is renewed, but the penitent is the same as the sinner. Sins before baptism come not into judgement--they belong to one who is no more, to one who died and was buried in baptism. But grievous sin committed after baptism, although remitted by absolution, is to be judged when the penitent comes before the judgement seat of Christ. [9]

For High Churchmen baptism implied the complete forgiveness of sins and union with Christ. Pusey believed and taught that apart from baptism there is no complete washing away of sin in this life and any sin committed after baptism has been conferred weakens the effects of the grace of baptism. Should the baptized fall away from the grace of baptism then he can nevermore reach the same position as the one who has kept the white robe of baptism unspotted. [10]

Many found Pusey's teaching unacceptable, including William Dodsworth, Perpetual Curate of Christ Church, St. Pancras, a zealous supporter of the High Church party, but who became a Roman Catholic following the Gorham Judgement. [11] He felt that Pusey was more concerned about baptism as the sacrament of cleansing from all sin than as the sacrament of incorporation into Christ.

F. D. Maurice saw Pusey's teaching as erecting a barrier which hindered the proclamation of the Gospel. Men know, said Maurice, that they cannot retain the baptismal purity of which Pusey speaks and writes. Fasting and prayer are the only consolation offered by the High Church party, as against the assurance that those baptized, having entered into a new covenant with God, are members of a spiritual kingdom, have the love of God continually brooding over them, and the grace of Christ given them, and the Spirit within them. [12]

Bishop Phillpotts followed Maurice's line, and Bishop O'Brien [13] declared Pusey's view not only unacceptable, but erroneous and contrary to scripture. Samuel Wilberforce, on the other hand, had mixed feelings, [14] not entirely agreeing with Pusey, but admitting that those "falling into a course of sinfulness after the purification of baptism may forfeit all hopes of a second chance".

The debate, however, did not abate the evangelistic zeal of the High Churchmen, but rather stimulated them to greater effort, both in proclaiming the Gospel and encouraging growth in holiness. Meanwhile, those who were very much opposed to the High Church view of sin after baptism, were equally active in teaching that baptism establishes a new relationship, one of constant union, in which growth in holiness and instruction in the faith are equally important.

NOTES

1. G. A. Denison, A Reply to the Committee of the Promoters of the Manchester and Salford Educational Scheme (1850) 10, 31-2. See also Pollen, op. cit. 144-5.

2. See The Guardian, April 27th 1853, 271.

3. Keble, Village Sermons: On the Baptismal Service 21-2.

4. How, Archbishop Maclagen 80-1.

5. W. J. Trower, A Pastoral Letter to the Clergy of the Diocese of Glasgow and Galloway, in reference to questions connected with the recent decision of the Judicial Committee of the Privy Council (Glasgow 1850) 13-4.

6. John Gibson, Nature and Effects of Holy Baptism viii-ix.

7. See Eugene R. Fairweather, The Oxford Movement (N.Y. 1964) 271-5.

8. E. B. Pusey, Parochial Sermons (1878) Vol. III, 20-2.

9. See E. B. Pusey, Scriptural Views of Holy Baptism 23-5, 33-6, 50-2.

10. See **Tracts for the Times** No. 68; 48, 53, 63.

11. Henry Parry Liddon, **Life of Edward Bouverie Pusey** (4 Vols., 4th ed. 1894-1898) Vol. III, 262-4.

12. Maurice, **The Kingdom of Christ** Vol. I, 95-8.

13. See Bricknell, **Tractarian Theology,** 381, 383-4, 386-405.

14. See Ashwell and Wilberforce, **Life of Samuel Wilberforce** Vol. I, 115, 153; also David Newsome, **The Parting of Friends. A Study of the Wilberforces and Henry Manning** (1966) 190.

D. The Problem of Sponsorship

"There shall be for every male child to be baptised, two godfathers and one godmother; and for every female, one godfather and two godmothers". Canon XXIX added further qualifications to this Prayer Book Rubric which stipulated the number and gender of godparents. This Canon forbids natural parents to fulfil the office and lays down: "Neither shall any person be admitted godfather or godmother to any child at christening or confirmation, before the said person so undertaking hath received the Holy Communion".

Securing duly qualified persons to fulfil the office of sponsorship in baptism was, for many living during the mid-Victorian period, becoming increasingly difficult. [1] Christopher Nevile in a letter to W. E. Gladstone expressed the opinion that: "It has become impossible to find three sureties or sponsors". He goes on to say that the bishops "like drowning men catching at a straw, are called upon, by altering a canon, to allow parents to stand, so as to reduce the number required from three to one--a mere temporary expedient". [2]

The debate surrounding the revision of Canon XXIX was to be abortive; some felt that such a revision was unnecessary and that what was required was an alteration in the appropriate rubric. Suggestions were made that only one sponsor be required; this, it was felt, would mean that the duties of a sponsor could be more easily fulfilled, but the one person should not be a parent and must be a communicant. [3] The idea of allowing parents to fulfil the office was completely unacceptable to many churchmen. A correspondent in the Church Times complained that if parents were allowed to stand as godparents for their own children, then the curate would have no reasons of objection to indifferent and ungodly parents. He went on to say: "If any objection is made they (the parents) will either write to the papers or complain to the bishop--of course the curate must go to the wall". [4] The very opposite view was taken by a correspondent in The Guardian, who felt that parents ought to be allowed to fulfil the office of sponsor for their own children. [5]

Complaints were made, from time to time, about the laxity of some clergy in allowing the unconfirmed to act as sponsors. It was felt that to allow such unqualified people to fulfil such a sacred office, offered less security that children would be brought up as Christians. Some felt that it was indeed better to allow the children of "heathenish parents" to be baptized without any sponsors whatsoever, rather than to go unbaptized.

There were also those who were very much aware of the seriousness of the office and felt that godparents should be chosen with great care, and only those who would willingly and conscientiously fulfil the duties were to be chosen; thus a few priests tried to carry out not only the letter of the law but also the spirit. [6] Practice, however, was far from the ideal, which must have dampened the spirits of the conscientious, for evidence suggests that in the mid-Victorian period the choosing of sponsors was generally done with little thought either about their functions or their suitability; indeed for many it was no more than a matter of convention. Parents were generally only too pleased to secure any relation, or person, willing to undertake the responsibility, or at least carry out the function laid down in the service of baptism. In such a situation they were hardly likely to quibble about the convictions of those whom they had secured, whatever a dedicated priest might suggest. In certain circles, mainly the middle class, social convention suggested that it was incorrect to refuse an invitation to act as a godparent, thus even those who took the office seriously felt that they had to comply, even when they believed that they were being asked for the wrong reasons. [7] In some areas sponsors were so difficult to obtain that cases were reported of people being paid at a fixed rate for their services in this capacity. [8] The accusation was often made that sponsors seldom, if ever, discharged their duties, that they gave little thought to the promises they made in the service and often had the feeling that no sooner had they made their vows than their job was done. There was little thought given to the future religious education of the children whose sponsors they were. [9] Sponsorship, in many cases, was simply a friendly act done for that day, primarily to the parents of the infant. But it must be acknowledged that the problems and abuses connected with sponsorship were not peculiar to this period, many of them existed prior to 1850 and still remain unresolved even to this day.

Greater commitment was also wanting among many parents. One anonymous writer of the period tells of the common practice of making the occasion of a baptism "little else than a day of extraordinary feasting, a day of vanity and ostentation, a day at least of mere worldly joy". In short, says the writer, "It must be acknowledged that Baptism, is on all sides neglected and profaned,...little else than a convenient ceremony, by which people bestow a name upon their children". [10]

Another anonymous writer of the time wrote that conscientious people were found to be unwilling to make solemn promises and vows for infants which they would hardly deem it right to make for themselves. [11] Inability to procure the necessary sponsors led, in some cases, to the administration of Private Baptism, thus postponing or perhaps entirely dispensing with, the obligation to provide godparents. [12]

For the conscientious godparent some useful pamphlets and books were published; these offered guidance and advice to enable a dutiful fulfilment of the sacred office. [13]

The unwillingness of the conscientious to make promises and vows raised once again the complex theological problem of vicarious faith. George Moberly, Bishop of Salisbury, saw the godparents as individual representatives of the Church and, as such, saw their expression of vicarious faith as agreeable to Christ. He had previously expressed the same idea in his Bampton Lecture of 1868: "The faith of the child, incapable of faith by age, is first that of the natural parents. But what if they are evil or unfaithful? There is the faith of the sponsors, but they too may lack faith". Baptism rests "upon the faith of the Church of Christ, whom the sponsors on the special occasion and for the special purpose represent". [15] Bishop John Kaye saw the duty of both parents and sponsors as being "to co-operate with the Holy Spirit in carrying on the work of sanctification in the soul of the baptised. They are pledged to bring up the child in the faith into which it has been baptised". But, he says, "Alas! how rarely is the education of the baptised infant conducted according to the pattern prescribed by the Church. Parents and sponsors do not co-operate with the Holy Spirit: they take no pains to prepare the child for the reception of his gracious influence".

The various factors which influenced the growing movement towards the revision of Canon XXIX in the Church of England at this period can be summarized thus: A general inability to obtain the required number of sponsors, or of sponsors who met the conditions of sponsorship, the abuses of paid sponsors, unsuitable sponsors, and the avoidance of sponsorship requirements by the administration of private baptism. There was also a growing conviction that sponsors were not essential for the efficacy of the rite. Parental influence was being recognized as playing a primary part in a child's Christian education and upbringing.

The Revision of Canon XXIX

John Mason Neale believed that the Church had many obstacles to overcome in her attempt to influence more parents to bring their children to baptism. He said difficulty arose "partly from our tripled population; then also from the system of registration (how many registrars make a point of telling the poor that it is just as good as Baptism)...also the low teaching of the Evangelicals on the benefits of the Sacraments". In addition to this, he mentioned the problem of obtaining three sponsors. [16] He told how, during twenty years, he had visited 3,000 churches: "Everywhere I hear of one great difficulty, that of the number of sponsors required at baptism". Many priests, he said, simply violated the rubric. Some admitted duly qualified parents to the office. In some parishes the clerk considered it a part of his duty to be sponsor in cases of need. Comparatively few, said Neale, strictly obeyed the Canon and the Sponsorship Rubric.

Violation of the rubric and Canon were also reported by an Evangelical, who wrote: "Most of the Canons are seen as defunct and obsolete. Why should not the twenty-ninth be allowed to share in the same indulgence? We ourselves have so treated it for many years; and we have done so at the suggestion of one who still adorns the episcopal bench". [17] Opinions varied on this point; some felt that such violation was the only way round the difficulties of sponsorship, but not all agreed with such disregard for ecclesiastical legislation.

Neale, a zealous High Churchman, suggested that one way out of the difficult situation was to allow parents to act as sponsors for their own children. The suggestion was not lightly made, for he believed that the problem of obtaining three sponsors had been a difficulty in England for at least 200 years. Sponsors, he felt, had little influence in seeing that the child was "brought up to lead a godly and Christian life", while those parents who were eager to accept the office, and who could keep the sponsorial vow, were not allowed to make it. Yet the fulfillment of the necessary qualification would, in some cases, lead to the confirmation of parents.

Neale's suggestions were most unacceptable in some quarters. Opposition prompted him to write another pamphlet on the subject, in which he maintained and defended his earlier position, remaining adamant that parents had the right to be sponsors of their own children and were indeed the proper and most suitable persons to fulfil the promises. [18]

On February 14th 1860 the Bishop of Lincoln brought a Petition for the repeal of Canon XXIX before the Upper House of the newly reformed Convocation. He listed a number of points in support of the petition: that when parents were unable to procure acceptable sponsors they would often take their children to the Wesleyan minister, who would baptize them without sponsors. That those most suitable for the office were usually most unwilling to take it unless they were satisfied that the parents would bring up their children in a religious and Christian way. This insistence usually led parents to accept others who were less demanding and at the same time less suited for the office. He also spoke of the practice of obtaining sponsors by means of giving a supper or dinner; finally he added that there was the feeling of some parents that sponsors relieved them of any responsibility for the Christian upbringing of their children. [19] In the course of the episcopal debate which followed the introduction of this petition (in which Samuel Wilberforce took a leading part and also wrote a number of letters on the subject to W. E. Gladstone [20]), it was pointed out that in large populous towns the Canon was often broken, for when large numbers were baptized it was difficult to know whether sponsors were parents or not. Episcopal comments during the debate indicate that some of the bishops had no clear idea of the exact content and meaning of the Canon. [21]

In its original form the Canon read: "No parent shall be urged to be present, nor be admitted to answer as godfather for his own child; nor any godfather or godmother shall be suffered to make any other answer or speech, than by the Book of Common Prayer is prescribed in that behalf; neither shall any person be admitted godfather or godmother to any child at christening or confirmation, before the said person so undertaking hath received the Holy Communion". During a further debate in the Upper House of Convocation in 1861 Wilberforce proposed the elimination of the words "parents shall be urged to be present, nor be admitted to answer as godfather for his child; nor any". Eventually the Upper House agreed to this proposal, but the Lower House were unwilling to accept, without question, what the bishops put before them. Debate in the Lower House turned on the second part of the Canon "neither shall any person be admitted godfather or godmother to any child at christening or confirmation, before the said person so undertaking hath received the Holy Communion". They felt that there was need for revision in the requirement that sponsors should be communicants. The Upper House were unwilling to consider any change in the second part of the Canon and asked the Lower House to confine themselves to the first part, which had been submitted for their endorsement. Unwilling to comply with the request, they asked that the matter be left over until the 1862 Convocation, but the bishops were not prepared to accept such a suggestion. Finally, a compromise was reached when the Lower House asked that the words "shall have received the Holy Communion" be altered to "shall be capable of receiving the Holy Communion". This proposed amendment to the second half of the canon was accepted by the bishops and after a joint meeting of both Houses on June 20th 1861, the revised Canon was signed. [22] The York Convocation simply recorded the decision made at the Convocation of Canterbury; indeed, compared with Canterbury, they had little to say on the subject throughout the years of debate. [23] Not all approved of the removal of the stipulation regarding communion; a Petition was in fact presented to the upper House of Canterbury by the English - Church Union in 1861: "That the whole E.C.U. deprecates any alteration of the 29th Canon, it most particularly prays their lordships not to repeal that portion of it which presumes that sponsors shall be communicants".

After a lapse of time, Government refusal to give Royal Assent to the suggested revision was made known, and strong objection was made to any change in the second half of the Canon. Convocations debated the issue further and it was agreed on 29th June 1865 to restore the second half of the Canon to its original form. [24]

On the following day Archbishop Longley sent the revised form of Canon XXIX to Sir George Gray, requesting approval and confirmation of the revision by Letters Patent from the Queen. Gray informed the Archbishop that the procedure would take some time; in fact nothing further was done and the Royal Assent was never given. [25]

Pastoral needs and insights, as well as abuse and neglect largely caused by the new urban situation and increasing population, contributed towards the move for the revision of Canon XXIX. Government refusal to allow the Established Church to carry out a reform, which she felt would be beneficial to her evangelistic outreach and pastoral ministry, thwarted the work of the Church. The factors which had influenced this move for reform in ecclesiastical law remained as though nothing had happened; sponsors of the right quality and qualifications were still difficult to obtain, in some cases impossible. The demands of the Church regarding sponsorship continued to deter people from having their children baptized, or forced them to go to the Non-conformists. But the debate and controversy had served a useful purpose in that it made many churchmen realize, perhaps as never before, that there was need for reform in this matter, both on pastoral grounds and because of the extent of violation, which many felt was justified on the grounds of expediency.

NOTES

1. See C. Perry, A Charge 1852 9-10.

2. Christopher Nevile, A Letter to the Right Hon. W. E. Gladstone, M.P. on the Present State of the Church Question (1863) 23-4.

3. See The Guardian, August 9th 1854. See also B. J. Kidd, **Selected Letters of William Bright, D.D.** (1903) 187-8.

4. Church Times, May 7th 1875, 232.

5. The Guardian, February 8th 1860, 119.

6. George Davys, **Village Conversations on the Liturgy and Offices of the Church of England** (1849) 98-100. Anonymous, Explanation of the Nature of Baptism; designed especially for all those parents who are about to bring a child to be baptised (n.d. c.1850) 3.

7. See Explanation of the Nature of Baptism 3-4.

8. The Guardian, February 8th 1860, 119.

9. See Proby, A Letter to the Right Rev. The Lord Bishop of Winchester 9-10. Also Explanation of the Nature of Baptism 3-5.

10. Explanation of the Nature of Baptism 2, 4.

11. Anonymous, Suggestions for a Revision of the Prayer Book: with the opinions of the Archbishop of Canterbury, the Bishops of St. Asaph, Chester and Limerick, etc. (1859) 8.

12. See Bricknell, **Tractarian Theology** 588. J. M. Neale, Additional Reasons for the Abrogation of the XXIXth Canon. A Second Letter to the Bishop of Oxford... (1861) 36.

13. See Anonymous, **A Serious Address to Godfathers and Godmothers** (1804). The duties of godparents are given in this pamphlet as: "To see that the children attend catechising and go forward to confirmation; to step into the place of parents if they die or fail to attend to the spiritual care of the children;

to see that they are taught to read, and to give them good books; and, if they go into service, to help them to a place in a godly family". Here the duties are set very high and it is impossible to know how widely they were fulfilled. See also John Venn, **The Office of Sponsors briefly and practically considered** (1844). John N. Woodroffe, **The advantages of Public Baptism and the Origin, Nature and Duties of Sponsors** (Cork 1841).

14. George Moberly, **Infant Baptism and Confirmation** 18-21.

15. George Moberly, **The Administration of the Holy Spirit in the Body of Christ; Eight Lectures: Preached Before the University of Oxford in the year 1868.** Bampton Lectures 1868 (Oxford 1883) 137.

16. J. M. Neale, The XXIXth Canon and Reasons for its Abrogation. A Letter to the Lord Bishop of Oxford (1860) 21.

17. The Christian Observer, April 1861, 285.

18. See J. M. Neale, Additional Reasons for the Abrogation of the XXIXth Canon. A Second Letter to the Bishop of Oxford. William J. Irons, A Reply to Mr. Neale's Second Letter against the Law of Sponsorship in Baptism. Being a second appendix to a pamphlet on that subject, lately addressed to Convocation (1861). J. M. Neale, Appendix, added to the Second Letter, February 11th 1881.

19. See Chronicle of Convocation, February 1860, 118.

20. Ashwell and Wilberforce, **Life of Samuel Wilberforce** Vol. II, 437-42.

21. For a report of the debate see Chronicle of Convocation February 17th 1860, 121ff., 190, 219ff; February 18th, 249; June 8th, 303.

22. On the Canterbury Convocations's debate see Chronicle of Convocation February 17th 1861, 338, 413, 443-4; February 28th, 510; June 19th, 706-7, 726, 770. See also Stephenson, **First Lambeth Conference** 97-9. Bishop Fitzgerald made the Canon the subject of his Charge of 1861.

23. See York Journal of Convocation 1861, 86; 1864, 214-19; 1865, 277; 1867, 31.

24. See <u>Chronicle of Convocation</u> June 29th 1865. The Appendix on 2411-13 gives all the correspondence on this issue. For the debate of the Lower House, see 2355-7, 2368-74; also **Rivington's Ecclesiastical Year Book,** 1865, 1866, 10-14, 71-4.

25. Some time later a move was made to revise all the Canons, see <u>Chronicles of Convocation</u> May 4th 1866, 373-5, and to this end a Committee was appointed, 617. The Committee felt that nothing should be done to interfere with the Colonial Churches, see 690-2. In 1873 there was published a <u>Code of Canons for the Use of the Church of England</u> agreed upon by the two Committees of Canterbury and York, submitted to their respective Convocations. Among the proposed canons was <u>Of Godfathers and Godmothers</u>: "No person of tender age shall be admitted Godfather or Godmother to any child, nor shall any Godfather or Godmother be suffered to make, during the Service for the ministration of Baptism, any other answer or speech than by the Book of Common Prayer is prescribed in that behalf; nor shall the Minister allow any person so to answer whom for immorality or other just cause he would refuse to admit to the Holy Communion".

III. THE ADMINISTRATION OF THE RITE

A. Public Baptism

Administration of baptism in the mid-Victorian period left much to be desired; there was a wide divergence on such matters as the day, time and setting of the rite. Rubrical directions in these matters were either disregarded or interpreted in a way which supported a particular practice. The rubric directs: "It is most convenient...upon Sundays and other holy days, when the most number of people come together...Nevertheless (if necessity so require) children may be baptised upon any other day". The time of baptism is given as: "Either immediately after the last Lesson at Morning Prayer, or else immediately after the last Lesson at Evening Prayer, as the curate by his discretion shall appoint". Disregard of these directions had invoked episcopal disapproval, before the period. [1] Some bishops suggested that clergy ought to baptize, as a rule, in public.

In 1844 Edward Bickersteth was able to comment on the far more general practice of public baptism. [2] Signs of a general improvement were also reported in some Episcopal Charges of the period. Edward Denison, Bishop of Salisbury, spoke of "a large increase in the number of places in which the Sacrament of Baptism is administered in the presence of the Congregation". Since his previous visitation, of 1842, three years before, there had been an increase of 57 parishes in the diocese, bringing the number which practiced public baptism to nearly two-thirds of the diocese. This increase can be attributed to Denison's constant recommendation of the practice, wherever circumstances would allow its adoption. Even though he believed the practice to be highly desirable, he did not recommend that it be enforced in all parishes as a universal rule, without consideration of local circumstances. He was willing to recognize the need to modify this strict rule where the population was very large. [3]

Failure to fulfil the rubrical requirements continued and was fairly widespread. Charles Thomas Longley, in his Primary Charge as Archbishop of Canterbury (1864), told his clergy that there were 126 churches in the diocese where the rubrics were not observed. He urged his clergy to follow the rubrics and to return to the regular usage. [4] Bishop Ollivant was not emphatic, but suggested that public baptisms should be carried out "occasionally at least". [5] In 1867 the Bishop of Gloucester in a Charge entitled 'Progress and Trials' observed, with justifiable satisfaction, that the baptismal rubrics were being fulfilled in "at least as many as 334 churches"; nevertheless, he felt that there was still room for further improvement. [6] Many bishops of this period, like their episcopal predecessors, realized that there was need for much improvement and reform in this matter, but at the same time believed that they could not be unduly rigorous. At least some of them acknowledged that there were cases of genuine difficulty, where strict observance of the rubric was impracticable. [7]

On the question of the time of administration, Bishop Ellicott suggested that every effort should be made to revert to what the rubric laid down. He went on to say: "In town congregations, where the greatest difficulties are experienced owing to the length of the Morning Services and the late hour of the Second Service, these difficulties might be to a great degree obviated by the administration, at the proper place in the service, on Holy days, and, when these might not be sufficient, by Afternoon Services on stated Sundays and even (if need be) on other appointed days which might be thus specially set apart for the administration of this holy Sacrament". [8]

William Jacobson, Bishop of Chester, complained in his Charge of 1868, that in the diocese the public administration of baptism "is far from being as large as could be desired". He thought that in pressing for compliance with the rubrics he was not recommending abrupt and sweeping changes--rather an improvement of a situation resulting from "the carelessness and slovenliness of the clergy in other days". Clergy, in compliance with the rubric, might begin giving baptism "its due place in the service on one Sunday regularly in the course of each month". [9]

Nevertheless, a letter written by Frederick Temple to one of his clergy reveals a different attitude: "Whether you have the Baptism on Sunday or weekday is a question not of law but of expediency. In these days I certainly should not press for a Sunday if I were a clergyman". [10]

Compliance with the rubrics could also raise other problems. Davys writes of how, when baptism was administered after the second Lesson, those present would often leave the service. [11] Some clergy complained of congregations who were unwilling to have the ordinary service interrupted and prolonged. The existing service of Morning Prayer was thought to be already too long, especially for the infirm. The service was lengthened by the custom, which still prevailed in many places, of uniting into one service Morning Prayer, Litany and Ante Communion.

There were some who objected to baptism being administered at Morning Prayer, not on account of the length of the service, but because they felt the service was unsuitable. James Hildyard, writing in favor of the abridgement of the Morning Service, recommended that: "Churching of Women, with the Baptismal Service, be limited by authority to the later hours of prayer, not Morning Prayer". [12]

With so many pastoral problems, often put forward as justifying an exception to the rule, the widespread clerical disregard of the rubrics and the strong lay objections, persistent episcopal pressure for reform may have seemed somewhat unreasonable. Addressing his clergy, in 1864, Archbishop Longley expressed the feelings of many churchmen of the period: "Surely we cannot be justified in depriving infants at their baptism of the united prayers of the whole assembled congregation". [13] The same sentiment was expressed by W. J. Conybeare who wrote in 1855: "The infant member is adopted into the Christian family with the sympathizing prayers of his assembled brethren". [14] George Moberly saw their presence as a theological necessity: "The whole Spirit-bearing Church, the Body of Christ, is engaged in the administration of the sacrament of Holy Baptism". He insisted that, except in cases of real emergency, baptism in the presence of the Church was both essential and necessary, for baptism is the work of the entire body. [15]

The congregation was, then, to be present at baptism, in order to carry out a very important function, to pray for those being baptized and also to witness the baptism. In witnessing baptisms they were reminded of their own baptism, and the baptismal vows were believed to stir up a more faithful performance of them in their own lives. Bishop Jacobson suggested to his clergy: "For the congregation at large, ought not the Office of Baptism to be as good as, if not better than, a sermon? The vows and promises, which they hear made for others, were once made for them". [16]

Thus many clergy looked upon the baptismal service as a real evangelistic opportunity, a sermon in action. They did not neglect sermons in words, however. Recognizing the widespread ignorance concerning the true meaning and purpose of holy baptism, at least some churchmen tried to enlighten the ill-informed and preached sermons on the subject. Bishops were attempting to educate and stir up clergy through their Charges, and clergy their people through their sermons, lectures, pastoral visits and catechetical instruction.

Works on the Book of Common Prayer and liturgical studies, produced in the mid-Victorian period, show a growing awareness and appreciation of ancient ritual and ceremonial practices which included the ancient baptismal ceremonies. To the majority of mid-Victorian churchmen these were, however, still symbols of superstition and 'popery', with which they had little, if any, sympathy. There are many examples during this period of how even conservative and limited ceremonial prompted outbreaks of violence and rioting. The use of an altar cross, the procession of clergy and choir to and from the vestry, bowing to the altar, the eastward position and frontals of the color of the season, roused so much fury and rioting at St. Barnabas, London, that a large body of special constables was required Sunday after Sunday to keep the peace.

In such a climate of opinion the use of ceremonial in the administration of the baptismal office was naturally limited in its extent and only attempted by the more ritualistically minded members of the High Church party and those with Romanistic tendencies. Those who wished to introduce such ceremonial into their services found that the Book of Common Prayer was an insufficient guide in matters of ritual direction. They argued that the Prayer Book was never intended as a complete <u>Directory</u> and that priests were right to seek elsewhere for guidance in these matters. Many of these more ritualistic High Churchmen felt that a manual of Catholic ritual, giving the real and ancient use of the English Church, was an urgent requirement. Such a manual was in fact produced by John Purchas and published in 1858 under the title **Directorium Anglicanum:** [17] it provides a valuable insight into the cermonial practices of not a few Victorian High Churchmen. While its long Preface illustrates how Purchas and his associates were acquainted with the usage of the pre-Reformation English Church, their final authority in matters of ritual tended to be the practice of the contemporary Roman Catholic Church. [18] They were apt to discard as incorrect and 'Anglican' old English customs which had survived the storms of the Reformation. Without careful leadership and the insights of the more scholarly churchmen, practices which were eccentric and even silly began to appear. Purchas, for instance, was accustomed to hang a stuffed dove over the altar at the Whitsuntide festival.

In spite of some of his odd ideas and practices Purchas' **Directorium Anglicanum** was in great demand and within six months of its publication it was completely sold out and further editions had to be produced. The third edition was published in 1866 under the editorship of Frederick George Lee. This edition was revised and the format completely changed. Additional material and comments added by Lee tend to be finicky and indicate an even less healthy development in ritualistic matters. An example of this finicky additional material is found in his opening statement, under the heading Baptismal Ritual. Here he states that if baptism is administered after the second Lesson at Evensong then the choir and priest should go in procession to the font. An acolyte is to walk on either side of the priest, one with the Service Book, and the other with the baptismal shell and napkin. This was a considerable embellishment on the direction by Purchas, who stated: "It is desirable always to have a lay clerk or chorister...in attendance to hold the service book, and silver-gilt shell (if the Priest use one), and to make the responses". Lee's direction was in fact outlining a practice already in use. A graphic description of the baptismal practice at St. Saviour's, Leeds, in 1850 illustrates a somewhat eccentric approach to baptismal ritual. [19]

St. Alban's, Holborn, under MacKonochie, had a similar but less elaborate baptismal practice. [20] Purchas gives the baptismal vestments as: "Cassock, surplice, [21] two stoles, one of violet and one of white silk...The ancient Sarum use was to wear a violet stole in the first part of the Office, and to lay it aside for a white one before the Interrogations...The Roman use is the same". He goes on to state: "According to the ancient form which was used at the door of the church, the male infants should be placed on the right hand of the officiating Priest, and the females on the left". Lee adds that when several children are being baptized the acolyte or parish clerk is to instruct the people with male children to stand on the priest's right facing east and the females on the left. The male candidates, he says, must always be baptized first. [22]

Concerning the water of baptism, Lee tells how it was the practice in some churches for an acolyte to fill the font with pure water, in the presence of the congregation, immediately before the administration of baptism. "It is proper for the Priest", says Purchas, "in celebrating this Sacrament, to make the sign of the Cross in the water, at the words 'Sanctify this water', in the prayer of Benediction, as he does upon the elements in the Sacrament of the Lord's Supper". He goes on to give careful instructions concerning the correct application of the water: "The custom of the Western Church, English as well as Roman, is to pour the water in baptism thrice--once at the name of each Person of the ever Blessed Trinity--on the head of the recipient (which is uncovered for that purpose)". Lee adds that the people are to be instructed to give the children into the priest's arms with their head towards his left shoulder. [23] Other points of practical information are also given. [24]

Only a passing reference is made to the ancient ceremonies of anointing with chrism and putting on the chrysom, but neither Purchas nor Lee makes the slightest suggestion concerning the use or re-introduction of these two ancient ceremonies. Among other subjects dealt with are private baptism; adult baptism; immersion and affusion, and emergency baptism. In cases of emergency baptism, if neither a priest nor a deacon can be found and "the speedy death of the child being apprehended" the parents had better get some friend to baptize the child. "If such cannot be procured, the father must administer the Sacrament; the mother may only do so if the father knows not the Sacramental words, or some other impediment exists". A final note states how it is irregular for a priest to baptize his own child in the church. In such cases a Deacon may baptize although in the presence of a priest.

NOTES

1. C. T. Longley, A Charge 1841. R. Mant, A Charge 1842. H. Phillpotts, A Charge, 1839; A Charge, 1842.

2. Bickersteth, **A Treatise on Baptism** (1844) xv.

3. E. Denison, A Charge, 1845 19-20.

4. C. T. Longley, A Charge, 1864 18.

5. See A. Ollivant, A Charge, 1866 22.

6. C. J. Ellicott, A Charge, 1867 18-19.

7. C. J. Ellicott, A Charge, 1864 21. W. Jacobson, A Charge, 1868 11-12.

8. C. J. Ellicott, A Charge, 1864 20-3. See also H. H. Norris, Ritual Conformity...A Sermon (1842) 15; and Michael Reynolds, **Martyr of Ritualism, Father MacKonochie of St. Alban's, Holborn** (1965) 49.

9. W. Jacobson, A Charge, 1868 11-12.

10. Sandford, **Memoir of Archbishop Temple** Vol. I, 457. In some 'High' churches baptism was in fact administered several times each week in the course of daily Evensong. See

Pollen, **St. Saviour's Leeds** 144; William Allen Whitworth, **Quam Dilecta: A description of All Saint's Church, Margaret Street** (1891); Table facing page I.

11. See Davys, **Village Conversations** 102-3.

12. James Hildyard, **Further Arguments in favour of the Abridgement of the Morning Prayer** (1856) 14.

13. C. T. Longley, A Charge, 1864 18. See also J. C. Ellicott, A Charge, 1867 19.

14. W. J. Conybeare, **Essays Ecclesiastical and Social** (1855) 111.

15. George Moberly, **The Administration of the Holy Spirit in the Body of Christ** 146-7; see also 132-3, 137, 140, 143; see also S. Waldegrave, A Charge, 1867 27-8.

16. W. Jacobson, A Charge, 1868 II; also Henry Blunt, **Directorium Pastorale: The Principles and Practice of Pastoral Work in the Church of England** (1st ed. 1864, revised ed. 1888) 161.

17. John Purchas, **Directorium Anglicanum: A Manual of Directions for the right celebration of the Holy Communion, for the Saying of Matins and Evensong and for the performance of other rites and ceremonies of the Church according to Ancient Uses of the Church of England** (1858).

18. See Purchas, **Directorium Anglicanum** v-xxx.

19. See Pollen, **St. Saviour's Leeds** 118-19.

20. See Reynolds, **Father MacKonochie** 119.

21. Lee adds the practical comment that a short surplice with close sleeves is more convenient for the administration than the ordinary surplice, "which is apt to get soaked at the sleeves".

22. Purchas, op. cit.,126. Lee, op. cit., 194.

23. Lee, op. cit., 194.

24. Purchas, op. cit., 126; Lee, op. cit., 196-7.

B. Ignorance, Irregularities, Abuses

Both clergy and laity were guilty of abuses and miscon-
ceived ideas in connection with baptism. In 1851 a priest wrote
to The English Churchman concerning an incident which had
occurred at a baptism: about to administer the rite he asked
the parents to remove the cap; they conferred with the nurse,
who said that the smallest drop of water put with the finger,
on the child's forehead, was all that was necessary. He pointed
out that the water was to be poured, at which point the parents
asked that the baptism be postponed till the child was stronger. [1] Clergy were sometimes asked to baptize without any
water because the child was too ill to bear it. [2] Such incidents
serve to illustrate the kind of ignorance which existed among
the laity concerning the purpose of the rite and the necessity
of water in its administration. The event recorded in The English
Churchman also shows how some clergy were unwilling to treat
the matter lightly. Others, however, were not so careful concerning the correct method of administration and the importance
of this to assure the validity of baptism.

Irregularity in the application of the water seems to
have been an abuse which was not limited to a minority. 'Public
Christenings' constituted a scandalous irregularity. At such 'Christenings' the persons to be baptized were arranged around the
communion rails and sprinkled from the font with a brush, like
a Roman Catholic asperging brush. Older candidates would stand,
while infants would be held in the arms of parents or sponsors.
The validity of such baptisms was held in question, even by
some who belonged to the Evangelical party. [3] But some Evangelicals had no scruples on such matters as their contempt for
everything external in regard to religion resulted in a very low
view of the sacraments. In his **Annals of the Tractarian Movement**
E. G. K. Browne records some of the abuses of the period. He
tells us how, in the winter months, some priests did baptize
without water. In large parishes when there were 60-70 baptisms
there was often carelessness and haste, and the use of a "drop
or two of water intended to sprinkle the child, merely touched
his cap or dress". He also tells of clergy just touching the forehead of the child with a wet finger. Although the Prayer Book
directs that the child be plunged under the water, most clergy
of the Church of England did not believe that this was the only
proper mode of baptism. Indeed Blomfield listed Trine immersion
as one of the practices to which he objected. [5]

Two ex-Anglicans, H. E. Manning and H. N. Oxenham who joined the Church of Rome, raised the question of the validity of baptism in the Church of England. Oxenham wrote to an Anglican friend of the carelessness with which baptism was frequently administered in the Anglican Communion and which, he said, made it "really impossible...to feel certain of its validity in any given case, without positive proof". Cases where no water was poured at all, or where its application did not synchronize with the sacramental formula, were not, he maintained, confined exclusively to Low Churchmen. "I cannot doubt the great frequency of invalid baptism among you". [6] Manning was in entire agreement with Oxenham and maintained that such carelessness had been great and frequent, and was sufficient reason for believing that many had never been baptized. However, he was willing to admit that there had been a revival of care in the administration of the rite on the part of Anglican Ministers. [7]

Inevitably such statements from the pens of ex-Anglicans converted to Rome tended to be somewhat polemical, and yet there is sufficient evidence from faithful members of the Church of England to substantiate such accusations. However, it is impossible to measure or estimate, with any degree of accuracy, the extent of such abuses and irregularities. They did exist and were not confined to one or two cases. Some priests did administer the rite in a hasty and often unintelligible manner, especially in the cases of large and over-crowded baptisms. Many lay people did look upon baptism as no more than a name-giving ceremony, or an occasion for a family feast and outward show. Obtaining sponsors created problems for many. The abuses which these led to produced an unhealthy situation which was all too common and left much to be desired.

NOTES

1. The English Churchman April 10th 1851, 225. See also Blunt, Directorium Pastorale 158.

2. See Edward K. Browne, Annals of the Tractarian Movement from 1842 to 1860 (3rd ed. 1861) 66-7.

3. Arthur Christopher Benson, The Life of Edward White Benson: sometime Archbishop of Canterbury (2 Vols. 1899) Vol. I, 6.

4. Browne, **Tractarian Movement** 66-7; also Blunt, **Directorium Pastorale** 158-9. See Pollard, **Charles Simeon** 42-3, also 125-6.

5. W. S. Bricknell, **Tractarian Theology** 526.

6. H. N. Oxenham, The Tractarian Party and the Catholic Church: A Letter to an Anglican Friend (1858) 4-5.

7. Manning, **The Workings of the Holy Spirit in the Church of England** 9-10.

C. Private Baptism

Provision is made in the Prayer Book for Private Baptism, but the second rubric to that office directs the curate to warn parents "that without...great cause and necessity they procure not their Children to be baptised at home in their houses". In the same office the curate is directed to admonish the people "that they defer not the Baptism of their Children longer than the first or second Sunday next after their birth". Davys tells of how many parents had their children baptized almost as soon as they were born "for fear that they should die, as they say, without a name". Other fears also influenced such speedy requests for baptism: There was the Church's doctrine of Original Sin and the fear that those tainted by such sin could have no certainty of eternal salvation. Indeed the rubric at the end of the rite of Public Baptism only asserts: "It is certain, by God's word, that Children which are baptised, dying before they commit actual sin, are undoubtedly saved". There could be no comfort offered should a child die unbaptized and it was the fear of what would happen to such children which influenced many to seek immediate baptism. Another influential factor, already mentioned, was the fear that, should their child die unbaptized, there would be no Christian burial by the burial rite of the Church or in her consecrated ground.

Some clergy had no scruples about administering private baptism when there was no just cause or necessity. Bickersteth, writing about abuse in this matter, tells of private baptisms being administered in drawing-rooms and cottages. Bishops often made reference to the abuse of private baptism and used their Charges to urge their clergy to avoid such baptism except in the cases of necessity. Where there were real cases of illness many clergy were willing to oblige, but even so, some seemed to treat the matter rather lightly.

For those who were willing to administer baptism in private, in cases of real necessity, it was not always easy to decide which were the genuine cases. Parents were not unknown to send for a clergyman to baptize in private "under the plea of the slightest indisposition which, whether real or imaginary, is thought sufficient to warrant them sending for the clergyman to administer the rite". Even if the clergyman had doubts about the urgency of a particular case he was disinclined to refuse the request. [1] The Queen felt nothing wrong in announcing that the new-born prince would be baptized in private. Objection to such a suggestion was raised by both Archbishop Howley and Peel, who felt that the interests of religion and propriety required baptism in church. [2]

While some spoke of a widespread abuse in this matter, the Bishop of Ripon, in 1867, was able to say: "My attention has been called to a practice which has prevailed in one or two parishes of administering baptism in private, without any necessity, on account of the health of the child". Such a practice was to be condemned as it tended to lower the estimate in which the sacrament ought to be regarded; it deprived the infant of the congregation's prayers, led to the neglect of sponsors and to the omission of the reception of the child into the congregation of Christ's flock. [3]

Private baptism was also sought in an attempt to avoid going to church and having to go through a long and public service. The wish to avoid this may have influenced the introduction in some places of "private baptisms, by appointment, in church", for at such services only parents and sponsors were normally present. Bishop Robert Bickersteth also reminded his clergy that the office "was intended to meet the special cases in which the child cannot, without imminent risk, be brought to the church for public baptism". A rubric in the rite lays down: "Nevertheless, if the Child, which is after this sort baptised, do afterwards live, it is expedient that it be brought into Church". The expression in this rubric 'if the child "do afterwards live"' seems to imply that danger of death was the situation under which private baptism could be administered. "It would", said the Evangelical Bickersteth, "be a dereliction of duty on the part of a clergyman, to refuse to baptise a child in private where necessity exists; but in the absence of such necessity no encouragement should be given to the custom of private baptism". In his Charge of 1867, he has so much to say on the subject that the accuracy of his statement of "one or two private baptisms" being carried out in his diocese, without necessity, seems open to question. Other bishops, including Blomfield, also wished to see the practice abolished.

Davys tells of how some people called private baptism having the child 'half baptised'. Such children were later taken to be 'christened', by which was meant public admittance into the Church. Sometimes this so-called 'christening' was left for a year or more, indeed two children in the same family were occasionally taken together. [4] In an attempt to avoid parental negligence in having those who had been baptized privately received into the Church, some clergymen began to give a certificate of private baptism. This certificate was given to the officiating clergyman when the child was presented to be "received into the Church". Such a practice was thought to serve a twofold purpose: it made the parents realize that the child had to be taken to Church, "thus interesting them in what is to follow", and secondly, it assured the clergyman that the child had been baptized.

Like many of the problems which surrounded baptism, that of private baptism did not disappear at the end of the mid-Victorian period. Theology, charity, carelessness and neglect of duty, in addition to such problems as that of obtaining Christian burial and many other social pressures, all encouraged the continuance of this particular abuse. Some bishops spoke out against the practice, others advocated expediency and discretion; but the position of the Established Church, and the freedom of her clergy, were large factors in its persistence. As with so many other problems which surrounded the sacrament of baptism, sound theological and pastoral arguments failed to establish the necessary reforms which many churchmen believed would lead to the ideal situation.

Notes

1. The Guardian September 10th 1851, 643.

2. See Chadwick, **The Victorian Church** Part I, 192-3.

3. R. Bickersteth, A Charge 1867 7-8.

4. See Davys, **Village Conversations** 1849.

CONFIRMATION

I. SOME RELATED ISSUES

A. Baptism and Confirmation

During the years 1850-75 the sacrament of confirmation did not provoke vexed controversy as did baptism. Deep theological differences over the relationship between baptism and confirmation were to emerge, but not until the end of the period, although the roots of this later controversy can, in some ways, be traced back to earlier years. However, the fact that the rite produced no deep theological cleavage or controversy does not imply that during this period the Church of England could claim to hold a common and undivided theological approach to confirmation. Differences there were, but not of such magnitude that the opposing parties or over-zealous individuals were willing to unchurch their opponents or charge them with heresy, as was the case with baptism.

Victorian churchmen were more or less united in the belief that the essentials of confirmation were prayer and the laying on of hands by a bishop. But concerning the doctrine of confirmation, where it is to be found and what it is, the picture is not so clear. Indeed, few churchmen seem to have given a great deal of time or thought to these issues, certainly nothing like as much as they had given to baptism.

When Mrs. John Mozley asked John Henry Newman for information on the subject of confirmation, he replied that he had nothing to offer and confessed "I am but partially informed on the subject". Was this modesty or a lack of interest on Newman's part? He expressed doubt "whether one should look to the service for the doctrine of the Church about Confirmation, though it might be there". [1] He went on, "The action speaks, it must be a gift. What else is meant by laying hands on?...laying on of hands is evidently a special kind of blessing". The confirmed are "strengthened by the Holy Ghost". Newman saw confirmation as "a deep fixing, establishing, rooting in of that grace which was first given in Baptism". [2] The grace of confirmation implies a perfecting, in it we become new men in Christ Jesus. When asked to recommend a book on the subject of confirmation he replied: "I know of no familiar book on the subject". This impression of a general lack of interest is also reflected by H. E. Manning when he wrote to Samuel Wilberforce on the close link between baptism and confirmation, and between regeneration and renewal: "I am convinced that neglect of confirmation is one of the great efficient causes of our present low state of religion in the Church. Regeneration without renewal is as a withered seed, and renewal without repentance and faith, i.e. the personal appropriation of God's mercies in Christ, is impossible".

The Cambridge High Churchman J. M. Neale saw confirmation as very much the "strengthening gift of the Holy Ghost" given to overcome the temptations of adolescence. [3] Moberly believed that confirmation was "closely connected with Holy Baptism, as being in some sort supplemental to it". The Church's task is "to link fast and true every part of the sacred chain that binds the first infant washing with the manly recognition of the vows and the seal of the gift of the Holy Spirit in Confirmation". [4] In his confirmation Charges Bishop W. W. How, the moderate High Churchman, emphasized that the gift of the Holy Spirit was bestowed in the rite of confirmation. For him the renewal of the baptismal vows was a preliminary to confirmation and not an essential part of the ceremony. [5] John Keble saw the Holy Spirit as being given both in baptism and confirmation; the Spirit is given, at confirmation, through the laying on of hands. To the newly confirmed of his parish he wrote: "The Holy Spirit has sealed you afresh as He had before sealed you in Baptism". He went on to exhort them to keep this seal unbroken, by being receptive to the prompting of the Spirit. [6]

Maurice saw a clear connection between the two parts of the fragmented initiatory rite: "Evidently the name (confirmation) points to a blessing already conferred. That which is not yet given to us, cannot be confirmed. Evidently also the confirmation must correspond in its kind and character to that which has preceded it...If confirmation raises itself to the level of baptism, it simply sets aside its own meaning...But there may be something in the nature of baptism which demands another act to carry out and fulfil its intention". Maurice saw confirmation as just such an act. [7]

Bishop Connop Thirlwall looked upon confirmation as both a public profession of faith and obedience and an admission into the full fellowship and the highest privileges of the Church of Christ. [8] Another Broad Churchman, Frederick Temple, expressed views about the sacrament which linked him with both High Churchmen and Evangelicals, providing an example of how on this subject there were no clear party lines. In a letter of 1850 Temple said that sufficient stress was not being laid upon confirmation; this was also the conviction of many High Churchmen. He suggested that the parish priest be empowered to admit fit applicants to Holy Communion after a short solemn service of admission; every three years those so admitted should be presented to the bishop for confirmation. "Confirmation might thus be made a solemn act; the sacrament (if I may call it) of conversion, as baptism of regeneration. It should be looked upon as the deliberate completion of baptism, and not simply treated as a matter of course that every one who was baptised was to be confirmed". Temple went on to say that such ideas were speculation and perhaps ought not to be indulged. [9] It is his idea of confirmation as the 'Sacrament of Conversion' that links him with Evangelicals, with their emphasis upon conversion as of prime importance.

One who is best described as a 'Catholic Evangelical', George Howard Wilkinson, both as a priest and successively Bishop of Truro and St. Andrew's, laid great stress on his confirmations, endeavoring to make them a real turning point in the lives of the candidates. Speaking of conversion he said "Our own Church seals this act of the individual soul at Confirmation". Nevertheless "Conversion and Justifying Faith are not indispensable presuppositions for confirmation for, just as in baptism, this ordinance confers a gift, even if it is despised and misused. If an unconverted person is already confirmed, pastoral care is concerned to teach not only Baptismal Grace, but the gift of the Holy Spirit in Confirmation".

During confirmation preparation the parish priest is to work, by God's help, for the conversion of candidates; such was the belief of Robert Wilberforce, who reminded his clergy that confirmation "is not only the Church's means to bless, but it is the Church's time for their conversion". He felt that unless there was true conversion and commitment and the resolve of habitual attendance at the Lord's Table, then it was better not to administer confirmation. [10]

The idea that Confirmation was a confirmation of baptismal vows was not confined to any one party. Archdeacon R. I. Wilberforce, speaking of confirmation candidates, said: "Unless they have not only a general faith in Christ's gospel, but an individual anxiety for their own salvation, how can they hon-

estly renew their vow of faith and obedience?" For George Moberly, the vicarious vows and promises of infant baptism were personally accepted and publicly acknowledged at confirmation.
For most High Churchmen, however, confirmation was far more
than the mere renewal of baptismal vows. William Maskell,
on leaving the Church of England, raised the question "Is it
a ceremony in which the candidates confirm the vows and promises made for them by others long before, when they were baptised, or is it an ordinance in which they receive also after
a sacramental and mysterious manner, by Laying on of Hands,
the gift of the Holy Spirit, never in like manner to be given
or received? and is this last the chief, or not the chief, end
and object of confirmation?" [11] Maskell's opinions on this
subject were representative of many members of the party to
which he had belonged before his secession to Rome.

Most Evangelicals on the other hand looked upon confirmation as no more than the renewal of baptismal vows. Bickersteth wrote: "Confirmation is the open and personal, ingenuous
and decided confession of the baptismal vow, on the part of
the confirmed". [12] This emphasis led Gilbert Elliott to say
that "the Church of England rite of confirmation could not
be used for the confirmation of those baptised outside her Communion, with no sponsors making promises on their behalf--
because they could not renew vows and promises which had
never been made for them". [13]

Thus these two fragmented parts of the initiatory rite
were generally believed to have some connection and this found
expression in a variety of ways. At the same time, many churchmen were not much concerned about the theological problems
raised by the fragmentation of the rite, such as: What takes
place at baptism? What takes place at confirmation? At what
point is the Holy Spirit given? Such questions were to be a cause
of controversy to churchmen of a later period, as baptism had
been in the mid-Victorian era.

NOTES

1. Anne Mozley, **Letters and Correspondence of John
Henry Newman during his life in the English Church** (2 Vols.
1891) Vol. II, 233.

2. Ibid., 234-5.

3. J. M. Neale, Lectures principally on the Church Difficulties of the present time (1852) 97-8. See also Moberly, Infant Baptism and Confirmation 35-6.

4. Moberly, Infant Baptism and Confirmation 42.

5. See How, Bishop Walsham How 293.

6. J. T. Coleridge, A Memoir of the Rev. John Keble, M.A., late Vicar of Hursley (3rd ed. 1870) 521-2.

7. Maurice, The Church a Family 75-6.

8. C. Thirlwall, A Charge 1854 64.

9. See Sanford, Archbishop Temple Vol. II, 505.

10. R. I. Wilberforce, A Charge 1848 4-5.

11. William Maskell, A Second Letter on the Present Position of the High Church Party in the Church of England (1850) 36-7.

12. See Bickersteth, A Treatise on Baptism 286. See also John Kaye, On Confirmation (1841) 10-11. Daniel Wilson, A Plain and Affectionate Address to Young Persons about to be confirmed (n.d.) 2-4.

13. Gilbert Elliott, Sermons on some of the Subjects of the Day, preached in Trinity Church Marylebone (1850) 260.

B. The Increase of the Episcopate

The Bishop is the Minister of Confirmation in the Church of England and she allows no exception to this rule. Many mid-Victorian churchmen recognized that the number of bishops was insufficient and the pastoral work of the Church inevitably suffered as a result. Therefore this period witnessed a growing demand among churchmen for more bishops. Most of the reports, pamphlets and debates saw the vastly increased population as justification for such an increase. It was generally agreed that new dioceses ought to be created to deal with the new centers of industrial population in the North of England. This move, together with the introduction of the office of suffragan bishop, is important to this study because alongside the suggestion that the large growth of population justified such an increase was the growing demand for an increase in the number of confirmation centers, and in the frequency of confirmations. Available literature shows how this pressure continued throughout, and indeed, long after, the mid-Victorian period.

Archdeacon Wilberforce believed that such an increase would remove a very real abuse which had grown up in connection with confirmation. He complained that because of the infrequent occurrence of confirmations clergy often submitted unsuitable candidates, rather than unduly delay confirmation, for this he said was often thought to imply rejection. Triennial and quadrennial confirmations resulted in large assemblies of young people gathered from over a wide area. Such confirmations were not regulated by a consideration of the spiritual wants of the young, but imposed by the shortage of episcopal manpower. He felt that the bishops were unable to increase the present number of confirmations; this could only be done through an increase in the episcopate, which would lead to more regular confirmations of smaller numbers of better prepared candidates. They would also give the masses more opportunities to witness this rite and thus bring home its meaning to them. [1]

The number of bishops required to meet the new situation was a cause of debate and disagreement. Lord John Russell suggested four and there were those who felt that a small increase in the number of diocesans, plus a large increase of suffragan bishops, was the best answer to the problem, but one writer suggested that nothing short of fifty or sixty additional bishops would meet the present exigency. On February 12th 1858, the Bishop of Oxford, Samuel Wilberforce, brought a petition with 217 signatures before the Upper House. This petition pointed out that in the last 300 years the population had increased from 4 million to nearly 20 million and the number of clergy had risen to nearly 18,000, yet the number of bishops had remained the same. The new situation, said Wilberforce, demanded an increase in the episcopate. A lengthy debate on the subject also took place in the Lower House. Canon Wordsworth suggested that the duty of sponsors to bring baptized children to the bishop to be confirmed was not being fulfilled as it ought; this, he felt, was a strong reason for increasing the episcopate. "How are we to have confirmation without bishops?" He suggested that six-sevenths of the whole number of children were left without the rite of confirmation. [2] Chancellor Martin suggested that, if confirmations were held regularly in every parish and the clergy impressed upon their parishioners the importance of the rite, the young people would be brought to be confirmed, and the numbers received into the Church increase beyond conception "and those vast masses which for want of effectual spiritual superintendence, are now driven to Dissent, or are without religion altogether, would be brought within the influence and pale of our own Church". [3]

In July 1862 a Petition was presented to the House of Lords by the English Church Union requesting that, in view of the increased population, clergy and parishes and "the large number of children to whom annually the ordinance of Confirmation ought to be severally ministered, it is impossible for the present very limited number of bishops to perform, in any adequate manner, the sacred function of their office". The Petition ended by appealing to the House to sanction any well-considered scheme for increasing the episcopate. [4] Twenty-five years later the E.C.U. was still petitioning, in the belief that such an increase would enable an annual confirmation to be held in every parish throughout the Kingdom. [5] The Upper House debated the issue once again, in 1863, when there was general agreement that something ought to be done to remedy the situation, but their good intentions failed to produce the necessary extra bishops. [6]

As an alternative solution a writer in The Christian Observer put forward a suggestion for non-episcopal confirmations. He supported both the need for an increase in the episcopate and in the number of confirmations, especially in large towns where it was generally administered in alternate years. "We should be glad if it were annual in every parish in the kingdom". He went on to claim that nothing in the rite of confirmation demanded that it be administered only by a bishop. "If the presbyter may baptise, why may he not confirm? If he may admit into the Church of Christ by the greater sacrament of baptism, why may he not administer the lesser one of confirmation? Why may he not publicly ratify his former act by admitting the baptised into full communion?" Bishops, he felt, could authorize and commission archdeacons and certain clergymen to administer confirmation on their behalf. [7] In spite of the obvious needs of the time and the zeal of most churchmen, the suggestion was too radical to be given any serious thought.

Although churchmen realized the need for reform in the system of the Church of England if she was to meet effectively the needs of the new society, as the national Church she was not free to implement such changes, however vital she thought them to be for her mission and well-being. State and secular influence, in the form of Crown, Government and politics, prevented such reform and this offered further ammunition to those seeking disestablishment. Where new dioceses were created, in Manchester and Ripon, experience supported the appeal for more such changes and pressure from churchmen did eventually result in a number of new dioceses being formed in the late 1870's and 80's. Among the various arguments used by the advocates of this policy, the need for more confirmations was certainly one of the most urgent. They constituted the part of the bishops' work which most nearly concerned the ordinary churchgoers for, as Owen Chadwick had written, "The most important occasions for the parish were confirmations". [8]

NOTES

1. See R. I. Wilberforce, A Charge 1847 10-11.

2. Chronicle of Convocation February 10th 1858, 52-3.

3. Ibid., 56.

4. Roberts, English Church Union 22-3, 45.

5. See Ibid., 292-3. The same plea was still being made at the end of the century; see Wilfred S. de Winton, "The Increase of the Episcopate" in Essays in Aid of the Reform of the Church ed. C. Gore (1898) 264-90.

6. Chronicle of Convocation 1863, 1001-17.

7. The Christian Observer April 1860, 262. See article on the subject on 257-64.

8. Chadwick, Victorian Church Part II, 342.

C. The Age for Confirmation

The Church of England has never laid down a particular age for confirmation and thus practice has varied widely. The Book of Common Prayer requires candidates to be of a 'competent age' having come to "years of discretion"--the deciding factor being the candidate's ability to repeat, in English, the Creed, the Lord's Prayer and the Ten Commandments, and also to be able to answer questions from the Catechism. Thus the Prayer Book emphasis is upon 'intellectual readiness' rather than 'moral and spiritual fitness'. Evangelicals tended to stress the need to be converted before confirmation, while High Churchmen emphasized the sacramental aspect of the rite which was not, they felt, dependent upon age, intellectual ability or conversion. These factors obviously influenced the approaches and aims of parochial clergy in preparing candidates for confirmation. In practice, the age at which candidates were confirmed depended upon the views and regulations of each diocesan bishop, which were influenced by churchmanship of the bishop and what he believed confirmation to be, but at the same time there was no party policy concerning the ideal age for its reception.

Pusey, an acknowledged leader of the Tractarian Party and their mentor on baptism, spoke of the usual age for confirmation as being fifteen or sixteen. He felt that if it was administered at an earlier age it might furnish the grace to resist temptation at a perilous time of life, or if later that it might seal repentance for the sins of an undisciplined youth. [1] W. E. Gladstone seems to have regarded fourteen as the usual age. In a letter of July 1854 he reminded his son Willy that having reached the age of fourteen he had arrived at a new stage in his Christian life: "The age of 14 is that which the Church very much recognizes as marking the passage from childhood properly so called to a state of fuller knowledge, judgement and responsibility. At that age, speaking generally, it is considered time to prepare young persons for their confirmation". Gladstone believed that those confirmed "received graces from God by the laying on of the Bishop's hands". [2]

Many Evangelical bishops looked upon the age of fifteen as the most suitable age and thus were at one with many High Churchmen. Bishop John Jackson, a tolerant and pious Evangelical, expressed the views of many of his episcopal brethren when he requested his clergy not to present candidates for confirmation under the age of fifteen, while the old-fashioned Evangelical bishop, John Thomas Pelham, could not agree with the opinions of some of the clergy that candidates ought to be confirmed at an earlier age because they were leaving school or the parish: "If at an earlier age a child is so ripe in understanding, and so proved to be faithful as to be, in the judgement of the clergyman, meet and in his own desire ready to attend the Lord's Supper, let him not be excluded because he is under the usual age. But such cases are rare and exceptional". He acknowledged that leaving school, and indeed the parish, to begin work were important factors, but not sufficient to constitute a reduction in the age of confirmation. [3]

Pelham was by no means the only bishop who felt that the parish priest was the best judge of the fitness of those who offered themselves. But the freedom given to the clergy in this matter by many of the bishops did not satisfy everyone. Evidence suggests that thirteen was the lowest age that even the most flexible bishops were willing to allow. J. M. Neale was not the only High Churchman who considered that the bishops were grievously wrong in refusing to confirm children at a much younger age for, by so doing, they were "prohibiting them from the grace of Confirmation". He firmly believed that all above the age of seven ought to be presented for confirmation. [4] Others agreed with Neale; as one of them expressed it, an "intellectual process has been substituted for the Divine Gifts of Grace, and it is held that a child is unable to be confirmed by the Holy Ghost until, intellectually, it can confirm itself. In other words, that a Sacrament is not, as the Church defines it, a Means of Grace, but an intellectual process". [5] For the advocates of an early age for confirmation the heart of the problem was: Is Confirmation primarily a sacramental or an intellectual event?

Scattered evidence from Broad Churchmen and other sources simply confirms the picture already outlined that, among mid-Victorian churchmen there was no common practice and usage concerning the ideal age for confirmation. Frederick Temple was confirmed at the age of twelve and never thought that this was too early. On one occasion he confirmed a group of boys and girls aged nine, after they had been fully instructed in the Faith. But while some argued for a lower age there were others who felt that an even higher age provided more satisfactory candidates. Bishop Charles Baring had some very strong views on this subject, indeed he was not only adamant in his position, but also somewhat intolerant both in expressing his views and in their implementation. His position was clearly expressed in his Charge of 1866, where ten printed pages are given to the subject. In his primary Charge he had appealed to his clergy in the diocese of Durham to endeavor "to raise, within reasonable limits, the standard of age and moral qualifications". [6] After much thought and consultation with others he came to the conclusion that those of seventeen, eighteen and twenty, and even older, were the most satisfactory candidates. [7]

Thus while some parochial clergy and even laity pleaded for a lowering of the age of confirmation, evidence suggests that the bishops of the period, from all parties, both in theory and practice, accepted and defended the age of fifteen to sixteen as the most suitable age to receive this sacrament. Some bishops were willing to allow rare exceptions to this rule, while others sought to raise the minimum age of confirmation even higher. The social reasons put forward in support of a reduction in the minimum age--the early age at which children left school and home to begin work--suggests that concern was primarily with the working classes. To reduce the age would, some believed, vastly increase the number of candidates who offered themselves from this social group. There is no evidence which suggests that the more educated, and the middle and upper classes, were confirmed at an earlier age, although those belonging to these classes were more likely to meet the stipulations laid down by the bishops concerning exceptions to the general rule. A more sacramental approach, which was not dependent on either the age or intellectual ability of the candidates, was put forward by some High Churchmen, but it cannot be said that these were the views of that party as a whole, and such views seem to have had little, if any, influence upon episcopal practice.

NOTES

1. Liddon, **Life of Pusey** Vol. I, 17. See also R. I. Wilberforce, A Charge, 1848 4-5. The Guardian February 28th 1853, 123.

2. D. C. Lathbury, **Correspondence on Church and Religion of William Ewart Gladstone** (2 Vols. 1910) Vol. II, 151-2.

3. J. T. Pelham, A Charge, 1865 16. See also C. R. Sumner, A Charge, 1850 27-8.

4. Neale, **Church Difficulties** 97-8.

5. Orby Shipley, ed. **Tracts for the Day: Essays on Theological Subjects: The Seven Sacraments** (n.d.) 149-51.

6. C. Baring, A Charge, 1866 43-4.

7. Ibid., 46-7.

D. Confirmation and Holy Communion

The need for more regular celebrations of the Holy Communion was one of the subjects most frequently mentioned in the Episcopal Charges of the nineteenth century. While High Church bishops tended to be the most emphatic on this point, encouragement and exhortations to the clergy came from bishops of every party. Clerical response to such episcopal appeals varied, but on the whole it was fairly good and in the mid-Victorian period there was a gradual, but very real, improvement. Instead of the majority of parishes having quarterly celebrations, the monthly service became the more regular pattern; in some parishes celebrations were even more frequent. Much depended upon the lead given by the bishop and thus practice varied from diocese to diocese. [1]

Tables of communicant figures and the number of celebrations began to appear more frequently as appendices to Episcopal Charges. An example of the kind of change which took place in many dioceses of the period is seen in that of York during the time of William Thomson. At his Primary Visitation in 1865, 276 parishes, almost half of the diocese, had less than twelve celebrations in the year. In 1884, the date of his last Visitation, there were only 53 churches with less than a monthly celebration, 128 with weekly celebrations, 24 with three each month, 122 with fortnightly Communion services and 261 with a monthly service. [2]

With this increasing emphasis upon the need for more frequent celebrations of the Holy Communion came a greater stress upon confirmation as the means of admission to the Holy Communion and an insistence that the confirmed should be regular in receiving the Sacrament. Some churchmen believed that the Holy Communion ought to be received as soon after confirmation as possible, but others felt this inadvisable and some even improper. While some at least of the Evangelical clergy began to emphasize the importance of this sacrament, it was of course the High Churchmen who insisted on the centrality and necessity of eucharistic worship. The priority they gave to their efforts to promote greater attendance at Communion led to some staggering results. For example, Lowder increased his communicants in Calvert Street Chapel from two in 1856 to 130 in 1860, while A. B. Goulden, who had seven Sunday services and three mid-week services, could boast of 8,257 working class communicants. All Saints' Church, Margaret Street with both Sunday and daily celebrations had 24,363 communicants in 1862, rising to 27,432 in 1869. There was in fact an increasing number of churches with celebrations more often than weekly, while those of the 'Catholic tradition' often had daily celebrations.

Unfortunately, while many Victorian churchmen were very conscious of the importance of statistics, others seem to have completely disregarded them. Communicant figures in the Visitation Returns during Thomson's time at York reveal that out of 638 parishes only 176 incumbents claimed to keep a list of communicants. Because of the lack of figures it is impossible to build up an overall picture of the situation. In any case it must be realized that attendance at the non-sacramental services of Morning and Evening Prayer were often enormous and far surpassing the number of recorded communicants. Exhortations to attend these services and records of the numbers who did attend found little place in the Charges of the period.

Returns from the dioceses of York and Ripon provide some insight into the kind of situation which must have existed in many other dioceses. The following furnish some useful examples of the situation in the diocese of York in the 1860's. [3] The communicant figures given are the average at each monthly or bi-monthly celebration: the average congregation are for other weekly Sunday services.

mid-Victorian period look upon the connection between confirmation and the Holy Communion? and, What was their teaching and practice?

			Average Weekly Congregation
Thorne	17	Communicants	200
Arksey	7	"	180
Wortley	16	"	150
Sprotborough	40	"	300
Tickhill	57	"	300–400 at Morning Prayer
			600–700 at Evening Prayer
St. John, Hull	110	"	1,000 at Morning Prayer
			700 at Evening Prayer

A very valuable manuscript Notebook compiled by Thomas Longley when Bishop of Ripon, from Parochial Returns of Visitation queries 1837-1856, supplies perhaps a unique source of illustration from northern industrial and rural parishes. The following is no more than a small selection of those recorded:

Rural Parishes		Communicants	Average Weekly Congregation
Boroughbridge	1853	40 monthly	250
	1856	34 monthly	514
Grinton	1850	22 monthly	200
	1856	12 monthly	200
Hawes	1850	25–30 4 times	200–300
	1856	36 a year	250
Market Towns			
Richmond	1850	40 twice monthly	200
	1856	30 monthly	200
Knaresborough	1850	145 monthly	900 adults, 600 children
	1856	120 monthly	1,000
Towns and Industrial Areas			
Bradford Parish Church	1850	200 monthly	2,000
	1853	200 monthly	1,400
Birstall	1850	65 monthly	800
	1856	50–60 monthly	800
Dewsbury	1850	70 monthly	900 adults, 500 children
	1856	90 fourteen times a year	1,000 adults, 500 children
Armley, Leeds	1850	60 monthly	600
	1856	40 monthly	650
Leeds Parish Church	1850	200 monthly 75 weekly	3,000–4,000
	1856	150 monthly 60 weekly	2,500

In many of the parishes the weekly average congregation at Morning/Evening Prayer was ten times that of the monthly communicant figures.[4] The figures suggest that many churchmen of the period did not feel that regular communion was intended to be the practice for church members as a whole. There was thus a gap between the official teaching of the Church of England and the popular approach to communion which may be taken as evidence of lay indifference or doctrinal ignorance, or perhaps both. But who was responsible for this inconsistency between official teaching and local practice? Was it really the ignorance and half-heartedness of the laity, or the contradictory views of bishops and clergy, plus the dilatoriness of some of the clergy? In view of the vast differences between attendance figures at the Holy Communion and at the non-sacramental services of Morning and Evening Prayer, consideration must be given to the questions: How did bishops and clergy of the mid-Victorian period look upon the connection between confirmation and the Holy Communion? and, What was their teaching and practice?

For many of the newly confirmed there was a considerable lapse of time between confirmation and first Communion; often this was due to pure negligence, either by the newly confirmed or the parochial clergy, or both, but in some cases the newly confirmed were deliberately encouraged by priest, parents and sponsor to delay receiving Holy Communion. Bishops of the period became more and more concerned about the vast difference between the numbers confirmed and the small numbers who became regular communicants. Many examples can be provided to show how, even after large confirmations, communicant figures remained unchanged.

The diocese of Oxford during the episcopate of Samuel Wilberforce had the largest increase of confirmation candidates of any diocese in the country--from 9,249 in 1846-8 to 20,028 in the period 1866-69--but communicant figures remained more or less unchanged. [5] Between 1858-60 Wilberforce confirmed nearly 19,000 candidates, but in his Charge for 1860 he records that the total number at ordinary celebrations of the Holy Communion was only 19,125 and at the greater festivals not quite 26,000. [6] Wilberforce became deeply concerned about this grave discrepancy and in his Charge of 1867 directed his clergy to keep an "accurate account of those who follow Confirmation up by that which is its proper conclusion--the coming to the Table of the Lord". [7]

Bishop Ellicott of Gloucester and Bristol put the question to his clergy in 1864 "Has the decorous Catechumen become a regular Communicant? Anxiously, most anxiously, have I looked at that part of your returns, in the case of all those parishes from which I have received candidates for confirmation". This examination revealed that out of 253 such parishes he was able to report that in 229, on average, "more than a fourth part of those confirmed have become communicants, or rather, to speak more carefully, have attended the Holy Communion since they were confirmed". He also noted that in 24 parishes those confirmed had not yet become communicants. [8]

Bishop William Jacobson's observation to his clergy in 1868 that "The proportion of those who, after being confirmed, become regular communicants varies very considerably", [9] was a fair comment on the position throughout the country.

The introduction of Evening Communion by many clergy was generally indicative of a growing concern over the general neglect of this sacrament. Many churchmen felt that the neglect of the Holy Communion ought to be dealt with at an early stage, namely at the time of confirmation preparation and first communion. Confirmation must be shown to be admission to communicant life within the Church. For A. C. Tait this was very much the case, for he looked upon confirmation as admission to the regular habit of Holy Communion month by month, a view shared by Charles Simeon, W. E. Gladstone and Julian Moreton.

There was widespread concern that so few confirmation candidates became communicants and Tait's idea of regular monthly communion was one shared by many of his contemporary churchmen. Indeed at least one manual of preparation was produced specially "for those who do not communicate oftener than once a month". This manual by W. E. Scudmore, **Steps to the Altar: A Manual of Devotions for the Blessed Eucharist,** first published in 1846, by 1867 went into its forty-first edition and in 1888 the sixty-ninth edition was published. This was typical of the continuous demand for such devotional manuals throughout the nineteenth century.

In some parishes all those confirmed proceeded at once to receive the Holy Communion; for these candidates the communicant life began immediately, even if it was not maintained. However, the idea of receiving the Holy Communion on the day of confirmation was thought to be somewhat unusual and it was certainly not a widespread practice. [10] In many cases the practicalities of the situation, when a large number were confirmed during the course of one service, would prevent, or at least make difficult, the administration of the Holy Communion, without inordinately lengthening the service.

Practice with regard to receiving Holy Communion after confirmation varied considerably. In some cases it took place on the Sunday following the Confirmation, in other cases candidates were advised to wait and some were expected to attend a prolonged Communicant Class, to prepare them fully to receive the Holy Sacrament. In such cases pre-confirmation preparation was seen as primarily instruction in the Chirstian life and faith and a preparation for confirmation, with preparation for Communion as something independent and to be carried out later. Bickersteth reflected the changing attitudes on the subject when he wrote: "There is an important interval between confirmation and going to the Lord's Table which may advantageously be shortened or lengthened according to the age, knowledge and character of those confirmed. But I believe increasing experience has led us to the conviction that it is desirable that the confirmed shall communicate as early as circumstances will allow after confirmation". The first part of this statement seems to imply that before receiving Holy Communion, the newly confirmed must have the right knowledge and moral qualifications. This attitude prompted Bishop John Jackson to say in 1867: "There are few as yet, who are prepared to advocate the admission of children generally under the age of fifteen to the Holy Communion". [11] In saying this he was reflecting the feeling of a number of his episcopal brethren that it was not right or proper for the young, who were spiritually immature, to receive the sacrament of Holy Communion. Bishop Wilberforce, however, urged the newly confirmed, whatever their age, not to put off coming to receive their Lord at the altar and appealed to them to be frequent and regular at the Holy Communion. In this he expressed a conviction which was gaining a much wider acceptance, but its implementation depended upon the parochial clergy, whose opinions on this subject also varied considerably. Archdeacon Wilberforce felt strongly that if candidates for confirmation did not intend to become regular communicants then they ought not to be confirmed and Keble refused to recommend for confirmation those who would not pledge themselves to be communicants.

The so-called 'Confirmation Rubric', "And there shall none be admitted to the holy communion, until such time as he be confirmed, or be ready and desirous to be confirmed", was taken by the majority of mid-Victorian churchmen to imply that confirmation was an essential pre-requisite to the Holy Communion. For some it was simply the introduction or gateway to the Sacrament, while others believed that without confirmation there could be no communicant membership of the Church. Some were extreme rigorists in the application of the Confirmation Rubric, while others took a very liberal approach.

An anonymous writer pleaded that the infrequency of confirmations in rural areas, which could lead to young people lapsing before the next confirmation came round, was a good reason "why clergymen should not teach so persistently as they do that the unconfirmed must not communicate". [12] J. M. Neale argued that, if bishops refused to confirm young candidates, then priests should allow those whom they felt fit and proper recipients to receive the Holy Communion.

Like so many other doctrinal matters in the Church of England this also was to remain a controversial issue and its application a matter of individual interpretation. It does, however, serve to illustrate the fact that for most churchmen, at the close of the mid-Victorian period, confirmation alone constituted admission to the Sacrament of the Lord's Table and that neither of these sacraments ought to be neglected or treated lightly.

NOTES

1. The following provide examples of episcopal exhortation to more frequent celebration of the Holy Communion and also figures regarding the actual frequency of celebrations:

Robert Bickersteth, Ripon, A Charge, 1867 11-13.
Edward H. Browne, Ely, A Charge, 1865 13-14.
R. Durnford, Chichester, A Charge, 1871 36-7.
C. J. Ellicott, Gloucester, A Charge, 1867 20-I.
W. K. Hamilton, Salisbury, A Charge, 1858 27-8.
J. Jackson, Lincoln, A Charge, 1867 17.
W. Jacobson, Chester, A Charge, 1864 11-12.
J. T. Pelham, Norwich, A Charge, 1865 13-14.
S. Wilberforce, Oxford, A Charge, 1857 20-2; 1860 11-13; 1863 14-15.

2. See H. Kirk-Smith, **William Thomson: Archbishop of York, His Life and Times, 1819-1890** (1958) 18-19. A Comparison between the two archiepiscopal sees shows a clear increase in the regularity of celebrations. Longley's returns for the diocese of Canterbury in 1868 (see Longley, A Charge, 1868 45-50) were as follows: 176 churches or 37% with less than monthly celebrations; 277 or 59% with monthly celebrations or oftener; 18 or 4% with weekly celebrations or oftener. While the compound figures for the diocese of York nearly 20 years later give the following: 53 churches or 9% with less than monthly celebrations; 407 or 69% with monthly or oftener; 128 or 22% with weekly celebrations or oftener.

3. See Kirk-Smith, op. cit., 19-25.

4. See Charles Thomas Longley, M. S. Notebook of Parochial Returns.

5. See Standish Meacham, **Lord Bishop: The Life of Samuel Wilberforce** (Cambridge, Massachusetts 1970) 143.

6. S. Wilberforce, A Charge, 1860 10-12.

7. S. Wilberforce, A Charge, 1866 4.

8. C. J. Ellicott, A Charge, 1864 26-7; see also 1867 24-5.

9. W. Jacobson, A Charge, 1868 16.

10. See F. Jeune, A Charge, 1867 9.

11. J. Jackson, A Charge, 1867 25. See also C. Baring, A Charge, 1866 47-9

12. Anonymous, Confirmation Considered with reference to the Holy Communion (n.d. c.1870) 8.

II. PREPARATION FOR CONFIRMATION

A. Religious Instruction in the New Society

For the majority of mid-Victorian churchmen some kind of preparation was looked upon as an essential prerequisite to confirmation. True, some were negligent in this matter, as was acknowledged by the conscientious, and often recognized by the offenders. Even so, for most of the clergy of this period, religious instruction implied something far wider than confirmation preparation. There was the feeling that the Established Church was 'England's Schoolmaster' and as such responsible for the religious teaching and training of the young in the Faith of the national Church. Her position in this area was so well established that few were willing to challenge it, at least until the nineteenth century. All this was to be changed through Nonconformist pressure, which resulted in the Parliamentary reform of English education and thus it was that the educational role of the Church of England underwent a radical change. By the end of the nineteenth century, although the Church still made a valuable contribution to the field of education, she could no longer claim to be 'England's Schoolmaster'. The privileged position which she had enjoyed for so long, and often taken for granted, was now curtailed and what remained had to be carefully guarded and often fought for.

Much of the Church's work of religious instruction took place in connection with confirmation preparation and was approached from numerous angles. For centuries the Catechism had been looked upon as the ideal form for such preparation and instruction in the Faith of the Church, indeed knowledge of the Catechism was felt by most Victorian bishops to be an essential prerequisite to confirmation. Generally, a bishop expected those presented to him for confirmation to be able to answer questions on the Catechism, and not always by rote. Catechetical instruction was given in all Church of England Day schools; it was this fact which enraged the Dissenters and inspired the agitation for the removal of education from the Church's control.

Catechetical instruction was also given in the parish church, at Sunday school and in some cases in the home. That which was given in the day schools was, by the nature of things, no more than a general religious instruction or, at the most, a pre-preparation for confirmation. The early school-leaving age of the period, and the later age of confirmation, generally at fifteen years of age, left a considerable gap between what had been taught at school and the knowledge of the Faith required before confirmation. The majority of children left day school at the age of eleven and 95% by the age of thirteen. Attempts to retain children during this critical period before confirmation, and the extent and quality of their preparation, depended very much upon the conscientiousness, convictions and ability of the parish clergy. Bishops were very much aware of this factor and many of the Charges of the period contain exhortations to make a greater effort in this area. Many of the clergy responded with great zeal and enthusiasm, although others remained as dilatory as ever. It must be admitted that the task which the bishops urged upon their clergy was not easily accomplished. Indeed, the social conditions of the mid-Victorian period made confirmation preparation more hazardous and complex than ever before. The nature and difficulty of the Church's task is appreciated when considered in the light of the sociological situation produced by industrial development, population explosion and movement, and mass urbanization.

In the new industrial areas clerical manpower was insufficient to meet the requirement of a widespread and thorough confirmation preparation. Alongside the development of these new urban areas there was a decline in the life and population of the old rural communities. Movement away from the rural areas to the new communities, in search of employment, led to a shortage of suitable confirmation candidates, while the preparation of the servants of large country houses also had its problems. Large town parishes, and the distances which had to be travelled in order to attend a confirmation group, acted as a deterrent to some, while home conditions, squalor and overcrowding did not encourage home preparation. Working conditions and long hours left young children little time or energy for confirmation preparation, even if they had the personal desire or parental encouragement. The early school-leaving age and the low level of education achieved during the short period of education had a limiting effect upon the extent and quality of confirmation preparation which clergy were able and willing to give. The drift of the masses from the Church meant that many children of the period had little, if any, contact with the Church and for such children confirmation preparation must have appeared both unnecessary and irrelevant. The geographical distances which had often to be covered to reach a confirmation center, and the long period between confirmations also created problems. Some parents were unwilling to allow their children to travel to such centers and thus did not encourage them to undergo preparation; moreover, lapse of time between confirmations meant that some candidates were lost because the confirmation was too far in the future to offer any real incentive to persist in preparation. Rather than have to wait for the next confirmation, candidates were sometimes prepared and presented before they were mentally and spiritually ready, but clergy felt that if they did not do this such children might be lost for good as far as the Church was concerned.

These were some of the mid-Victorian problems which militated against confirmation preparation, but perhaps the greatest which the Church had to face in this connection was child labor. This was no new phenomenon, for children had been made to work hard in the countryside and in domestic industry even before the new industrial age, but it raised unprecedented difficulties in those areas where, unfortunately, the Church was at her weakest, i.e. in the new industrial towns of mills, mines and factories. Agricultural labor, domestic service and apprenticeships had always made it difficult for working children to attend any kind of religious instruction, but the appalling conditions of employment in industry made it well-nigh impossible. When considering the failure of the Church to retain the working class we have to remember that it was not until 1874 that children under ten were satisfactorily barred from all forms of regular wage-earning labor, and only in the same year the ten-hour day was secured. Kingsley's **Water Babies** was inspired by a Parliamentary Report of 1863, in the middle of our period.

Apart from this, the vast increase in the number of domestic servants alone must have removed a large proportion of potential candidates from direct contact with their parish priest, for although some employers sent their servants to church and would arrange for them to be prepared for confirmation, the majority did neither and the children who went into service, sometimes as young as nine years of age, grew into adulthood quite out of touch with the Church. Moreover, it was not only children who suffered thus. Adults also faced long hours, appalling working conditions and often tyrannical employers. Gradually, through Parliamentary reform, their working hours were shortened and they found that they had increasing time available for recreation.

Much has been said about the degrading pastimes and vices of the period, but there was also a growing use of truly recreational activities: bands, musical teaching, choral groups, general entertainment, penny reading, games and sports, the free use of parks, libraries and galleries, also excursions; these activities tended to take the place of the social life which had previously been provided by the local church. Such was the environment in which the State was attempting to improve and widen the educational system of the nation, and in which the Church had to fulfil her mission in the field of religious education and the instruction of the young.

Addressing the House of Commons in 1867, the Right Hon. H. A. Bruce expressed the opinion that there ought to be 2 million at school and not the recorded 800,000 to 900,000. When attendance figures are examined on a regional basis the nature and extent of the problem is seen in its true light--the new industrial areas were the most neglected and yet the most needy. It is true that many of the ignorant working class masses cared little for the education of themselves or their children, but at the same time there were real signs of a growing interest in, and desire for, education. There was a growth in the number of Mechanics' Institutes, Working Men's Colleges, Reading Rooms, Working Men's Clubs and Institutes; more books were being borrowed from public libraries than ever before; there was an increase in the number of cheap newpapers and in the amount of general literature available. All this indicates the increasing demand for, and appreciation of, adult education among the working classes. Between 1850 and 1861 the issues of the Religious Tract Society increased from 11,090,259 tracts and books to 41,710,203, an increase of 270%. This thirst for education and the increase in religious publications and instruction gained the full approval of Queen Victoria, who expressed the desire that "the youth of her kingdom should be religiously brought up". Many members of Parliament concurred with the Queen and were actively working for a more effective and wide-embracing educational system. There were some however, like Lord Melbourne, who saw no reason for educating the masses and his advice was: "Why not leave it alone?"

A nineteenth century writer saw evidence of a general improvement in education and the intellectual ability of the masses in the fact that there were fewer and fewer candidates for confirmation who were unable to sign their names. Such was the social setting in which parish clergy were being urged to carry out confirmation preparation and religious instruction. Unfortunately, little record has been left of the practical implications of this aspect of their work in the new industrial areas, in prentice houses, workhouses and the like, for which they were often responsible and where, in many cases, chaplains were appointed. In spite of this lack of documentation, the Church's preparation of candidates for confirmation must be seen in the context of the sociological situation in which this work was being attempted: Child labor, involving long hours and bad working conditions, leading to exhaustion and ill-health; bad and overcrowded housing; poor clothing; lack of money; the growth of secularism and non-religious interests; the increasing numbers of those in domestic service; the problems and difficulties raised by prentice houses, workhouses and parish poor houses; the movement of young agricultural laborers. All these issues created many new problems which the conscientious clergy had to face and somehow overcome, if they were to be effective in gathering the young of their parishes together and adequately prepare them for confirmation and communicant membership of the Church.

The Neglect of Confirmation Preparation

We have been considering some of the daunting problems faced by the mid-Victorian church; we have also to admit that some of the neglect of confirmation preparation was due to negligence on the part of the clergy. Francis Goddard, curate of Winterbourne Bassett, wrote in 1840 of a visit to a fellow curate, E. W. Tuffnell of Broad Hinton: He was shown into the drawing room which was full of girls, a confirmation class, and was moved to remark, "It is a fact that I had never before heard of classes for instruction for confirmation; the only mode adopted by me and others was a sort of house-to-house visit to those we could pick up after their work was done". The vicar of Alfriston strongly disapproved of confirmations and always evaded them if he could. When his bishop arranged a confirmation in his church he even contrived to be away from his parish. [1]

Bishop Wilberforce wrote to reprimand one of his clergy who, at the last confirmation, had fixed a note on the door of the church giving notice of the date of the forthcoming service and telling those interested to prepare themselves. [2] Again, to the rector of Heyford he wrote "It is...my painful duty to blame you for the manifest want of preparation for the holy rite of Confirmation manifested by several Catechumens appearing with your ticket of approval whose levity obliged me to dismiss them from the Church". [3] Years before, H. E. Manning had written to Wilberforce expressing his view that the neglect of confirmation was "One of the great efficient causes of our present low state of religion in the Church".

In a book **Duties of the Clerical Profession** we are told of clergymen who, after hearing each of the children utter a few sentences in haste and by rote, gave them tickets for confirmation as a matter of course. An even worse situation was referred to by Bishop George Moberly, when preaching in Salisbury Cathedral. He told of a boy of fifteen who was sent for by the rector, asked his age and received his ticket for confirmation without a word. Moberly expressed the opinion that he did not think this a solitary case of a parish where no preparation was given.

At the end of the mid-Victorian period Bishop Durnford raised the question: "Why is it that in parishes of equal population the proportion of children presented for confirmation should so widely differ?" "Why in one are all the youths and maidens of suitable age, and even many adults, brought forward; in the other but a sample, so to speak of each? Make reasonable allowance for adverse circumstances, the prevalence, for instance, of local non-conformity, and hence of ingrained prejudice and even hostility to the ordinance; still there remains the fact that the rising generation do not come under their pastor's teaching, when that teaching may be most fruitful and most blessed".

During the period there was a considerable improvement in the field of confirmation preparation and this was being continually extended, but neglect and abuse were still to be found in many places; there was still a long way to go before the Church of the nation could be satisfied that she was doing all that was possible to gather suitable candidates together and offer them adequate preparation before confirmation.

NOTES

1. See Edward B. Ellman, **Recollections of a Sussex Parson** (1912) 164.

2. Pugh, **Letter-books of Samuel Wilberforce**, 58 fn.

3. Ibid., 159-60.

B. Catechetical Instruction

The Book of Common Prayer gives the Catechism the sub-title 'An instruction to be learned of every person, before he be brought to be confirmed by the Bishop'. At the end of the Catechism are four rubrics, which leave priest and people in no doubt about what Mother church expects of each of her members, whether clerical or lay. The first two rubrics state:

"The Curate of every parish shall diligently upon Sundays and Holy-days, after the second Lesson at Evening Prayer, openly in the Church instruct and examine so many children of his parish sent unto him, as he shall think convenient, in some part of his Catechism". "And all Fathers, Mothers, Masters and Dames, shall cause their Children, Servants and Apprentices (which have not learned their Catechism) to come to the Church at the time appointed, and obediently to hear, and be ordered by the Curate, until such time as they have learned all that is here appointed for them to learn".

These rubrics presuppose a common aim between clergy, parents and employers--the Christian instruction of the young in the Faith of the Church, with their confirmation as its object. Generally speaking, bishops, clergy and people accepted the injunctions of the Book of Common Prayer in this matter and believed that knowledge of the Catechism was an indispensable condition for confirmation. Evidence shows that there was considerable variation in the practice of catechizing. On the one hand the directions of the Book of Common Prayer seem to have been completely disregarded, for in many parishes there was a complete neglect of public catechizing, while in many others the practice was inconsistent. This neglect can in fact be traced back to the seventeenth century. [1] John Kaye, in his Charge of 1828, speaks of how catechizing "has been allowed to fall into disuse". He suggests two reasons for this: pluralism leading to non-residence and the fact that instruction in the Catechism constitutes a part of the teaching of both National schools and Sunday schools. Having indicated the reasons for the neglect, he then urged his clergy to re-introduce the practice. [2] In a letter written to his clergy twenty years later he still had to admit: "We have allowed the public catechising of children...to fall comparatively into disuse". [3] During this period Churchwardens were required, every year, to say whether children were being catechized or not. [4] Archdeacon Wilberforce carried out an enquiry into the practice of catechizing in his archdeaconry and found that in many parishes it was often carried out only before confirmations (this was in fact the practice in many parishes throughout the country); that in some cases it was carried out only in Sunday school; that on the whole the duty was frequently left entirely to the schoolmaster and seldom brought to the notice of the congregation. Wilberforce tells of one set of Churchwardens who reported that they "never saw the clergyman instruct the children". [5] His brother Samuel in 1857 was able to report that in his diocese there were 173 churches where public catechizing was carried out, but this did not prevent him from appealing for an increase in the practice. [6]

The general picture seems to be that in many parishes the formal method of catechizing, as directed by the Prayer Book, was much neglected. A letter to The Guardian, in March 1865, could well reflect the national situation: "It is much to be wished that the old custom of catechising at our Church services on Sundays were revised". But in spite of this general neglect at parochial level, many of the bishops seemed to feel, although in some cases with certain qualifications, that catechizing was a laudable practice and much could be said in its favor.

Samuel Wilberforce was an avowed advocate of public catechizing and his enthusiastic recommendation of the practice had the support of his own experience and success in this field.[7] He felt that it could be used as an alternative to the sermon, while Bishop Short even suggested that it was more valuable than instruction by preaching.

The Prayer Book directs that catechizing should take place after the second Lesson at Evening Prayer on Sundays. Although this appointed time and place were probably the most widely used, there were those who did not think these suitable; some felt that half-an-hour before Evening Prayer was ideal and others that Sunday School was the best place. There was also some diversity in methods of catechizing and much depended on the abilities and convictions of the individual clergyman. Bishop Phillpotts was not alone in insisting that catechizing should not only be constantly, but intelligently taught.

The mere formal repetition of the words of the Catechism was a widespread practice, which many felt was grossly inadequate. Detailed and varied explanations and illustrations of each part of the Catechism, followed by questions and a familiar practical lecture at the close, was the method recommended by Edward Denison. [8] W. F. Hook's practice was to begin by making the children repeat the whole of the Catechism "which takes about ten minutes; I then cross-examine them, leading them by my questions from the Catechism to the lesson of the day, which takes another ten minutes, and then I apply what they have been taught in a short address". [9] Keble was a most conscientious catechist, but did not confine himself to the Church Catechism. He would prepare the children beforehand in the questions he meant to ask publicly; those unable to answer were carefully helped and encouraged. When the catechizing was ended he lectured from the pulpit on the subject of his questioning. His general practice was to take boys and girls on alternate Sundays. [10] There were many other clergymen who were equally conscientious, consistent and considerate as Denison, Hook, Keble and Wilberforce.

Many saw the catechizing of the young as an opportunity to reach and teach parents and employers. Keble made a practice of repeating the answers given by the children in order that parents present might follow the subject intelligently. Masters and Dames were expected to encourage their servants and apprentices to go to church to learn the Catechism. The Victorian period witnessed a phenomenal growth in the number of those in service from 600,000 in 1801 to 2 million in 1881; unfortunately, this increase was not accompanied by an increasing sense of responsibility among employers, or in the number of those who were faithful in the discharge of their godly duty towards those in their employment.

The work of children in mills, mines and agriculture was seen by some churchmen as a real problem in the religious instruction of the young. Some millowners were not averse to taking their apprentices to Sunday worship and encouraging their religious instruction on Sundays. Bishop Phillpotts believed that one way to be sure that children in employment would be catechized and receive religious instruction was "to find and to retain a proper master: one who is on principle a churchman, and will on principle teach in due subordination to his pastor", but he admitted that to secure such a master was no easy task. A letter to the Gentry, Yeomen and Farmers of the archdeaconry of the East Riding, from Archdeacon Wilberforce, reminded such people of their responsibility to send the young to church every Sunday to be catechized. He suggested that lack of knowledge concerning their duty to God was the reason for their unruliness in their employment. He recommended that the latter should "revive the custom of bringing the younger class of servant to catechetical instruction and those of riper years to public worship". Wilberforce went on to write: "On this head especially I will entreat every proprietor of landed property to use his influence with his tenantry and every master to remember the responsibility with which he is invested". [12]

The ever-increasing number of servants raised a very

real problem for the Church regarding their catechetical instruction and confirmation preparation. The religious instruction
of servants was largely dependent upon the encouragement of
their employers and their willingness to allow servants time
off their duties. There were those who felt little sense of responsibility towards the religious well-being of their servants and
others who had genuine concern in this matter, and who felt
responsible for the moral training of those in their service.
Victorian literature has preserved numerous accounts of how
master and mistress would take their servants to the parish
church and delight in hearing them being catechized. Horace
Mann, however, in the introduction to the Religious Census
of 1851 states that the duties and responsibilities of servants
were a preventive measure against their church attendance.
There can be little doubt that the long hours and physical demands of work in the case of both adults and children, which
often left Sunday as the only free day of the week for rest
and relaxation, was a real deterrent against making any effort
of their own volition to attend either public worship or catechizing.

The spiritual well-being of workhouses, of which there
were 650 in 1864, was largely the responsibility of the Established
Church. In 1861 it was estimated that the workhouses had a
total of 122,644 inmates, of which 106,224 claimed to belong
to the Church of England. Guardians of these workhouses were
responsible for the appointment of a Chaplain. One of the chaplain's duties was "to examine the children and to catechise such
as belong to the Church of England, at least once a month",
reporting on their progress to the Guardians. Although the Church
was aware of its responsibility in this field and indeed at the
time of the Religious Census claimed that her thousands of
adherents in these institutions had not been taken into consideration, nevertheless there was said to be room for much improvement in her work in this area. [13]

Prentice houses in general left much to be desired;
however, in at least some the education and religious instruction
of the children was undertaken, sometimes by members of the
owner's own family. Unfortunately, no real evidence of the
actual work of the church in these places has been discovered,
especially in relation to catechetical instruction. The genuine
pastoral concern of an increasing number of churchmen towards
the masses living in heathen darkness, suggests that the needs
in these quarters cannot have gone unnoticed and that some
attempts must have been made to meet the spiritual needs
of those apprentices who lived in such establishments.

During the Victorian period, manuals on the Catechism
were produced in large quantities and even larger editions; ecclesi-

astical newspapers of the time carried many advertisements of such manuals, tracts and leaflets. There were books on the Catechism in general, on the Creed, the Lord's Prayer and the Ten Commandments. Some were produced with the aim of helping those responsible for the catechetical instruction of the young, while others were intended for use by the serious minded candidates. The literature for candidates seems to have been produced mainly with the middle and upper classes in mind, or at least those of reasonable education. Among such churchpeople careful home training in religious matters such as the Catechism, Bible reading and prayer was a feature of the period, which partly accounts for the very great demand for religious publications, especially devotional manuals and works of religious instruction. The High Church party produced a number of 'Catholic Catechisms', but manuals were produced by all parties, and to meet the need of every brand of churchmanship. Not all churchmen felt that these manuals were of value, indeed Phillpotts believed that while they might help the catechist, they only tended to confuse the learner.

Churchmen were more or less united in the conviction that the school played an essential part in the religious instruction of the young people of the nation. Bishop John Kaye in 1847 expressed an opinion widely held among mid-Victorian churchmen--"Viewed with reference to the moral and religious character of the rising generation, the schoolroom is scarcely a less essential part of the parochial establishment than the house of God itself". [14] With such an exalted view of the school, one can understand the fight to maintain more than a foothold in the field of education. The moral and religious instruction of the young was of paramount importance, for they were seen as the parents of the future and upon them would depend the moral and religious upbringing of their offspring. Bishops were constantly urging their clergy not to neglect the education of the young, or regular attendance at the local school; the early age at which children were induced to withdraw from school in order to begin work, and the age at which many left home and the supervision of their parents, made early religious and moral instruction all the more essential and urgent.

Catechizing at day school was more widely practiced and more willingly accepted by the clergy than the public catechizing in church. Such catechizing, either by the local clergyman or the schoolmaster, was seen as an essential part in the educational programme in the majority of Church schools. Bishop Phillpotts roundly declared that he could not see any circumstances "which can justify a faithful clergyman in having to do with a school in which the Book of Commmon Prayer and the Church Catechism are not regular, necessary and main parts of the matter taught". [15] Phillpotts sometimes expressed views which gained little support among his episcopal brethren, but in the matter of the clergyman's duty and right to teach the Faith of the Church in schools, he was expressing the firm conviction of the majority, if not all, of the bench. Pressure to implement a conscience clause began in 1852 and resulted in a conflict between its supporters and the National Society. [16] Dissenters were divided in their attitudes towards the Established Church's insistence on teaching the Catechism in her schools. Not all Dissenters felt the need for the 'Conscience Clause' and while some used it to prevent the teaching of the Catechism to their children, others did not think that the situation warranted such action. [17] and were content with the instruction given.

The Education Act of 1870 struck a decisive blow at 'England's Schoolmaster'. This Act laid down that for schools to receive State aid they must accept the Time-table and the 'Conscience Clause', which meant a divorce between religious and secular education, which the Church had always opposed. From this time onward religious instruction no longer formed the pivot of teaching, it became a mere adjunct, a subject which had to compete for a place on the time-table.

As the Church's privileged position as 'England's School-master' was threatened, and gradually weakened and undermined, she was forced to re-examine her role as the Religious Instructor of the nation's young, for whom she still felt a deep responsibility.

Public catechizing and catechetical instruction in schools had provided the Established Church with a valuable opportunity to teach the Christian Faith, as understood by the Church of England, to the children of the nation. The decline in, and lack of enthusiasm for, public catechizing and the pressures which were being put on religious instruction, created a new situation, both in the country as a whole and in the Church in particular. Through catechetical instruction in both parish church and parish school the Church had had a very real hold and influence upon the young, prior to their beginning work or leaving home. True, the early school-leaving age had meant that such religious instruction was no more than a preliminary grounding in the Christian Faith, and that there was a very critical period between leaving school and/or home, and confirmation, but whatever the problems and difficulties in bridging this, the Church always knew, at least in rural areas, that many of the children had had some instruction in the Faith and thus some kind of a religious foundation had been laid.

The new situation in the schools, and the general decline of public catechizing, meant that the Church's age-old method of confirmation preparation was no longer the general practice and was in any case felt by many to be inadequate; it challenged churchmen to discover new means and new methods of gathering the young together and instructing them in the Faith of the Church.

NOTES

1. See W. K. Lowther Clarke, **Eighteenth Century Piety** (1944) 8-9. See also Charles J. Abbey and John H. Overton, **The English Church in the Eighteenth Century** (new ed. 1887) 469-70. F. V. Thornton, **Public Catechising**...(1850) 9-11.

2. J. Kaye, A Charge, 1828 13, 21-2.

3. J. Kaye, A Letter to the Clergy of the Diocese of Lincoln (1847) 8.

4. Thornton, op. cit., 11.

5. R. I. Wilberforce, A Charge, 1842 6-7.

6. S. Wilberforce, A Charge, 1857 16-17.

7. Ashwell and Wilberforce, **Life of Samuel Wilberforce**, Vol. I, 171. Also Pugh, **The Letter-books of Samuel Wilberforce**, Letters 148, 279, 411, 717.

8. E. Denison, A Charge, 1845 39-40.

9. W. R. W. Stephens, **The Life and Letters of Walter Farquhar Hook** (2 Vols. 1879) Vol. I, 19.

10. See Coleridge, **Memoir of John Keble** 572-3, 594-5.

11. H. Phillpotts, A Charge, 1845 44.

12. See R. I Wilberforce, A Letter to the Gentry, Yeomen and Farmers of the East Riding (Bridlington, 1842) 5, 11.

13. The Church in the Workhouse was the subject of a Paper read at the Church Congress at Bristol on October 15th 1864.

14. J. Kaye, Letter to the Clergy 1847, 7. See also A. C. Tait, A Charge, 1862 92.

15. H. Phillpotts, A Charge, 1845 44-5.

16. See Henry James Burgess, **Enterprise in Education: The Story of the work of the Established Church in the Education of the people prior to 1870** (1958) 163-7.

17. See C. Thirlwall, A Charge, 1860 26-9, 40. Thirlwall had a great deal to say about the Conscience Clause in his Charge of 1866, see pp. 20-42.

C. Confirmation Preparation

However dilatory and negligent clergy may have been in the past with regard to serious confirmation preparation, of which, apart from catechizing, little, or often none, was given, in the mid-Victorian period there was a growing awareness of the importance of this aspect of the priest's work. With the reform of the administration of confirmation, bishops were becoming more and more aware of the need for a careful preparation of candidates for confirmation and the subject was touched upon in many Episcopal Charges of the period, and also in those of some archdeacons.

Robert Isaac Wilberforce in his Primary Archidiaconal Charge urged the clergy of his archdeaconry, "Let preparation for the approaching confirmation be a main part of our care during this present season". [1] A Synodal Address by Bishop Charles Wordsworth gave him the opportunity to remind his clergy, "There is no better test of pastoral faithfulness and efficiency, than the diligence with which you seek out and prepare candidates for the administration of that holy rite"--confirmation. [2]

Past confirmation preparation had often been extremely inadequate and in many cases children had been made to learn the Catechism by heart, without ever being given a clear notion of the connection between it and confirmation. [3] It was felt that those presented for confirmation ought to have a more intelligent hold upon the principles of the Christian faith, and also a more intelligent conception of their position as members of the Church of England. [4]

Bishops realized that such preparation would demand a great deal of time and labor from their clergy; but it was, after all, one of their chief functions and a most important and worthwhile task which could make a deep and lasting impression upon those prepared. Indeed, Tait, when Bishop of London, expressed the view that it was impossible to exaggerate the importance of confirmation work, "for it brings children of all ranks under the Pastor's eye and if done effectually there is no estimating its value". He went on to say that the number of confirmation candidates was for him a good test of the pastor's earnestness. [5]

During this period bishops were putting forward numerous

suggestions for a more thorough preparation of candidates: the need to seek out and know the young people of the parish, ascertaining their general habits of life; recommending useful books for instruction and Scripture reading; encouraging candidates to give much time to fervent prayer. Various meeting places for confirmation groups were proposed--the vicarage, the school, the church, cottage meetings, night schools. It was suggested that the priest ought to have a group of candidates always under systematic instruction, rather than rely on some set occasion, with immediate preparation just before the confirmation. Even a three-group system, covering three years, was suggested, the first group being distant preparation at Sunday School; the second spoken to more frequently and gradually prepared; the third those about to be confirmed, who were given thorough and formal instruction. To the meetings of this latter group the second could be invited, to hear what would be expected of them a year later. At these groups instruction should be given in the Bible and Prayer Book, private prayer, Creed, Commandments, Lord's Prayer and Catechism. Private and individual counselling and prayer, immediately before the confirmation, was also suggested by many of the bishops. [6] Some, however, remained traditional in their approach to confirmation preparation and simply stressed the need for a more intensive teaching of the Catechism. On the whole there was no lack of enthusiasm and encouragement among the bishops, but in this matter, as in so many others, they were entirely dependent upon the diligence of the parochial clergy.

The numerous Episcopal Charges of the period give some indication of the transformation in the attitudes and actions of many of the bishops in connection with this area of their work. At parish level a radical change had also taken place. What the bishops were exhorting the clergy to do was in fact being applied with great zeal in many of the parishes of the land. Parish clergy realized the great opportunity which was given to them in preparing parishioners, both young and old, for the rite of confirmation. They too appreciated that it could be a turning point in the lives of those who were carefully prepared. They too recognized the need for improvement and experimentation in methods of confirmation preparation. They too were beginning to realize that the new society, with its increasing standards of education and amount of leisure time, in addition to the growing amount of employment, especially among children, and the ever-increasing population, all made new demands upon them and not least in the field of confirmation preparation.

Evangelicals and Tractarians tended to differ in the importance which they attached to confirmation and its preparation. The seriousness with which High Churchmen looked upon this subject is seen in the considerable preparation given, and the trouble they were willing to take, to assure such preparation. This does not mean that all High Churchmen were equally dedicated, or that Evangelicals lacked, or were generally negligent in confirmation preparation, or that Evangelical bishops did not take the matter as seriously as others. But with these qualifications, available evidence suggests that confirmation preparation was more widespread and more intensive both in content and length among High Churchmen than among those of other parties.

Charles Simeon, whose example and teaching was to influence later Evangelicals, saw confirmation as giving ministers a valuable contact with their flocks, "opening their minds, at a peculiar season of life, and with the power of specific duty, to instructions which also would come sleepily upon them"; [7] personally he was regular in catechizing and in preparing the young for confirmation. [8] John Venn usually gave a seven-week confirmation preparation, giving a lecture in church on seven successive Friday evenings. His classes were large and he usually presented 200-250 candidates at each confirmation; these large numbers were, however, mainly due to the infrequent administration of confirmation. During his 20 years at Clapham he had only five opportunities to present candidates for confirmation. [9] W. W. Champney, an Evangelical slum priest, looked upon confirmation as a real turning point in a person's life; he believed that a deep impression upon the faithful begins during preparatory instruction. For Champney, such courses of instruction were an annual event of which he felt the clergyman must take full advantage. He was convinced that the time devoted to such instruction, however considerable, is never wasted. For him and, he believed, for others such courses gave the opportunity for systematic teaching of the great doctrines of the Christian faith. [10]

Churchmanship inevitably came into confirmation preparation and when a Tractarian bishop insisted that clergymen could only prepare and examine confirmation candidates residing in their own parish, this resulted in Evangelical opposition. It was felt that such a rule would confine everyone in a parish to accept the ministration of their clergyman, whatever his views. Evangelicals, it was claimed, ought to be able to instruct candidates from other parishes who accepted their doctrinal position.

John Keble provides, perhaps, the best example of one fully dedicated to this aspect of the priest's work. When one confirmation was over he would ask for the names of all those who wished to be confirmed at the next. On at least one occasion he gave notice at the beginning of Lent that there would be a confirmation at the end of Lent in the next year and he would like the names of those who wished to be confirmed. Keble looked upon such preparation as a priority, and one of the most essential parts of his parish work. He too was convinced that it was a turning point in the lives of many candidates. His methods of preparation varied according to the needs of the candidates: to some he gave only oral teaching, to others questions in writing, directing them as to the books they were to consult; those whom he considered capable he directed to study the ancient Latin and Greek Liturgies. He also gave private preparation in special cases, where the candidates were either too slow or too intelligent for the rest. His general method, however, was weekly instruction of a period of six months to a year before the actual confirmation. This was lengthy compared with the three to four month courses given by many others. Older boys were instructed at the vicarage, so as not to offend their dignity by having to attend the village school. Those unable to get to the vicarage were prepared in their homes. The content of his preparation courses was wide-ranging; first, he went through the baptismal service, then the Catechism, after that the service of confirmation and lastly that of Holy Communion. He usually gave three or four passages of Scripture, bearing upon the subject of the next lesson, which he required to be learned by heart.

As a parish priest, George Howard Wilkinson, later Primus of Scotland, had said: "Of all the anxious work none is so anxious as preparation for confirmation; so much depends upon it". He normally held classes for about seven weeks, after which he would see candidates privately. When vicar of St. Peter's Eaton Square, London, he gave confirmation addresses on Sunday afternoons; these were open meetings and were attended, and appreciated, by many already confirmed. To intending candidates he put the question on a printed paper, "Why do you wish to be confirmed?" Various reasons why people were confirmed were then given, and each found wanting. If confirmation was sought for the wrong reasons, then Wilkinson would tell his candidates: "It will only do you harm to be confirmed at present". He suggested that if they had turned to God with all their heart, then it was right that they be confirmed; for him the condition of the 'heart' was of vital importance for confirmation. [11]

An unusual book by a Mrs. Sherwood, **The Lady of the Manor: Being a series of conversations on the subject of Confirmation. Intended for the use of the Middle and Higher ranks of Young Females** (1823), tells of how a country clergyman in the summer months gave lectures on confirmation after the Sunday evening services and every Thursday evening. He would privately examine the young men of the parish in his own home, while the village schoolmistress did the same with the young women of the lower orders (classes). The Lady of the Manor undertook the confirmation instruction of the "young females of higher rank" in the parish. The book goes on to give an interesting account of the instruction given to these young ladies of higher rank; there is no indication whether or not such a practice was widespread.

Children living in workhouses, Homes and orphanages were also prepared for confirmation. Where there was an official chaplain he was responsible for such preparation or, if not, it was the responsibility of the priest in whose parish the institution was situated.

Robert Wilberforce when speaking to the clergy of his archdeaconry in 1841, mentioned the practice of distributing appropriate books. Literature produced as helps for those preparing for confirmation abounded in great quantities during the mid-Victorian period. Such literature offered help and advice to candidates, parents and sponsors, and provided a means of private preparation, by way of reading.

Personal interviews with each of the candidates, sometimes at the outset of the course and always before presentation for confirmation, was the practice of many clergy and highly recommended by a number of bishops. But what did the mid-Victorian clergyman seek to achieve at these private interviews? W. W. How, writing on the "Private Life and Ministration of the Parish Priest" provides the answer to this question. Having insisted that the parish priest must, above all else, be thorough in his confirmation preparation, How goes on to write: "He will ascertain in private interviews the habits of his candidates as to prayer, the reading of the Bible and self-examination...These private interviews must be very kind, loving, gentle and encouraging. In them the parish priest must take every care to set the moral preparation of his heart infinitely above intellectual preparation of the head. Every endeavor must be made to get the candidates to speak frankly and openly...they should look upon him as a friend whom they may fearlessly consult in any trouble or difficulty. It need scarcely be added that every private interview should be ended with prayer". [12] For J. M. Neale, confirmation preparation constituted another difficulty which the church had to face; he wrote: "You shall see a parish priest labouring even beyond his powers to prepare the younger part of his flock for confirmation...and yet they shall be as ignorant of the nature of the rite as if it existed not". Neale was not alone in feeling that over-preparation could still be inadequate preparation and as such miss the whole object of the exercise.

In an attempt to avoid inadequate preparation there was a real danger in going to the opposite extreme and rendering the instruction given no more than an intellectual exercise, making sure that the candidates had an academic knowledge of the Faith, but overlooking the need for personal faith and commitment. Bishop Kaye reminded parents and sponsors that confirmation preparation was not so much of the understanding as of the heart, while Bishop Wilson stressed that personal preparation was of prime importance. [13] Gladstone looked upon such personal preparation as being essential, and with this in mind wrote to each of his sons before their confirmation. To Henry he wrote in 1868: "It is in the preparation of the heart that the surest promise as to this and every other ordinance is to be found: in humility and self-mistrust, in the continual looking up to God, the silent prayer of the soul, for help and strength, in the manifold resolution...to follow right, conscience, honour, duty, truth, holiness". [14]

Confession before confirmation was seen by at least some High Churchmen as desirable, and by others as essential. When Samuel Wilberforce was asked for his views on this subject he wrote: "It seems to me to belong to the Roman School and not the teaching of the Church of England". [15] Charles Lowder was one who encouraged this practice and often heard confessions before confirmation, but he was not so rigorous as the clergy of St. Saviour's, Leeds, who insisted on it. Their teaching on this matter led to a controversy with their bishop, C. T. Longley, and ultimately to a number of secessions to Rome. [16] Because of the confidential nature of the practice, and lack of information in general, it is impossible to say how widely confession was practiced as a means of final preparation to receive the sacrament of confirmation, but we know that it persisted in spite of episcopal opposition and injunctions. Perhaps Mandell Creighton's view on the subject is fairly representative of how many mid-Victorian churchmen felt on the matter; he wrote to one of his clergy: "(1) That you should not give candidates for confirmation any literature concerning confession; (2) That you should not urge upon them confession as preliminary for confirmation; (3) That you should not give them any teaching on the subject beyond what is contained in the Book of Common Prayer". [17]

Extremists did exist, but others were more discreet in the matter. W. W. How, a representative of the moderate High Church group, writing on the subject of private confession admits that it can and has been abused. Enforced confession is seen by him as evil, habitual confession tends to become unreal; with these reservations he felt that private confession was allowed by the Church of England and at certain times and occasions it could be of considerable help and value. One such time, he believed, was during confirmation preparation. [18] Such a moderate approach found acceptance among many who were very conscious of the possible dangers and abuses of confession and yet, in spite of these, saw it as a valuable asset in their pastoral ministry and especially prior to confirmation.

Having undergone such preparatory instruction, reading and perhaps confession as their parish priest felt necessary, candidates before being presented to the bishop were generally asked questions, often from the Catechism or based on it, which they were expected to answer correctly; they were also expected to be able to repeat the Creed, the Lord's Prayer and the Ten Commandments. Conscientious priests who took their confirmation preparation seriously were sometimes quite ready to refuse confirmation tickets, if the candidates were felt to be either unprepared or unworthy.

Post-confirmation Groups

A comparison between the large numbers being con-firmed and the communicant returns showed a considerable discrepancy, which alerted the bishops, or at least some of them, to a very grave problem. Those being confirmed were either failing to become communicants or were drifting away from the Church very rapidly. In an attempt to rectify this alarming trend some of the bishops began to exhort their clergy to introduce some kind of post-confirmation meetings or groups. William Jacobson of Chester told his clergy: "The proportion of those who, after being confirmed become regular communi-cants, varies very considerably, but is, generally speaking, lamen-tably small...Any pastoral attention and superintendence continued after confirmation, is often extremely valuable. The effort made during the time of preparatory instruction is very apt to be followed by a sort of collapse...It is distressing to find that, in some of the Returns, ignorance, more or less absolute, of the number of those who become Communicants, is avowed without any apology or expression of regret". [19]

The hard-working Bishop of Gloucester, C. J. Ellicott, expected his clergy to be equally diligent in their cure of souls. He suggested that they endeavor to keep up, for a time at least, some connection with those recently confirmed. A realist, he admitted "it is certain that many will drop away; some will evade; some will soon pass into service". But still, he felt, a remnant would remain and these the pastor should gather together that they might be strengthened so as to continue faithful. In this way some of those prepared for confirmation and ulti-mately confirmed would be kept together for at least a time. [20]

For some parochial clergy, post-confirmation instruction consisted of a single lecture; others realized that something of an ongoing nature was required. W. W. How was such a priest, believing that clergy ought to be concerned about "the retention of an influence over the newly confirmed. Communion Class, Bible Class, Sunday School and Night School must suffice as suggestions of instrumentalities which are too well-known to need detailed description, and which the faithful Parish Priest will not despise". However successful such groups might be, How was convinced that the only way to maintain a real and effectual influence over the confirmed was by private interviews from time to time, which should follow some systematic plan. Faithful parish priests were not unaware of these needs, but long continued preparation classes, sometimes of twelve months' duration, would for some leave little time for post-confirmation groups as well. Some did find time, especially those High Churchmen who saw the Holy Communion as the center of the Christian life; in such parishes communicant classes were an essential feature of the Church's life. Under such men as Charles Lowder these classes sometimes continued for the greater part of the year. A vital feature in parish life, they were intended to give full instruction concerning the sacrament of the altar, so that none approached unworthily, and all were able to make some devotional preparation. In this period numerous manuals were produced with the aim of preparing the newly confirmed for the reception of the Holy Communion. Some provided a detailed course of preparation, others spiritual and devotional assistance, and yet others sympathetic encouragement to those who were reticent about receiving their First Communion.

But post-confirmation groups were by no means the prerogative of High Churchmen. Francis Jeune, Bishop of Peterborough, a strong opponent of the Oxford Movement, urged his clergy to give special attention to post-confirmation instruction and to initiate adult classes. [21] Tait, when Bishop of London, had expressed the view: "If communicant classes developed into meetings for prayer and reading of the Scriptures, the pastor in the largest parishes would thus find himself at the head of a compact body of coadjutors, selected from his congregation, who would greatly aid his missionary labours, among the surrounding crowd". [22] No mid-Victorian clergyman ministering in a large parish in one of the new, densely-populated, industrial areas would have despised or frowned upon such a group to assist him in his missionary activities. Was this just a dream? Tait was no mere dreamer, but unfortunately this vision did not materialize on any realistic and worthwhile scale.

By the end of the period, the problem of making the newly confirmed into active communicant members was fully realized and the gap between the large numbers confirmed, and the poor increase in the number of communicants was a recognized and established fact. Unfortunately, the numerous attempts to stem the tide failed and the decline continued. In the end, the Church had to accept that all her attempts seemed doomed to failure and the discrepancy between confirmations and communicants had to be accepted as somewhat inevitable.

NOTES

1. R. I. Wilberforce, A Charge, 1841 17.

2. Charles Wordsworth, A Synodal Address: The Ministry of the Church historically considered with reference to the circumstances of the Church of Scotland (1866) 6.

3. See C. Thirlwall, A Charge, 1854 62.

4. See J. Fraser, A Charge, 1872 92-3.

5. A. C. Tait, A Charge, 1862 92-3.

6. On suggestions regarding confirmation preparation and confirmation classes, etc., see the following Charges:

    E. H. Browne - 1865, 11.
    R. Durnford - 1871, 19-20.
    C. J. Ellicott - 1864, 29.
    W. Jacobson - 1868, 28.
    T. V. Short - 1859, 22-3.
    A. C. Tait - 1862, 91-4.

7. See Pollard, Charles Simeon 112-13.

8. George W. E. Russell, A Short History of the Evangelical Movement (1915) 50.

9. Michael Hennell, John Venn and the Clapham Sect (1958) 122.

10. W. Weldon Champney, Spirit in the Word: Facts Gathered From a Thirty Years Ministry (1862) 56-7.

11. Mason, Memoir of George Howard Wilkinson Vol. I, 84-5, 138, 223-4, 268.

12. William Walsham How, Essay "Private Life and Ministration of the Parish Priest" in Archibald Weir and William Dalrymple MacLagan (eds.) The Church and the Age, Essays

on the Principles and Present Position of the Anglican Church (1870) see 220-1.

13. Kaye, **On Confirmation** 10. Wilson, A Plain and Affectionate Address to Young Persons about to be confirmed 5-7.

14. Lathbury, **Correspondence of William Gladstone** Vol. II, 185, see also 15-16.

15. See Pugh, **Letter-books of Samuel Wilberforce** 183-5.

16. See C. T. Longley, A Letter to the Parishioners of St. Saviour's, Leeds, with an appendix of documents (1851). See also Pollen, **St. Saviour's, Leeds** 88-98. C. T. Longley, A Charge, 1868 20.

17. Creighton, **Mandell Creighton** Vol. II, 365.

18. W. W. How, in **Church and the Age** 217-20. An anonymous manual was produced to help would-be penitents: **The Ministry of Consolation: A Guide to Confession for the use of members of the Church of England** (1854). The availability of sacramental confession prior to confirmation and as a part of the preparation was emphasized by Nathaniel Woodard; see Brian Heeney, **Mission to the Middle Classes: The Woodard Schools 1845-1891** (1969) 64-5.

19. W. Jacobson, A Charge, 1868 16-17.

20. C. J. Ellicott, A Charge, 1864 30-1.

21. F. Jeune, A Charge, 1867 10-11.

22. A. C. Tait, A Charge, 1862 94.

D. Confirmation at Public Schools

As with the parishes of the nation, so it was with Public Schools, in that the practice and quality of confirmation preparation varied considerably, being ultimately dependent upon the convictions and abilities of those to whom the task was entrusted. Public Schools, therefore, like parishes, present a varied picture; some were very good and others extremely bad. In the end, the system was largely dependent upon the Headmaster.

Charles Wordsworth tells of how, when he was confirmed at Harrow in 1824, he had no preparation. "All that my tutor did for me was to ask whether I could say my catechism, to which I answered in the affirmative". Eton in those days also left much to be desired and there was a general indifference to religion. [1] However this may have been, it could not suppress an innate religious feeling in many of the boys. Scott Holland wrote to his mother from Eton in 1860, sharing his thoughts about his pending confirmation. He told of his preparation through regular Bible reading, prayer and self-examination, and of a resolve to avoid trivial acts of wrongdoing. He was also deeply concerned about receiving his first Communion. Such were the religious feelings and activities of a thirteen year-old boy at Eton. Eventually he was confirmed: "My confirmation, illuminated by the majestic power of Samuel Wilberforce, left a deep and life-long impression on my soul". [2]

Writing about his confirmation at Eton in 1854 Charles Lindley Wood said that he received no preparation beyond being told by his tutor to read a book Laneton Parsonage, a story turning on confirmation; he had also to copy out some hymns and religious extracts from a notebook and was told that it would be a worse scandal to be whipped after confirmation than before. [3]

William E. Gladstone, who went to Eton in 1821, had told his father that he did not wish to be confirmed at the school, but somehow he was included among the candidates. Part of the preparation was to read a book of sermons, which was paid for but never arrived, and upon which no question was ever asked. Three visits to his tutor, who read a couple of pages of Sinclair's Sermons to him, shut the book with a snap and said, "You can go", was the extent of the young Gladstone's preparation: "Not a word of help or advice was given". [4]

Smaller schools seem to have varied in quality. Frederick Temple was prepared for confirmation in 1834 while at Blundell's School, Tiverton. Of the clergyman who carried out the preparation Temple said: "He did not pay much attention to those under his preparation; all he did was to bring us together in one room and make us say the Catechism all round". Dissatisfied with this preparation, Temple's mother had him travel home for several weeks beforehand and personally undertook the task of preparing him for the sacrament. Edward Thring, appointed Headmaster of Uppingham School in 1853, had preparation classes for his scholars and even post-confirmation meetings. He was convinced that the school suffered by not having an annual confirmation, a complaint which was also voiced at other schools.

Woodard Schools (the first being built in 1847, Lancing in 1848) were often more fortunate and had a strong religious ethos and confirmation was not treated lightly. Nathaniel Woodard rooted the religious instruction of his scholars firmly in the Catechism, the three Creeds, the Bible and in an English Primer specially drawn up for use in the Schools. The aim of all religious instruction was confirmation. No one was exempt and when a boy reached fourteen or fifteen, if he was considered fit, he was confirmed. Parents who did not agree with the system had either to accept it or to withdraw their child. Not only did Woodard insist upon confirmation preparation as an essential part in the life of all his schools, but such preparation was decidely Anglo-Catholic. With such a dogmatic approach to confirmation it is not surprising that impressively large numbers were confirmed annually at the Schools. The pupils of the Woodard School of All Saints, Bloxham, were fortunate that in their early days they were blessed by the presence of the second master and chaplain, the Reverend A. D. Crake, who remained at the school from 1865-1878. Crake prepared a valuable devotional manual specially for use at public schools which contains prayers and some most helpful instruction in the Christian faith and way of life. He was but one example of those who were seeking to establish a living faith in the lives of public school boys. [5]

At the turn of the century F. D. How wrote an interesting book, **Six Great School Masters,** which covers the period 1835-1865 and deals with Eton, Winchester, Shrewsbury, Harrow, Rugby and Marlborough. He shows how, in varying degrees, religious instruction and Christian worship played a real part in the lives of these schools during the period he covers. How's conclusions are supported by the Report of the Royal Commission on Public Schools, which was set up in the 1860's under the chairmanship of the Earl of Clarendon. Over a period of three years the Commission enquired into the state of the nine public schools of the nation. The Report revealed that the public schools were considered to be the Church's institutions; the senior members of the staff, at least, were clergymen of the Established Church and there was no opposition to the strong ecclesiastical atmosphere which prevailed. Regular attendance at chapel was the rule; boys were prepared for confirmation by the school and most of them received Holy Communion regularly. [6] Obviously things had greatly improved, but the reminiscences of Charles Lindley Wood and others raise the question whether the situation was quite as satisfactory as the Report of the Royal Commission implied.

Thomas Arnold, whose reign at Rugby ended before the mid-Victorian period, must be considered, because of his influence upon public schools both in his own day and during the years which followed. Arnold looked upon education as primarily the religious and moral training of boys: "He is not well educated who does not know the will of God, or knowing it, has received no help in his education towards being inclined and enabled to do it". Arnold was an exceptional man, but there were others of his time, and certainly in the mid-Victorian period, who shared his educational objectives. As Headmaster of Rugby, Arnold was anxious that boys should be confirmed and he and the other masters prepared their own boys for confirmation and presented them to the bishop on the day. His method of preparation was to issue a printed list of questions, more as a guide to their thoughts than a test to be passed. He interviewed each boy individually, seeking from them a promise to pray and emphasizing that the Bible provided a law for life; for Arnold the Bible was of tremendous importance in Christian education and growth. He encouraged all boys who were serious to attend the Holy Communion.

Frederick Temple, as Headmaster of Rugby, believed that preparation for confirmation and the service itself had a great effect in raising the tone of the school. Temple's method of preparation was to address the candidates collectively every week, while he made the housemasters (lay and clerical alike) responsible for the special preparation of their own boys, whom they presented to the bishop. He firmly believed that an annual confirmation would be in the best and general interest of the school--this he in fact eventually obtained for Rugby. He would help boys in their preparation for Holy Communion, but never made a personal appeal for them to attend the service.

Neglect and abuse were still to be found in the religious life of the public schools of the period, but some Headmasters and masters felt a serious obligation to encourage the growth of the Christian faith in the boys committed to their care. This included a careful and adequate preparation for confirmation and encouragement to practice their communicant membership of the Established Church. Thus the mid-Victorian Church witnessed not only an increase of dedicated parochial clergy, for whom confirmation preparation was an essential part of their ministry, but also an increase in dedicated schoolmasters, both lay and clerical, who also felt that they had obligations to meet in their own special sphere.

NOTES

1. William Hill Tucker, **Eton of Old: 1811–22** (1892) see e.g. 121, 125.

2. See Stephen Paget, ed. **Henry Scott Holland: Memoir and Letters** (1921) 11,15.

3. J. G. Lockhart, **Charles Lindley, Viscount Halifax** (2 Vols. 1935) Vol. I, 79, but see 40–41.

4. See also W. E. Gladstone, **Gleanings of Past Years** (1897) Vol. VII, 138.

5. See A. D. Crake, **The Bread of Life: A Manual of instruction and devotion for the Blessed Sacrament** (1875). See K. E. Kirk's Preface to the 1939 edition. Crake also compiled a "**Book of Private Devotion for Boys**" which at one time was bound with **The Bread of Life**.

6. A number of valuable contributions have been written on the subject of public schools. See: Newsome, **Godliness or Good Learning**; Heeney, **Mission to the Middle Classes**; Bowden, **Victorian Church,** which has a section on public school life, 211–22; Smyth, **Simeon and Church Order:** chapter "Religion and the Schools" 46–96. Articles: "Christianity and the Public School", Theology, June 1939, XXXVIII, 438–46; "Public Schools of England", Edinburgh Review, 1830 Vol. LI.

IV. THE ADMINISTRATION OF THE RITE

A. Episcopal Reform of Confirmation

Bishop Samuel Wilberforce provides perhaps the best example of the change which had taken place among many of the bishops in their attitude towards confirmation. Not a few bishops had looked upon the endless round of confirmations as a tiresome duty which was seldom properly carried out. Vast numbers of candidates, and disorderly behavior, may have caused episcopal concern, but not sufficient to stimulate any active attempts to reform the system. More and more of the mid-Victorian bishops were beginning to realize the valuable opportunities which were offered to them through this aspect of their work and with this, there went an increasing feeling that some reform was needed if they were to take full advantage of the pastoral opportunities which these occasions offered. It has been shown how many of the bishops of this period were continually appealing to their clergy for more satisfactory confirmation preparation, and even post-confirmation instruction. Episcopal administration of the rite of confirmation provides valuable insight into what the bishops felt about confirmation and how much, apart from exhortations to their clergy, they were actually willing to do in order to improve the system and take full advantage of this part of their own ministry.

Wilberforce saw confirmations as a tremendous pastoral and sacramental opportunity and there are numerous accounts which indicate how he gave of his best in the administration of the rite. To read through his diary during his episcopate reveals how this part of his duties was anything but a tiresome chore; for him it was a responsibility of great privilege and one which made a deep impression upon him and upon those present at his confirmations, both candidates and observers. The atmosphere which existed at such services was something which he seemed to feel at a deep and personal level. In his diary he writes of confirmations as being "cold", "nice", "very nice", "very interesting", "striking", "pleasant", "a little chilled", "a poor confirmation with wretched attendance". [1] His attempts to make the service more meaningful were not always appreciated by the clergy. At one confirmation, during the laying on of

hands, he asked the clergy to kneel down and join in intercession--
a request to which some took exception.

During one of his confirmation tours he wrote to his
sister: "There is so much deep interest in a confirmation that
it takes a great deal out of one. The present interest is intense:
the single opportunity of making, if God will, a dint in a character". The effect of the rite upon those being confirmed was
something about which he was deeply concerned. How serious
were the candidates in their promise? Would they remain faithful?

Another interesting aspect of confirmations, at least
for Wilberforce, was the insight they gave into the state of
the parishes and their clergy. He was acutely aware of the importance of a confirmation in the life of a parish and events which
would have caused some bishops to change or cancel a confirmation date, would not influence him in this way. To put off a
confirmation would, he believed, cause considerable inconvenience
and disarrange the whole parish. Clergy were often commended
by Wilberforce for their obvious devotion in preparing candidates:
"The bearing and demeanour of those whom you have brought
before me has, moreover, as a whole borne undoubted and most
grateful evidence of the greater seriousness and understanding
of the rite with which your candidates have come to confirmation. Let me take this fresh opportunity of encouraging your
hearts in this eminently useful portion of your labours...For
myself I grudge no labour which is needful to give the fullest
effect to this ordinance". [2] Ten years later, he commented:
"Nothing can be more marked than the difference between confirmations of these last years, and those of twenty years ago".
He attributed this reform, and the quality of candidates, to
the prayers and labors of the clergy. He went on to point out
the importance of securing, at confirmation, the attendance
of the parents and godparents of those being confirmed. [3]

Wilberforce was not the only bishop who felt prompted
to commend the clergy for their obvious labors in this work;
many of the Episcopal Charges of this period contain statements
on this matter and clergy were urged not to relax their efforts
in this most valuable work. [4]

In some areas, approaching confirmations were seen
as a signal for renewed efforts to prejudice the poor and unedu-
cated against the rite, in an attempt to induce them to keep
their children away from it; clergy were sometimes exhorted
to counteract such attempts by the circulation of tracts and
through oral instruction. [5]

Among the bishops there was a growing concern that
the service should not be unduly long and tiring for children.

Careful instructions about the service, which in some cases went into minute detail, were sometimes sent by the bishops to their clergy, in an attempt to avoid abuse and to get the best out of the service.

Confirmation Tours and Centers

A bishop's willingness to play a part in the growing reform which surrounded confirmation could be partly judged by his attitude to Confirmation Tours and his willingness to increase the number of places at which he administered the rite. Parochial clergy often complained about the infrequency of the rite, the inconvenient times at which it was administered, the considerable distances which many candidates had to travel to the nearest center and the extraordinary numbers confirmed, which seemed to prevent any real dignity at the service. The vast numbers presented at one service are beyond the comprehension of later churchmen: Bishop Sparke recorded that at his last confirmation in the diocese of Chester in 1812 he confirmed 8,000 children in Manchester in one day--between 8 a.m. and 8:30 p.m.

An anonymous writer of the mid-Victorian period tells of how parents were often extremely anxious about their children having to travel a long way for a confirmation, especially when they were unable to accompany them. Sometimes mothers felt that it was improper for their daughters to go alone: "The harm which ensues from the gathering of so many young persons, at what they consider a kind of rural festival, is well-known to every country clergyman". This genuine concern by parents for the well-being of their children sometimes led to confirmation being deferred and this occasionally resulted in candidates lapsing in the ensuing three years before the next confirmation. "The infrequency and sparseness of confirmations in rural districts is the cause why so few are confirmed there. In towns the rite is more accessible. But even there, young men and women can only attend at the convenience of their employer and if they happen to be in the service of other than religious people they never hear of the rite at all". [6]

To charge the bishops of the eighteenth and early nineteenth centuries with responsibility for all the problems which surrounded confirmations during this period, would be grossly unfair. It must be acknowledged that the difficulties of travel at that time prevented many of the reforms which were implemented at a later date. The remote regions of some dioceses could only be reached on horseback and this influenced both the time and the frequency of confirmations. Travel by coach was the most usual method used by the bishops during the early nineteenth century, but this also had its problems. Steam locomotion opened up new possibilities for the bishops, which would have been unthinkable, as well as impossible, for their episcopal predecessors. The ease, comfort and increased facilities of travel by railway, which enabled more frequent and widespread confirmations, was mentioned in at least one Episcopal Charge of the period. [7] Rail travel revolutionized the whole of British life, not least in speed and convenience. The mid-Victorian period witnessed a vast extension of the railway network, reaching out to every corner of the nation; in 1850 British railways carried 67.4 million passengers, and in 1875 490.1 million. Although pastoral care and reforming zeal were the prime factors which contributed towards the new attitude and understanding of confirmation in the Victorian period, the new mode of travel undoubtedly made an important contribution. Bishops could, and did, travel more widely and more quickly and were thus able to increase the frequency of their confirmations and the number of their centers. The same travel facilities also assisted candidates in getting to distant confirmation centers, when these were not in their own parish.

Once again Samuel Wilberforce provides an illustration of the radical transformation which had taken place: his predecessor, Richard Bagot, had 9 confirmation centers in 1840; by the 1860's Wilberforce had increased these to 188, each of which he visited triennially. [8] Increased centers did, however, bring other problems, in that when several confirmations were arranged in one day (and Wilberforce often fitted three into the same day), it inevitably meant that some confirmations tended to be rather hurried affairs and in this they shared one of the failures of the past. But even with this vast increase in the number of centers, Wilberforce still felt that exceptional cases could still arise and so, in 1857, he told his clergy that should they have any urgent cases for confirmation before the next circuit in their own county, these could be taken to the most convenient place, even if in another county. "Besides this, I am ready to arrange to visit biennially or annually any parish in the diocese, as I have already done to many parishes". He went on to tell his clergy that in the previous three years he had confirmed in 200 churches and ministered in 89 others: "I trust that during the next 3 years, if it pleases God...so long to spare my life and health, those 289 common services in various parishes may be yet further multiplied". [9] His prayer was granted, for between 1857 and 1860 he confirmed 18,747 candidates in 217 places. [10] Further increases were reported in his own diocese between 1860 and 1863, when he confirmed on 225 occasions, but with fewer candidates--a total of 18,570.[11] Obviously Wilberforce took great pride in this aspect of his work and one cannot help feeling that sometimes his pride borders on boasting over the increasing number of confirmation candidates and centers. Entries in his diary reflect the importance which he placed upon this sacrament, for often the only notes recorded were facts about his confirmations, the places at which they were held and his assessment of the service.

Other bishops were not lacking in apostolic zeal. William Thomson, as Archbishop of York, had a vast diocese containing both rural and industrial areas; his practice was to hold annual confirmations in large towns, biennial in smaller ones and less frequently in villages. Whenever possible he would willingly meet the requests of his clergy for more frequent confirmations. Indeed he went so far as to promise that he would hold a confirmation in any village which could muster ten candidates. In 1865 he shared his reasons for increasing the number of centers with his clergy: "You are aware that the number of places has been greatly increased because I desire to shorten as much as possible the weary journey which, in former days, was the usual preparation for that solemn rite, and also to prevent the over-crowding which often distracted the attention from the real work of the day". [12] Nevertheless, confirmations must still have been somewhat crowded, for he wrote of "2,000 confirmations in a week and still two more places to come". Like Wilberforce, Thomson seems to have gained much satisfaction from the visible improvement in this area. He wrote to his wife on one occasion in 1882 of "9,192 confirmations this year; our highest previous year had been 8,463. It is a great and encouraging rise".

Pressure on these tours was considerable; during one in 1867 he wrote to his wife of three confirmations in one day, and went on to complain: "I have not read a paper since I left you, and know nothing except that the tone of confirmations is improving". During his time at York he increased the confirmation centers from 32 to 76 and in the same period confirmed 200,000 candidates.

Bishop Ellicott of Gloucester and Bristol sought to reform the confirmation system in his own diocese, but in doing so tried to be realistic about what he could effectively undertake, refusing to act like some of his episcopal brethren in making rash promises of additional confirmations. "I shall" he said to his clergy, "endeavour to reduce our confirmations to an orderly and regular system, and then, having done so, to multiply as far as I am able, and to change, as far as it can conveniently be done, the various centres". Some places, he pointed out, would always be annual centers while others, because of difficult access and limited accommodations "can hardly ever count on being regularly adopted as places to be periodically visited".

These places might well be appointed for Sunday Confirmations: "But on this point I will not make any definite promises". [13] Three years later Ellicott was still endeavoring to adjust his circuit and change his centers, in an attempt to offer an opportunity for clergy to present candidates twice in three years, instead of triennially.

There were some bishops who felt very strongly that the smaller places ought not to be overlooked. In a Pastoral Letter on the subject of confirmation Walter Kerr Hamilton, Bishop of Salisbury, expressed his deep conviction that centers should be made as convenient as possible, especially for those living in rural areas. [14]

A few of the bishops had very definite guidelines which they applied in deciding on confirmation centers. John Pelham, of Norwich, said: "I propose to confirm throughout one Archdeaconry each year, and in the principal towns annually. I shall also be ready to hold Sunday Confirmations in parishes with a population of 500 and upwards, only stipulating that on such occasions I cannot admit Candidates from other parishes, whose churches are more than two miles distant from the one in which the Confirmation is held". [15] Richard Durnford of Chichester also had definite guidelines: "Wherever the population reaches 2,000 and does not exceed 5,000 I shall be ready to confirm every second year, where the population is above 5,000 an annual confirmation is indispensable". [16] James Fraser of Manchester resolved that he would never exceed the limit of 500 candidates at any one confirmation. [17]

Whatever the bishops did, they could not possibly satisfy everyone; some tried to do so, others were more realistic. John Jackson, Bishop of Lincoln, admitted to his clergy what many of his episcopal brethren refused to recognize, that the increasing number of confirmations resulted in a neglect of other duties. [18]

This examination of some of the available evidence reveals that there was no common episcopal policy in this matter, but there was a common feeling that the inherited system of administering confirmation, through a limited number of tours and centers, left much to be desired. Unceasing labor by many of the bishops rectified much of the former neglect and abuse but, even at the end of the mid-Victorian period, there was still room for considerable improvement, and the move to increase centers continued.

NOTES

1. See Ashwell & Wilberforce, **Life of Samuel Wilberforce** Vol. III, 46, 180, 221, 296-7, 363, 401.

2. S. Wilberforce, A Charge, 1857 5-7.

3. S. Wilberforce, A Charge, 1866 3-4.

4. See, e.g., R. Bickersteth, A Charge, 1867 9-10; C. Graves, A Charge, 1867 9-12; W. Jacobson, A Charge, 1864 9-10.

5. See C. Thirlwall, A Charge, 1854 61-2.

6. Anonymous, **Confirmation Considered with reference to the Holy Communion** 7-8.

7. F. Jeune, A Charge, 1867 11.

8. R. K. Pugh, **The Episcopate of Samuel Wilberforce,** unpublished thesis, Bodleian Library Oxford, 1959, 116-17.

9. S. Wilberforce, A Charge, 1857 7-8.

10. S. Wilberforce, A Charge, 1860 9.

11. S. Wilberforce, A Charge, 1863 4.

12. W. Thomson, A Charge, 1865 18-19.

13. C. J. Ellicott, A Charge, 1864 23-4.

14. W. K. Hamilton, A Charge, 1858 11.

15. J. T. Pelham, A Charge, 1858 16-17.

16. R. Durnford, A Charge, 1875 14.

17. J. Fraser, A Charge 1872 93-4.

18. J. Jackson, A Charge, 1867 16.

B. Confirmation Statistics

Confirmation statistics for the mid-Victorian period are far from complete, but those available provide some indication of the success resulting from the dedicated pastoral ministry of the parochial clergy, especially in the field of confirmation preparation, and the reforming zeal of many of the bishops in the administration of the rite.

A number of the bishops of the period quoted confirmation figures in their Charges, but this was by no means the common practice of the episcopate in general, nor the invariable practice of individual bishops. Some made no more than a passing reference to the number of candidates they had recently confirmed, others occasionally compared the figures with the numbers quoted at another time; a few carefully prepared tables of the figures and tried to make analytical observations. This irregularity in recording, publishing and preserving confirmation returns during the period means that only a very general picture can be drawn.

C. R. Sumner, who was fascinated by facts and figures, records the confirmation figures of Hampshire as increasing from 8,249 in 1835 to 9,663 in 1844. Those in Surrey increased from 4,390 in 1836 to 8,174 in 1845, denoting a progressive increase and nearly doubling the number of confirmands in ten years. "I admit", says Sumner, "that figures taken alone, afford no certain criterion of the state of parishes...But none will deny that a good attendance on the ordinances of the church is a hopeful sign--that it negatives the supposition of a careless or repulsive ministry--that it affords at least a strong presumption of diligence, zeal and efficiency on the part of the pastor, and of edification on that of the people". [1]

The increase did not satisfy Sumner, for five years later he told his clergy "While ever the population increases according to its present ratio, we have no leisure for relaxation of efforts". [2] His brother, John Bird Sumner, when Bishop of Chester attributed in 1841 the increased number of confirmation candidates to an increase in Church schools and in the education of the poorer classes. Speaking of his own diocese he said that confirmation candidates had increased far beyond the growth of population, having trebled since his first returns in 1829. [3]

In 1861 numerous letters in the correspondence columns

of The Guardian expressed concern over the small percentage of people being confirmed, when compared with the increasing population. Comparison of some of the available figures helps us to judge whether or not such anxiety was justified. It must be borne in mind that considerable variation in a diocese from year to year was often due to the system of confirmation tours used, and the frequency at which confirmations were administered, as also the regional variations of population.

Rivington's Ecclesiastical Year Book for 1865 provides a valuable list of the Confirmations in England and Wales during that year. The list provides the number of persons confirmed, the number of confirmations and, in a few cases, the number of male and female candidates. Unfortunately, the details given are neither consistent nor complete; nevertheless, an analysis of the figures provides some interesting facts. The figures and percentages are rounded off to the nearest unit. The average number of candidates per center throughout the country was 130.64. Of the total number confirmed there was an average of 58.93% females per diocese, and their was an average of 45.74% more female than male candidates per diocese throughout the country.

Diocese	No. of Confirma- tions	No. of Persons Confirmed	Ave. per Ctr.	Percentages of Total Candidates				% Female above Male
				Male	%	Female	%	
Canterbury	20	2,732	137					
York	28	4,204	150	1,622	39.0	2,582	61.0	59.00
London	57	11,154	196	3,844	34.5	7,310	65.5	90.00
Durham***	53	4,582	87	1,766	38.5	2,816	61.5	59.45
Winchester***	66	13,299	202	5,458	41.0	7,841	59.0	43.66
St. Asaph	22	1,595	73					
Bangor	23	1,081	47					
Bath & Wells	25	3,642	146	1,502	41.0	2,140	59.0	42.47
Carlisle+++								
Chester	70	17,325	248					
Chichester	70	8,900	127					
St. David's+++								
Ely	61	7,086	116					
Exeter	76	10,170	134	4,746	47.0	5,424	53.0	14.28
Gloucester & Bristol	55	4,300	78					
Hereford+++								
Lichfield	7	1,090	156	397	36.0	693	64.0	74.55
Lincoln	37	4,701	127	1,880	40.0	2,821	60.0	50.00
Llandaff	60	4,108	68					

Diocese	No. of Confirmations	No. of Persons Confirmed	Ave. per Ctr.	Percentages of Total Candidates				% Female above Male
				Male	%	Female	%	
Manchester	27	8,821	327	3,386	38.0	5,435	62.0	60.51
Norwich	32	3,833	120	1,483	39.0	2,350	61.0	58.46
Oxford	67	5,457	81	2,512	46.0	2,945	54.0	17.23
Peterborough	25	5,288	212					
Ripon	36	5,471	152	2,086	38.0	3,385	62.0	62.27
Rochester	72	8,461	118	3,849	45.5	4,612	54.5	19.82
Salisbury	103	6,491	63	2,852	44.0	3,639	56.0	27.59
Worcester	11	1,012	92	489	48.0	523	52.0	6.95

*** The Rivington total figures do not correspond with the numbers given for each sex and thus has been adjusted to the figures given.
+++ No figures were given for this diocese.

The figures also reveal a considerable variation between the dioceses; compared with the average of 130 candidates per center, Bangor had only 47 and 13 of the dioceses had less than the overall average. Manchester had the highest number per center with 327 candidates. In every diocese the number of female candidates was higher than the males presented. London had the highest difference, with 65% of the total number confirmed being female; in 10 of the dioceses more than 59% of the total were female. The percentage of female candidates above male varied considerably; there were 90% more in London, but only 6.95% more in Worcester. These figures provide insight into a complex situation which is difficult to explain.

In the case of some dioceses further details are available which, although fragmentary, do help to enlarge and clarify the picture:

St. Asaph

Between 1869-1879, 15,437 candidates were confirmed, an average of 1,543 per annum; [4] compared with the Rivington figure they show a 3% decrease. [5]

Bangor

Between 1866-1869 a total of 1,727 candidates were confirmed over the three-year period, an average of 575.6 candidates per annum, a considerable drop in the Rivington figure of 1,081, which could have been a high figure at the end of a triennial period. Nevertheless, in presenting these figures in his Charge of 1869 Bishop J. C. Campbell commented that they were very small, even in proportion to the population of the district from which they were taken which, he said, at the last census amounted to 195,390 people. [6]

Chester

The Rivington figures for the number of persons confirmed in the diocese of Chester are considerably higher than for any other--17,325 candidates. The figures available for the subsequent years suggest that the Rivington figure could be a compound one for a triennial period, or that there was a considerable drop in the corresponding triennial year of 1868; indeed, 3,329 less candidates were confirmed in that year than in 1865; a decrease of nearly 19%.

1865	70	Confirmations	17,325	Candidates:	Average of 248 per center
1866	14	"	2,238	"	"	" 160	"
1867	19	"	3,665	"	"	" 193	"
1868	81	"	13,996	"	"	" 173	"

An average over the four years of 9,306 per annum, with an average of 202 per center. [7]

Chichester

1870	533	male	731	female	Total	1,264
1871	3,847	"	4,971	"	"	8,818
1872	730	"	1,343	"	"	2,073
1873	1,157	"	1,884	"	"	3,041
1874	3,847	"	4,430	"	"	8,277
1875	909	"	1,577	"	"	2,486

Over the six-year period recorded there were 11,018 male candidates and 14,936 female, an annual average of 1,886 males and 2,489 females. The total number of candidates for the period 1870-1875 was 25,954, an annual average of 4,325, of which 57.5% were females and 42.5% males. Over the six-year period covered by these returns there were 35% more female candidates than male. [8]

Durham

1858-1862: 82 confirmations, 11,730 candidates, an annual average of 2,932 candidates with an average of 143 candidates per center.

1862-1866: 161 confirmations, 13,365 candidates, an annual average of 3,341 with an average of 83 candidates per center. The average over the eight years 1858-1866, was 3,137 candidates per annum, with 103 candidates per center.

Of the 161 confirmations held between 1862-1866 55 were held on Sundays and were limited to the candidates of the parish where the confirmations were held. Sunday confirmations were felt to meet the needs of the working classes, who were often prevented from being present at mid-week confirmations. The increase of nearly 100% in the number of centers was largely due to Bishop Baring's willingness to meet the needs of his clergy for more frequent confirmations, which led to an increase of 1,635 candidates, an average of 408 per annum and an overall increase of nearly 14%. [9]

Gloucester

1864-1867: 130 confirmations: 7,511 females, 4,841 males, total 12,352 candidates, an average of 4,117 per annum with an average of 95 candidates per center. Of the total number presented, 61% were female, 39% male, and over the three years 55% more female candidates than male. Ellicott in his Charge of 1864 expressed the hope that the number of male candidates might increase; in that year there were 6,490 candidates, of which 4,102 or 63% were female. He felt that on the whole the figures were fair, but hoped that there would be an overall increase in view of the growing population. In his Charge of 1867, he said he was pleased to see an increase of 11% in the number of male candidates. The analysis shows that there was a slight discrepancy in his figures, for out of the total number of those confirmed in the three-year period there was in fact only about a 4% increase in the number of males. [10]

Lincoln

1859-1861: 6,028 male candidates, 8,583 female; a total of 14,611, an annual average of 4,870. Of the total number of candidates 58% were female, and there were 42% more female candidates than male.

1862-1864: 6,093 male candidates, 8,347 female; a total of 14,440, an annual average of 4,813. Of the total number of candidates 57.8% were female, and there were 36% more female candidates than male.

1865-1867: 6,116 male candidates, 8,504 female; a total of 14,620, an annual average of 4,873. Of the total number of candidates 58% were female, and there were 39% more female candidates than male.

These figures reveal a reasonably static figure in the

overall picture, with a slight increase in the number of male candidates. In his Charge of 1864, Jackson said that the regional variation was difficult to explain. He rejected suggestions that a reduction in the age of confirmation candidates, or an increase in the number of centers, would result in a growth in the number of candidates. [11]

Manchester

Within two months of his consecration, in 1870, Bishop James Fraser had confirmed nearly 4,000 young people; he observed that they were almost all from the "respectable classes". He felt that the Church ought to try to reach the working classes. [12] By the end of 1876 he had confirmed 71,000, an average of 10,142 per annum. Of those confirmed 27,000 were male and 44,000 female. Of the total number confirmed 62% were female and there were 63% more female candidates than male. Fraser expressed grave concern over the disparity between the sexes, which was largely confined to the town parishes and not so much a problem in the country. Some of his clergy had told him of the increasing difficulty of getting young men to come forward for confirmation. [13]

Norwich

1856-1858: 14,547 candidates were confirmed, an annual average of 4,849; of these 14,547, 6,500 were confirmed in 1858 in the course of 29 confirmations--an average of 224 candidates per center. Pelham commented that although candidates were numerous, they were few when compared with the number of baptized persons. [14]

Oxford

Wilberforce provides the fullest and most useful figures:

1846-1848	9,249	candidates, an	annual	average	of 3,083
1851-1854	14,057	"	"	"	"	" 4,685
1855-1857	16,586	"	"	"	"	" 5,528
1858-1860	18,747	"	"	"	"	" 6,240
1860-1863	18,570	"	"	"	"	" 6,190
1866-1869	20,028	"	"	"	"	" 6,675

Between 1846-1869 Wilberforce had a 116% increase in the number of candidates he confirmed. He attributed this tremendous increase largely to the "greatly increased exertions of the clergy". During the period 1855-1857 he records the confirmation of 9,429 female candidates and 7,187 male, a total of 16,616 (this figure is a little higher than that quoted above from another source). Of the total confirmed, 56% were female and there were 31% more female candidates than male. During the period 1858-1860 he confirmed in 217 places, with a total number of 18,747 candidates, an average of 86 per center. Wilberforce was confirming an increasing number of male candidates, which he found especially encouraging; indeed of those confirmed in the period 1858-1860, 10,239 were female and 8,508 or 45.4% were males and there were only 20% more female candidates than male, a drop of 11% on the previous three years. He firmly believed that confirmation returns offered the most accurate gauge of the real effect of the Church's work. Six years later he was able to express further satisfaction in the growing equality of the two sexes among those confirmed; this he felt was a hopeful sign. The Rivington figures do show a further increase of male candidates in 1865, when 46% of the total number confirmed were male and there were only 17.23% more female candidates than male. [15] Unfortunately, the sign which offered encouragement to Wilberforce was not so evident in other dioceses.

Peterborough

1864-1867: 113 confirmations with a total of 18,304 candidates, an annual average of 6,101, with an average of 162 candidates per center. Bishop Jeune made some attempt to analyze his confirmation returns and commented: "The returns, carefully analysed, show that about one half of the parishes contributed candidates to the amount of 3% of their population: and that many parishes fell grievously short of that average. Two populous parishes there were, which presented catechumens to the amount of only 1/4%. Daventry exhibits the largest proportion of any town parish. In several country parishes a much higher average has been reached. Unavoidable causes, my brethren, may cause great fluctuations; but can unavoidable causes account for failures so complete?" [16]

Ripon

1862-1864: 90 confirmations with a total of 12,788 candidates, an annual average of 4,262 candidates, with an average of 142 per center.

1865-1867: 101 confirmations with a total of 16,181 candidates, an annual average of 5,393, with an average of 160 per center. Over the six years an average of 4,828 candidates per annum and 152 candidates per center.

Salisbury

1856-1858: 207 confirmations, 12,842 candidates, an annual average of 4,280, with an average of 62 per center.

1859-1861: 219 confirmations, 12,559 candidates, an annual average of 4,186, with an average of 57 candidates per center.

1862-1864: 217 confirmations, 12,460 candidates, an annual average of 4,153, with an average of 57 per center.

1865-1867: 220 confirmations, 11,715 candidates (this decrease in the number of candidates was due to internal changes in the diocese), an annual average of 3,905, with an average of 53 candidates per center.

During this period of 12 years Hamilton confirmed 49,576 candidates, an annual average of 4,131, with 57.4 candidates per center. In his Charge of 1858 he commented that the increased number of those confirmed "does not bear any proportion to the increase in the number of places at which I have confirmed. I find that when 100 confirmations were held in the year, the bishop confirmed 12,115 persons". But he went on to say that he had never believed or expected that the mere multiplying of the places of confirmation would make any great change in the numbers of candidates. [17]

Winchester

Bishop Charles Richard Sumner witnessed a considerable improvement in the number he confirmed in his diocese which, he believed, was an indication of a renewal, and increasing spiritual life. [18] The figures for Hampshire for the triennial period ending 1835 were 8,249, rising to 9,663 for the triennial period ending 1844. For the 12 years 1833-1844 he recorded 35,949 candidates confirmed in Hampshire, an annual average of 2,995. The figure for Surrey, while lower, shows a regular and progressive increase; for the triennial period ending 1836, 4,390 candidates were recorded as confirmed, rising to 8,174 for the period ending 1845. During the 12 years 1834-1845 he confirmed 25,723 candidates, an annual average of 2,143 candidates. This was partly due to the increase in the number of his confirmation centers. Hampshire in 1822 had 16 confirmation centers; by 1832 Sumner increased them nearly 200% to 45. Surrey in 1830 had 24 centers, which he enlarged to 56 by 1863. [19] His general increase in both candidates and centers is seen in the Rivington records; in 1865 he had 66 centers and confirmed 13,299 candidates.

Conclusions

Incomplete, inconsistent and inadequate records prevent the drawing of any definite conclusions in the area of confirmation statistics; nevertheless, the figures considered and analyzed, and an examination of the table which follows, does indicate some trends, and useful facts do emerge, and a few general conclusions may be drawn.

General Analysis of Diocesan Returns

Diocese	Period	No. of Years	Total Number Confirmed	Annual Average	No. of Centers	Annual Average Centers	Average per Center	Percentages		
								Male	Female	Female above Male
St. Asaph	1869-79	10	15,437	1,543						
Bangor	1866-69	3	1,727	575						
Chester	1865-68	4	37,224	9,306	184	46	202			
Chichester	1870-75	6	25,954	4,325				42.5	57.5	35
Durham	1858-66	8	25,095	3,137	243	30	103			
Gloucester	1864-67	3	12,352	4,841	130	43	95	39.0	61.0	55
Lincoln	1859-67	9	43,671	3,407				42.0	58.0	39
Manchester	1870-76	7	71,000	10,142				38.0	62.0	63
Norwich	1856-58	3	14,547	4,849						
Oxford	1851-69	18	87,938	4,888						
Peter-borough	1864-67	3	18,304	6,101	113	38	162			
Ripon	1862-67	6	28,969	4,828	191	31	152			
Salisbury	1856-67	12	49,576	4,131	863	71	57			

This table covers 13 out of the 27 dioceses, thus nearly 50%. The annual average number of candidates is 5,171; only four dioceses are above this average. Out of the 13 dioceses listed, 6 had an annual average in the 4,000-5,000 group, with 3 below this group and 4 above. The annual average of centers varied considerably. Durham over a period of 8 years had 30 centers per annum, with an average of 103 candidates, while Salisbury over a period of 12 years had 71 centers per annum, with an average of 57 candidates. The figures do not show conclusively that an increase in the number of centers resulted in an increase in the number of candidates, although in many dioceses fragmentary evidence seems to indicate that this did happen.

There was considerable variation between diocesan returns relating to the number of male and female candidates and the diocesan disparity between the percentage of female candidates above male. The analysis of Rivington shows that of the total number of candidates confirmed 52% were female in Worcester, and 65.5% in London; in 8 of the dioceses listed in Rivington over 60% of the total confirmed were female. Of female candidates above male there were 6.95% more females than males in Worcester and 90% more in London; the analysis in this field reveals an incomprehensible picture. This variable pattern may have been due to a variety of factors, such as occupations, and the female percentage of the overall population; the fact is that some bishops became very much aware of the disparity and urged their clergy to seek out more male candidates. It is felt that this latter point was a very influential factor in increasing the number of male candidates in at least some of the dioceses.

One conclusive fact which emerges from the analysis of the fragmentary figures is that in every diocese there were always more female candidates than male.

Even in the areas where there was a notable increase in the number of candidates, it was generally admitted by the bishops that this was not really satisfactory when compared with the increasing population. But not all dioceses were able to report a marked increase in the number of candidates; in some it was only marginal; in others, the situation was fairly static and when compared with the increasing population was in fact indicative of a decline in the percentage of candidates against the population.

John Dowden (1840-1910) who lived through the mid-Victorian period and was Bishop of Edinburgh from 1886 to his death, had some interesting things to say to his clergy in 1888, on the subject of confirmation statistics. These comments offer wise guidance when examining the kind of statistics which have just been considered and analyzed:

"The statistics of the Confirmations of a diocese afford some valuable material, by help of which after due precautions a bishop may, with a fair measure of accuracy, estimate the progress of the Church generally, and also (after allowance for the peculiar circumstances of particular congregations) the faithfulness and energy of the clergy in their respective posts of duty. Of course he will not fail to perceive that a small settled congregation in the country is not afforded the same scope for expansion as may be found in a mission church, planted in a populous and neglected district of a great city. Again, he will readily acknowledge that in an undermanned city charge, where all the varied labours of the pastorate, visiting the sick, attending the schools, superintending guilds and classes, preparing for the pulpit, and a score of other duties, equally diverse, fall to be discharged by one priest, it is inevitable that seeking out the candidates of due age for confirmation, and their careful preparation when found, must sadly suffer. A bishop may, in such cases, deplore a state of things which he may be unable to censure. Yet, after all due allowance for peculiar circumstances in particular cases, he will, I think, be justified in believing that a want of interest in his Confirmation classes may be taken as a sufficient indication of a careless priest. Certainly no part of a clergyman's duty can, if carried out with prayer and with care, be made more fruitful of lasting spiritual good".[20]

Perhaps not all the members of the mid-Victorian episcopate had Dowden's wise insight into the peculiar factors and circumstances which must be duly considered in relation to confirmation returns, but there is good reason to believe that most of the bishops of the period shared his feelings in relation to the clergyman's duty in this respect, namely that the seeking out and preparing of confirmation candidates was a pastoral priority and gave some indication of the spiritual life and growth of parishes, and the faithfulness and energy of the clergy, and of the life of the diocese as a whole.

NOTES

1. C. R. Sumner, A Charge, 1845 9-11, 28-30.

2. C. R. Sumner, A Charge, 1850 37-9.

3. J. B. Sumner, A Charge, 1841 12-14.

4. Alfred George Edwards, **Landmarks in the History of the Welsh Church** (1913) 270-1.

5. When Rivington figures are given they refer to the tabulation of the figures shown from the **Rivington Ecclesiastical Year Book 1865.**

6. J. C. Campbell, A Charge, 1869 8.

7. W. Jacobson, A Charge, 1868 5-6.

8. R. Durnford, A Charge, 1875.

9. C. Baring, A Charge, 1866 42-3.

10. C. J. Ellicott, A Charge, 1864 25; A Charge, 1867 23.

11. J. Jackson, A Charge, 1864 9, 56; A Charge, 1867 10-12, 55.

12. Thomas Hughes, **James Fraser, Second Bishop of Manchester: A Memoir 1818-1885** (1887) 209-10.

13. J. Fraser, A Charge, 1876 26.

14. J. T. Pelham, A Charge, 1858 16, 24.

15. See Meacham, **Lord Bishop** 143; S. Wilberforce, A Charge, 1857 5-6; A Charge, 1860 9-10; A Charge, 1866 3-4.

16. F. Jeune, A Charge, 1867 11.

17. W. K. Hamilton, A Charge, 1854 11-12; A Charge, 1864 92; A Charge, 1867 134.

18. C. R. Sumner, A Charge, 1845 28.

19. See G. H. Sumner, **Life of Bishop C. R. Sumner** (1876) 215-20.

20. J. Dowden, A Charge, 1888 5.

C. Confirmation Day

Confirmation Tickets

Tickets were presented, by a priest, to the candidates whom he had prepared and found acceptable for presentation to the bishop. Even after episcopal reform in the administration of the rite, confirmations were sometimes still attended by very large numbers of candidates, and these tickets acted as a guide, telling the bishop, or the officials on duty, the candidate's name, parish and the priest who was supposed to have prepared him, but the system was not without its abuses. In practice some priests were particular about those to whom they issued tickets, while others seemed willing to do so even when little, if any, preparation had been given.

John Skinner, incumbent of Camerton, Somerset, was one of the conscientious. Two classes of collier boys, fourteen in all, "were so very ignorant and ill-behaved I did not think that I could in conscience give them tickets for confirmation". The only boy whom he felt fit to receive a ticket was the schoolmaster's son. Of eighteen girls who received tickets, one who had behaved improperly received her ticket only on her promise of amendment. Two years later collier boys were still a problem to Skinner; two were not only ill-behaved, but grossly ignorant, having entirely forgotten their Catechism and could not say the Lord's Prayer: "When I expostulated with them, both laughed in my face, and I was obliged to beg them to leave the room". At a later confirmation, two of his candidates lost their tickets and he had to certify that they had been examined. [1]

The English Churchman tells of a clergyman who refused to issue a confirmation ticket to a female candidate of twenty-seven, because she had refused to promise never to attend a Meeting-house service. Two days before the confirmation he had a change of mind and issued the ticket, although still uncertain whether he was right to do so. [2] Edward King tells of how he received his confirmation ticket from his father, who at the time was an Archdeacon. He was called into the study and asked if he knew the Catechism, his father then gave him a card and told him to get on his pony and ride to where the confirmation was to be held by Archbishop Howley. [3]

Some bishops insisted that details of candidates should be sent to them before the confirmation; they required not only the name and age of candidates, but also some description of the class to which the candidates belonged.

Tickets presented by ill-prepared or badly behaved candidates enabled the bishop to ascertain who was responsible for issuing the ticket and to reprimand the clergyman concerned; Samuel Wilberforce was one who used the tickets to this end. [4]

The method of presenting confirmation tickets varied. There were some bishops who refused to confirm candidates who had arrived without their tickets; others were not so rigid and did confirm such forgetful candidates. At some confirmations tickets were presented to the bishop's chaplain or to the church-wardens before the candidate was allowed to enter the chancel--and none were admitted without tickets.

The Day of Confirmation

For the majority of churchpeople the day of confirmation was an occasion of tremendous importance, not least for the clergy and candidates, for whom it was the end of a period of serious preparation. More bishops were coming to look upon it as a unique opportunity, which could have a profound and lasting effect upon those confirmed, and upon others present at the service. For the parish in which it was administered it was an occasion of great honor and importance and, as such, a memorable event. But there were cases which left much to be desired: unspiritual clergy, ill-prepared candidates, unreformed bishops, unscrupulous parishioners. Further problems arose from the necessity of using a single confirmation center for a wide area; among these were the long journey which candidates had to undertake and the large numbers confirmed at a single service.

Country people tended to regard Confirmation Day as a convenient excuse for a trip to town. When children had to travel a long way to a central confirmation the churchwardens often provided wagons to take them to their destination. If the distance was considerable, then most of the day would be spent in travel. The boys and girls were generally mixed together on the wagons; the fact that they were often unaccompanied usually resulted in much frivolity on the way, laughing and playing and in some cases it is suggested worse misbehavior took place, which made some parents apprehensive about allowing their daughters to travel to a confirmation without an adult companion. There is evidence to suggest that many young people looked upon the day as offering a riotous holiday. It was a usual practice to take the candidates to an ale-house for bread, cheese and beer before the journey home. But while the day was open to misuse not all abused the situation.

There were parish clergy, like Kingsley, who were very much aware of the type of misdemeanors mentioned and who carefully planned and supervised the excursion of their candidates, so as to avoid such abuses. Hamilton, Bishop of Salisbury, urged his clergy to accompany their candidates both to and from the confirmation "and thus by your presence to guard them from such evil that may befall them". Samuel Wilberforce worked hard to bring an end to the revelling which had often taken place on the confirmation days in his own diocese. Through the efforts of men like Wilberforce, Hamilton, Kingsley and others confirmation days in many dioceses were gradually transformed, but it was a slow process and not always easy or appreciated. One publican is said to have requested compensation from Bishop Wilberforce for loss of trade, since the confirmations had become a matter of religion and not carousing. The Ball, provided by Wilberforce's predecessor, on the evening following the confirmation and given in honor of the occasion was abandoned by Wilberforce.

For some it was not only the distance which was a problem, but also the time of the service. This was generally held mid-week. The times of mid-week confirmations were spread throughout the day, at 8, 11, 11:30 a.m., 12 noon and 3 p.m., both time and place sometimes being advertised in ecclesiastical newspapers. There were very real problems for many working class people and working children in getting time off in order to be confirmed. During the mid-Victorian period bishops became more willing to confirm on Sundays, which suited the working classes much better, and gradually the practice became more widely accepted and implemented. Lack of suitable clothing was also a problem for the working classes and there were occasions when candidates failed to appear at a confirmation because of this. [5]

Vast crowds were an inevitable feature when candidates were being confirmed in their hundreds; with such large numbers it is not surprising that there were complaints of disorder and a lack of quietness and respect. This fact alone was seen by many bishops as a sufficient reason for increasing the number of confirmation centers and setting a limit to the number of candidates to be confirmed at any one service.

Accounts of disorderly confirmations are too numerous to cover in full, but fortunately this widespread failure had begun to decline in the mid-Victorian period. Even Wilberforce records in his diary details of disorderly confirmations: "some trouble in keeping order", "Confirmation at first unruly", "disorderly confirmation", "mob--got it quiet". [6] Some clergy in the Welsh Church are said to have hired people for the day, to be present at confirmations in order to make a good show for the bishop; in such cases the bishop seems to have been unaware of the reason for the large crowd and went away delighted. [7] Bickersteth believed that if candidates had the right reason for being confirmed and really meant from their heart all that the service required, then the problem of disorder and abuse would be overcome. But it was not only the candidates and the laity in general who needed to take the service more seriously; Kilvert tells of a youthful looking curate who, with a girl candidate, arrived late at a confirmation. When the curate brought the girl to the rail the bishop thought that he was a young farmer candidate. Pope, the curate, tried to tell the bishop that he was a clergyman and the girl his candidate. The bishop, comments Kilvert, was "over-bearing and imperious", and thought that he was a refractory ill-conditioned youth. In spite of the curate's pleas, either unheard or unheeded, the bishop insisted that he knelt down; no one intervened to save him and the whole church was in a titter--and the curate was confirmed. An amusing incident and yet a serious reflection on the attitude of the time, 1870. The curate was not properly dressed in his gown and thus partly at fault, the clergy standing by could have stepped forward and prevented the incident, and the bishop ought not to have been so hasty and overbearing. [8]

During a confirmation service at Beverley, the clergy disgraced themselves by gossiping to each other throughout the service and actually laughing during the laying on of hands; their conduct was described as "wretchedly irreverent". [9] There were some clergy of the period who felt that too much "extraordinary pomp and circumstance was thrown over the rite". Thus, in spite of reform, mid-Victorian confirmations could still be occasions of abuse; irreverent behavior and various other failings, both among laity and clergy could be encountered. Nevertheless, many bishops of the period complimented their clergy on the vast improvement in the general conduct and behavior of candidates. When William Maclagan was Bishop of Lichfield he told his clergy that part of the confirmation preparation given to candidates should be to "instruct the candidates as to their duties and demeanour at the time of confirmation itself. Candidates must be told what is expected of them at the Confirmation". Not all large confirmations were occasions of disorder, for many were conducted with decency and little noise. The Church Times reporting a confirmation conducted by Wilberforce told of "the reverent demeanour of the congregation and the devout behaviour of the candidates, the evident earnestness of the youth and the modesty of the girls". Bishop Ellicott expressed to his clergy his deep thankfulness that the general behavior and deportment of those confirmed had been uniformly good and edifying. Three years later he mentioned two matters in this connection: firstly, the increased seriousness of manner and behavior in those confirmed, and secondly, the almost strikingly increased interest shown by the congregation. Such comments as these are typical of what many bishops of the period were saying on this subject, although of course there were some exceptions, where bishops condemned rather than commended. [10]

The Setting of the Rite

The liturgical setting in which confirmation took place was largely dependent upon each diocesan bishop, thus practice varied from diocese to diocese. Many administered the rite as complete in itself, while others administered it after Morning or Evening Prayer. Charles Wordsworth always prefaced the rite with the Litany, if this had not already been said. The Litany was followed by a hymn, then an address, then another hymn which was followed by the rite of Confirmation in its entirety. Sometimes Confirmations were immediately followed by the Bishop's Visitation; this was usually because the bishop felt that he ought to take advantage of all the clergy being together. Morning Prayer, followed by Ante-Communion and then Confirmation was also a practice used by some.

The laying on of hands was administered in a variety of ways. Maclagan would sit and had the candidates brought before him two at a time; both hands were first laid on each of the candidates and afterwards one hand on each as he said the words of administration. George Wilkinson had candidates presented to him singly by their own priest, who gave their names to him; he then signed each one with the sign of the Cross and laid hands upon them. Some bishops stood and administered confirmation to each candidate individually. John Hull stated in 1840 that neither the Archbishop of Canterbury nor the Bishop of London laid their hands upon the head of each candidate. Such a deviation was, said Hull, advisable: "Bishops do not confirm, and from the multitudes of candidates, could not confirm, according to the rubric. [11]

There is little available evidence of ceremonial at confirmations during this period, either of the use of lights and incense or of the dress used by the bishops. Purchas in his **Directorium Anglicanum** provides clear details on the subject which, no doubt, influenced the practices of the more Catholic Anglicans. It is impossible, however, to give any indication about the extent of their use. The proper vestments for the bishop, states Purchas, should be prepared in the sacristy. He lists the following: "A rochette, an amice, a surplice, a white stole, a white cope, a gold embroidered mitre, and pastoral staff, and the usual surplices, hoods and cottas for the Priests and assistants. The pastoral staff may be carried in his hand, or else borne by his chaplain".

Concerning the furniture, Purchas writes: "During the administration of this Sacrament the throne should be adorned with white hangings, and the arms of the diocese may be suspended behind. Seats should be prepared for the chaplains, one on each side of the throne". Of the altar, he states: "The altar should be vested in white, and vases of white flowers may be placed upon the super-altar".

Of the rite and candidates he says: "The rite itself consists in the laying on of hands. The question asked before is intended to satisfy the congregation that the candidate is in earnest. The first Book of Edward VI does not contain the renewal of Baptismal vows".

"The candidates in order to be confirmed come up and kneel either at the footstep of the Sacrarium; or, so that the Service may be both seen and heard, sometimes at the step of the chancel".

"It is a Catholic custom for females to be dressed in white, and to wear veils without caps".

The practice of preaching a sermon, or giving an address at confirmations, was another matter on which episcopal practice varied. Wilkinson generally gave three addresses: the first to the congregation, the second to the candidates, the third after the Confirmation. Maclagan and Phillpotts usually gave two addresses, the majority only one. Many of the bishops took these addresses very seriously and what they said often had a deep and permanent effect upon the hearers.

A sermon preached by Bishop George Moberly in 1876 sums up well the changes and reforms in the administration of the rite during the mid-Victorian period: "That things are in this respect greatly changed for the better within the last forty or fifty years in our dioceses, I most thankfully acknowledge. Having myself been engaged continually, for more than thirty years, in preparing public school boys for Confirmation, and having, during the last six years, confirmed upwards of twenty-eight thousand candidates, in almost every case singly (as is, I believe, now the general practice of all the bishops), and having witnessed the great care and pains taken by the parochial clergy in the preparation of the candidates (and not only in a few exceptionally well-ordered parishes, but in almost every parish in my diocese), I feel able to testify, in the clearest

and most unhesitating way, to the wonderful improvement that
has taken place in the church of England since the time when
I was myself confirmed in the year 1820...I verily believe that
there is no agency at work in our beloved Church which has
upon it clearer tokens of the blessing of God than that of Confirmation as it is now administered, not in one or two dioceses
only, but I believe in every single diocese of the Church of
England".

NOTES

1. See Howard Coombs, **Journal of a Somerset Rector
1803-1834. John Skinner, A. M. Antiquary 1772-1839, Parochial
Affairs of the Parish of Camerton** (Bath 1971) 241, 284, 350.

2. The English Churchman May 8th 1851, 293; May
15th 1851, 318.

3. George W. E. Russell, **Edward King, Sixtieth Bishop
of Lincoln: A Memoir** (1912) 3.

4. See Pugh, **Letter-books of Samuel Wilberforce** 159-60.

5. See A. Hume, **Thoughts unspoken...Sunday School
Teachers' Conference** (1880) 18, 42-3, 52-4, 64-6. See also How,
Archbishop Maclagan 244.

6. Ashwell and Wilberforce, op.cit., Vol. III, 374-5,
410.

7. See Henry T. Edwards, **Wales and the Welsh Church**
(1889) 344.

8. See William Plomer, ed., **Kilvert's Diary, 1870-1897**
(1964) 350.

9. See Newsome, **Parting of Friends** 279.

10. See C. J. Ellicott, A Charge, 1864 25-6; A Charge,
1867 22-3; A. Ollivant, A Charge, 1866 19; J. C. Campbell,
A Charge, 1869 8-9.

11. John Hull, **Observations on a Petition for the Revision
of the Liturgy** (3rd Ed. 1840) 6, 13. See Henry Blunt, **The Book
of Church Law, being an Exposition of the Legal Rights and**

Duties of the Parochial Clergy and Laity of the Church of England: Revised by G. F. Phillimore 1876, 77.

LITURGICAL REVISION

Serious nineteenth century agitation for the revision of the Prayer Book began in 1828; [1] by the mid-Victorian period dissatisfaction with the Prayer Book and attempts at its revision had gained considerable momentum. Early attempts at revision have been described as "scissor and paste schemes"; liberal in outlook and lacking in liturgical knowledge; seeking to accommodate widely held Low Church theological ideas and at the same time to encourage Dissenters to join the Established Church. As the nineteenth century progressed, the number of pamphlets on, and petitions to Parliament for, Prayer Book Revision increased considerably. Both the Gorham Judgement and the Religious Census gave encouragement and support to the advocates for revision. The two main aims of the revisionists were first, the comprehension of Dissenters and secondly, the accommodation of a particular theological outlook. There were other lesser causes which influenced attempts at revision, but examination of a large number of mid-Victorian pamphlets on liturgical revision reveals that the two main points mentioned, especially their connection with the initiatory rites, were recurring themes in many of the publications. But, however valid these two points, however vocal their advocates, however numerous their publications and petitions, in the end their attempts to revise the Prayer Book in order to satisfy and win over Dissenters, or to calm the doctrinal controversy of the period within her own ranks, were doomed to failure; the suggested revisions, at least in the mid-Victorian period, never received the official acceptance for which their advocates had worked so hard and so long.

The revival of Convocations provided the opportunity for official debate and action in this field. Reports of the Convocation debates provide a valuable insight into opinions, ideas and pressures of the period. Concern over the vastly increased population and the accompanying social conditions prompted, in 1854, the appointment of a Committee to consider some adaptation of the Church's rules appropriate to meet their spiritual necessities. This Committee presented its report in 1854; it suggested: "The twenty-ninth Canon should be relaxed to allow parents to stand as sponsors for their children at baptism". The report, described as "a pedestrian and unoriginal composition", caused many to lose their confidence in the ability of the newly revived Convocation to deal with the problems of worship. In spite of this setback the revisionists continued their work towards their desired ends.

In 1858 Samuel Wilberforce reminded a meeting of the Upper House of Convocation that they could not shut their eyes to "the fact that there is a movement afoot for introducing marked changes into the Prayer Book". Such attempts, however, failed to gain his approval or that of many of his episcopal brethren. Thirlwall seems to have changed his mind on the advisability of such revision, for he expressed the view that such revision would only increase the dissensions in the Church and lead to formal and visible disruption. [2] Others also used the possibility of disruption as an argument against revision. Tait, in the same debate, expressed the opinion that such revision would endanger "the unity which we have been able to preserve in the midst of the diversity of our opinions". In the same year Ollivant of Llandaff felt that the unanimous opinion of the bishops was: "that we are convinced that any attempt to alter the expressions or the doctrinal bearing of our services, so as to make them more comfortable to the particular views of any separate persons in our Church, would be most injurious, and that to any attempt of that kind we are most determinedly opposed".

In 1859 Bishop Wilberforce declared: "The position of safety for the Church of England is, where we can preserve great principles untouched, to make changes which will supply the wants of the people". He went on to say: "I have come to the distinct conviction that this is a time in which to be bold is to be wise, to be bold is to be safe". [3] In addressing his clergy during the following year Wilberforce said: "Another cloud which hangs over the future is the threatened revision of our Book of Common Prayer"; and in 1862 we find Bishop C. R. Sumner speaking about the continuing agitation for the Revision of the Liturgy. [4] Touching upon the subject of the Prayer Book Revision in his Charge of 1864, Hamilton told his clergy: "I trust that all true lovers of the Church of England will steadily resist such an encroachment of their common inheritance". During an Upper House debate on the subject of liturgical revision, the Bishop of Chichester reported how his clergy were, with one or two exceptions, unanimous in their rejection of Prayer Book Revision: "They all objected to any interference at this present time". [5] There were many who believed that some form of revision was required, but felt that it was not the appropriate time to undertake this. Not all the bishops were against liturgical revision; nevertheless, when Lord Ebury put his proposals for Prayer Book Revision before the House of Lords, it was the bishops who rejected it. [6]

Members of the Lower House were equally divided on the issue. The object of Prayer Book Revision was not, said Archdeacon Bickersteth in a debate in June 1859, the alteration of doctrine, "but in some degree to relax the stringency of the Book of Common Prayer, so as to make it more available for the wants of the common people". Others, however, were in no doubt that the alterations being put forward did involve doctrinal alterations, indeed some felt that very many of them "strike at some of the essential doctrines of the Church". [7] Archdeacon Denison believed that what they should seek was not an alteration of the existing Book of Common Prayer, but to supplement the Prayer Book with certain services which are required--and which enable the Church of England to do her work among people much more efficiently than she is able to do in the present state of the Prayer Book. He advocated that they should not interfere with the Prayer Book or infringe its doctrines. The argument that the revision of the Prayer Book at that time would disturb the peace and unity of the Church was rejected by the dean of Norwich, who said that the peace and unity was already very much disturbed. He spoke of the "most appalling fact which came out of the Census of 1851" that 5 million people never attend worship; he felt that this fact supported the many small alterations in the Prayer Book which would, he believed, be highly beneficial and would remove a great many difficulties. [8] It is not surprising to find that many of the points raised in the Convocation debates, both for and against revision, found much fuller expression in the pamphlet warfare of the period.

Horace Mann's disclosure in the Religious Census of 1851 of the "labouring myriads" outside the Church and the vast number of practicing Dissenters, was used by both sides to support their position. An anonymous pamphlet argued: "Many... and cogent, are the reasons for preserving our Liturgy as it is and let us trust it will be long, indeed, before any alteration be permitted by our legislature". The writer was not unaware, or unconcerned, about the disclosures of the Religious Census, but he felt that the growing opposition of the masses towards religion and their estrangement from the Church of England, was due to her failure to care for their souls, and her failure to instruct them. While he approved of the various schemes put forward to make up for this neglect he did not think that Prayer Book revision was the answer to the problem. [9]

Another writer, Isaac Taylor, having examined the findings of the Religious Census, argued that in the light of the facts contained in it "as an act of plain justice to the Dissenters, certain minute liturgical changes in the Prayer Book should be carried out...we must expect that the advancing tide will continue to advance; we must expect that the Dissenters will become more dangerous in their hostility, and more powerful in their political attitude. Surely on the lowest grounds of expediency, if on no higher ground of Christian charity, even the highest of High Churchmen might consent to surrender betimes points which they themselves admit to be indifferent or non-essential". [10] The conviction that revision of the Prayer Book ought to take place in order to win over Dissenters, or to satisfy some of their difficulties, was the starting point of several of the pamphlets published. Taylor was convinced that wise liturgical concessions would eventually win over the Dissenters, not in his own day, but the children of the present generation of Dissenters; in this he was more realistic than some, who felt that visible results would become apparent almost overnight.

The idea of revising the Prayer Book in order to comprehend the Dissenters, or to ease the tender conscience of some churchmen, was opposed by the leaders of the Tractarians, who demanded loyalty to the Prayer Book as it stood. Some felt that any compromise to win over the Dissenters could be a real threat to those already within the Church of England and to her existing unity, but Taylor felt that liturgical revision need not cause or even offer a "pretext of disruption". The Bishop of Chester, J. B. Sumner, said that if he were allowed to alter 20 words in the Prayer Book he could at once bring 20,000 Dissenters into the Church of England; there is, however, no evidence to substantiate such a bold claim.

Not all churchmen were as optimistic as Taylor and Sumner. The Reverend Samuel Minton, writing to the Bishop of London, argued that there were too many things against a migration of Dissenters on a large scale. [11] The Reverend M. F. Sadler contended that a very small fraction of Dissenters were likely to be won over by the alterations suggested. No alterations, he said, would win over the Baptists; in the case of the Wesleyan Methodists they were uncalled for; the Independents or Congregationalists offered the only reasonable hope and such alterations could win over only a small fraction of these. [12] Bishop Ollivant was also realistic on the matter and expressed the view that if liturgical revision were to win over Dissenters then it would have to be so radical that it was out of the question. [13] Longley expressed the opinion that to expect to move any large body of Non-conformists into the pale of the Church by means of liturgical revision was a "visionary expectation". [14] The <u>Christian Remembrancer</u> took the line that no amount of concession to the prejudices of the Dissenters, and no amount of mutilation to the Prayer Book, however ruthless, would satisfy them. [15]

While the opposing factions debated the possible merits and results of such revision, there were others who were impatient and felt that delay was dangerous. One such person was William Peace, who believed that the present state of the Church was forcing the issue, and immediate action, in the form of liturgical revision, was demanded. [16]

Whatever the advocates of revision believed about the urgency of the problem, and the good results which they were confident would be achieved by such action, there were 10,000 clergy who saw fit to sign "A Declaration Against Altering the Prayer Book". The Petition stated that any attempt at that time to alter the Book of Common Prayer would be attended with great danger to the peace and unity of the Church. [17]

In 1860 the Christian Remembrancer raised the question: "The Revision of the Prayer Book--is it, or is it not, desirable?--is a question in itself most momentous and, at the present time, of pressing importance...The time has come for those who desire the welfare of the Church of England to form an intelligent opinion, and to take a decided part for or against revision". The paper posed three possible courses of action: (i) Doctrinal revision (this was dismissed); (ii) Preserving the Prayer Book and adding a Supplement of re-arranged services (this it was felt was tantamount to having two Prayer Books and found unacceptable); (iii) The safest course, to leave the Prayer Book exactly as it was (the Christian Remembrancer advocated this as the best possible course of action). [18] It was this latter approach which won the day, for whatever the reasons put forward for revision--to win Dissenters; to obtain doctrinal compromise to suit one party; to win the masses, or simply to improve the Prayer Book--opposition remained sufficiently strong throughout the mid-Victorian period to prevent the implementation of any of the suggested revisions. Suggested revisions connected with the initiatory rites were clustered round a few major points, based upon doctrinal and practical differences rather than liturgical improvements. The chief of these abortive suggestions were as follows:

The Baptismal Office

The Edinburgh Review of January 1861 published an article in which the writer examined the suggested revisions of the Book of Common Prayer; he wrote: "We...now come to the last and most important point of all, that of the Baptismal Office...It cannot be denied that this, which is the most important, is also by far the most difficult point to settle...". For this writer the crux of the problem was the application of the term 'regeneration' to infants.

One of the avowed aims of the 'Prayer Book Revision Society', formed in 1855, was the alteration of the words in the Baptismal Office which asserted the spiritual regeneration of each recipient. [19] Another group, 'The Association for Promoting a Revision of the Book of Common Prayer', which was an anti-Tractarian body formed in 1859, had among its aims: A revision of the Baptismal Services; the removal of everything which can be held to imply regeneration by the Holy Spirit as inseparably connected with the rite; a review of the sponsorial system, and generally the omission of any statement or assertion as to the effects of baptism. The Catechism was to be revised in harmony with these amendments of the services and some questions and answers on the great fundamental truths of Scripture to be inserted. The Confirmation Service was also to be similarly revised.

Pressure to remove all references to baptismal regeneration from the Baptismal Office, on the grounds that it was both unscriptural and unacceptable to the Dissenters, was both strong and consistent throughout the mid-Victorian period. For many the crux of the problem lay in the words: "Seeing now that this child is regenerate" and similar phrases expressing the same doctrine. There were those who felt that the best way to resolve the difficulty was simply to omit the offending words 'is regenerate'; such advocates seemed to believe that to omit these words would not offend anyone's conscience, and would satisfy many, and at the same time leave all free to teach their own views on the subject. [20] In 1859 an anonymous author produced services of Infant Baptism, the Baptism of those of Riper Years, Catechism and Confirmation, which had been systematically purged of the offending word 'regenerate'. [21] This same author put forward an alternative solution, which was also suggested by others, a bracketed Prayer Book in which the controversial words would be bracketed and could be said or omitted according to the conscience of each individual priest. Some churchmen could see no reason for such changes or omissions and felt that the term 'baptismal regeneration' ought to be left and the services remain intact. Evangelical attempts to purge the services of this term were partly motivated by the use which Tractarians made of the Prayer Book in support of their teaching.

Sponsors

The 'Association for Promoting a Revision of the Prayer Book' suggested the optional use of the vicarious stipulations on behalf of the children baptized; they also suggested that permission be given to parents to undertake all needful responsibilities for their own children. Behind these suggestions lay the problem of obtaining sponsors and a strong objection to the idea of vicarious faith which many believed to be unscriptural. [22] In 1870 the Royal Commission on Ritual issued its fourth and final report, in which it recommended that provision be made for only one godparent and that parents be allowed to act as sponsors for their own children.

Rubrical Revision

Suggestions in this field were put forward by James Hildyard in 1856. They were anything but revolutionary, but serve to illustrate how some churchmen were concerned with small and often uncontroversial points, such as references to "the vulgar tongue" which were no longer necessary and ought to be removed. [23] Another somewhat pedestrian suggestion related to the Prayer Book's declaration respecting the salvation of deceased infants; it was felt that this rubric ought either to be omitted or amended to infer that Christ's universal redemption is effectual to save all infants "dying before they commit actual sin" much more those who are dedicated to God by their baptism. [24] Robinson composed a revised rubric: "Although we charitably hope that all infants who die before they commit actual sin are made partakers in the benefits of Christ's death, it is certain by God's word that children which are baptized, dying before they commit actual sin are undoubtedly saved". [25]

A Convocation Committee on Rubrics published its Report early in 1876, but it offered very little by way of rubrical revision in the service of infant baptism. The sponsorship problem was recognized and it was suggested that the second rubric be extended thus: "Nevertheless, when three sponsors cannot be found, one Godfather and one Godmother should suffice". It was also recommended that parents be allowed to act as sponsors for their own children. The Committee recommended that a new rubric be added at the end of the service: "It is most expedient that such as are admitted to be Godfathers and Godmothers be communicants". They suggested that the following words be inserted into the third rubric: "or Evening Prayer, or at the conclusion of the Litany, if the Litany be used as a separate service, or, with the sanction of the Ordinary, at any other time". A new insertion was suggested relating to the reception into the Church of those privately baptized. They suggested a new rubric to meet the needs of those of riper years not baptized in infancy in extreme danger; the rubric gives the form in which such emergency baptisms should be administered. It was suggested that the Catechism include a rubric: "And it is expedient that every one have a Godfather or a Godmother as a witness of their Confirmation". At the end of the Service of Confirmation it was suggested that a new rubric be included relating to those presented to the bishop for confirmation who have had no sponsors. These suggested revisions, which were never to materialize, were nothing radical; although they did attempt to meet some of the practical problems which had been raised from time to time, they avoided those issues which were points of doctrinal conflict. [26]

Catechism

On the whole, suggested revisions of the Catechism centered upon what is said about baptism and the sacraments in general. Those who made suggestions regarding the revision of the rite of infant baptism simply sought to bring the Catechism into line with suggested revisions in the services. Some amendments and omissions were also put forward for revising the latter part of the Catechism, which deals with the Sacraments. Francis Russell Hall was one who objected to the first person being used in the Catechism, feeling that the object of a Catechism should not be a profession of faith but rather to teach children. His view was that the Church ought to have a short Catechism for little children and another for those from nine to thirteen. [27] Bishop Charles Wordsworth believed that the Catechism needed certain additions, especially on the Ministry of the Church and Confirmation. He had in fact intended putting suggestions forward on this matter to the Lambeth Conference of 1867, but was prevented from doing so. [28]

Confirmation

Connop Thirlwall believed that the Preface to the Confirmation Service was in need of revision and improvement. [29]

C. H. Davis believed that the language of the first Collect, which speaks of the forgiveness of all the candidate's sins, was too strong and that a more general language would be safer and better. James Hildyard felt that the rubrics at the confirmation should read, "saying over them, 'Defend, O Lord, these thy servants...' ". He believed that this was necessary in view of the great numbers of candidates for confirmation and was in fact already being practiced by many of the bishops.

The Confirmation Service was seen to be applicable only to those baptized in infancy and did not anticipate those baptized as adults. It was felt by some that those who had had no Godparents could not ratify the promises which the bishops say they must renew. They could not renew what had not been made, and so some alteration in this part of the service seemed necessary if the service was to be realistic and honest; this problem was dealt with by the recommendation made by the Convocation of Canterbury Committee on Rubrics. This Committee proposed that the following rubric be inserted at the end of the service: "If any persons are presented to the Bishop, to be confirmed by him, who have been baptized and have had no sponsors, it shall be lawful for the Bishop to ask them these questions; viz: Dost thou renounce, &c; Dost thou believe, &c; Wilt thou then, &c; as in the Order for the Baptism of such as are of riper years; and they shall answer these questions instead of the questions contained in this Office". [30]

Any modification in the Service of Baptism with regard to baptismal regeneration and sponsors demanded a number of changes in the rite of confirmation, but there seemed little concern about this, although some did realize the need and made appropriate suggestions for revision.

High Church proposals were somewhat limited. Littledale suggested the restoration of the Chrism and the use of the sign of the Cross; one anonymous writer in the Church Quarterly Review for October 1876 suggested a return to the rite of 1549, with the emphasis upon Confirmation by the bishop rather than the renewal of baptismal vows.

Suggested liturgical revision, so far as the rite of Confirmation was concerned, was then most meager. But it was not such a burning issue as infant baptism and even the pedestrian suggestions for revision were either unacceptable or unheeded.

The Reverend C. Robinson's approach to the subject of liturgical revision, and the conclusions which he drew, were somewhat typical of many mid-Victorian churchmen who advocated the revision of the Book of Common Prayer. Robinson concluded: "I have now most carefully gone over the occasional offices to see what can be done to remove the conscientious scruples of Dissenters without interfering with the recognised doctrine of the Church; and in order that it may be clearly understood how slight a revision of our dearly cherished Book of Common Prayer is really needed to do away with every reasonable objection, I subjoin the following summary". In this summary he lists:

The Office of Infant, Private and Adult Baptism:

> Omission 25 words
> Alteration 18 words

Catechism:

> Alteration 6 words,
> Omission 6, and
> Addition of other questions and answers. [31]

It was a typical attempt to remove what caused offence to some and then to rationalize the attempt to others, by indicating how small and insignificant were the suggested changes, especially when compared with the tremendous amount of good that it was claimed such a slight revision would achieve. If such attempts had been implemented, it is more than likely that they would have satisfied very few.

Mid-Victorian attempts at Prayer Book revision do not really deserve the exalted title of 'Liturgical Revision', for on the whole liturgical scholarship and ideals, certainly in the field of Christian Initiation, did not enter into this movement to revise the Prayer Book. The approach of the period was indeed very much that of 'scissor and paste schemes', the alteration or omission of the offending words and phrases in a vain attempt to offer something acceptable to Dissenters, in the hope of winning their loyalty, and to satisfy those who found certain aspects of the Prayer Book incompatible with their doctrinal position. The possible improvement or enrichment of the liturgical aspect of the Prayer Book was something almost entirely overlooked in the heated controversies of the time.

NOTES

1. See R. C. D. Jasper, **Prayer Book Revision in England 1800–1900** (1954) 1–5, 12–16.

2. See Chronicle of Convocation 1858, February 8–9, February 1860, 189–90. But see Jasper op. cit., 9; in 1832 Thirlwall had advocated the Revision of the Prayer Book for the stability of the Church and winning Dissenters. Also see C. Thirlwall, A Charge, 1860 43–79.

3. Chronicle of Convocation February 11th 1859, 29.

4. See S. Wilberforce, A Charge, 1860 56–7; C. R. Sumner, A Charge, 1862 51–3.

5. Chronicle of Convocation, February 16th 1869, 189.

6. See Jasper, op. cit., 65–6. Also Lord Ebury, **On the Revision of the Liturgy: The Speech of Lord Ebury in the House of Lords** (3rd ed. 1859).

7. See Chronicle of Convocation February 16th 1860, 188. Also T. E. Espin, Our Want of Clergy: Its causes and suggestions for its cure: A Sermon preached...March 1st 1863 (1863) 17.

8. Chronicle of Convocation February 14th 1860, 154–5.

9. Anonymous, **The Book of Common Prayer: A National Bond of Peace** (1855) 3–5, 30–2, 39–41.

10. Isaac Taylor, **The Liturgy and the Dissenters** (2nd ed. 1860) 9.

11. Samuel Minton, A Letter to the Lord Bishop of London in favour of Liturgical Revision (1863) 5.

12. M. F. Sadler, **Doctrinal Revision of the Liturgy** (1861) 38–44.

13. A. Ollivant, A Charge, 1860 53–4. See also A. C. Tait, A Charge, 1862 38–41. C. R. Sumner, A Charge, 1862 51–3.

14. C. T. Longley, A Charge, 1864 34-5.

15. Christian Remembrancer, XXXXIX, No. I, 1860, 212.

16. William Peace, **Cogent Reasons for Entertaining the Question of Revising the Prayer Book** (1859) 3-4.

17. See The Guardian, May 2nd 1860, 388-9; May 9th 1860, 413-14; May 16th 1860, 445. The Guardian of May 2nd expressed the view that many other signatures could have been added.

18. Christian Remembrancer, XXXXIX, No. I, 1860, 208-12. See also letters in The Times December 2nd 1859; January 4th 1860; January 30th 1860.

19. See J. B. Lowe, **The Case as it is, between the Rev. J. Baylee, D.D. & The Liturgical Revision Society** (Liverpool, 1855) 3, 5-6.

20. William Deane Ryland, A Letter to the Lord Archbishop of Canterbury, on certain alterations which are required in the Liturgy and Offices of the Church of England (1856) 19-20. Taylor, op. cit., 37. C. Robinson, **Church Questions...** (1859) 30-1. Also C. H. Davis, **Liturgical Revision: Illustrated and vindicated on Orthodox Principles** (1859).

21. See Anonymous, Suggestions for a Revision of the Prayer Book (1859) 20-3.

22. Anonymous, The Necessity of Liturgical Revision demonstrated from Canonical Subscription (1859) 8-9. Davis, **Liturgical Revision** 46-7. Philip Gell, **Thoughts on the Liturgy** 40-1. Edward Shirely Kennedy, **The Liturgy and the Laity** (1860) 16-18. Ryland, op. cit., 21.

23. James Hildyard, **A Revision of the Rubrics and Liturgy** (Grantham 1856) 41-2.

24. See Davis, **Liturgical Revision** 47.

25. Robinson, **Church Questions** 31.

26. See Chronicle of Convocation July 1876, 29-39. See also Kennedy, op. cit., 10-11. Anonymous, **The Necessity of Liturgical Revision** 7-8.

27. Francis Russell Hall, **Liturgical Reform Defended** (Cambridge 1834) 25-6.

28. John Wordsworth, **The Episcopate of Charles Words-worth, Bishop of St. Andrews, Dunkeld and Dunblane, 1853–1892. A Memoir** (1899) 353-60.

29. C. Thirlwall, <u>A Charge, 1854</u> 63-4.

30. <u>Chronicle of Convocation</u> July 1876, 39.

31. Robinson, **Church Questions** 35.

CONCLUSION

The Gorham Judgement was intended to resolve an entangled doctrinal dispute concerning the official baptismal theology of the Church of England. Instead of resolving the issue it provoked further controversy and division. Because of the fundamental importance of baptism and its relation to many other aspects of church life, the issues raised during the Gorham controversy could not be treated lightly. Unfortunately, the conflict disturbed the life of the Church at a most crucial period, thwarting the full participation of many churchmen in constructive and much needed evangelistic enterprise.

Ecclesiastical parties were a prominent feature of the period and attest to an important facet of Anglicanism, her comprehensiveness. Such comprehensiveness was only possible because of the lack of doctrinal precision in many of the Church's formularies, as exemplified in the field of initiation. But while this comprehensiveness enabled the Church of England to contain within her ranks churchmen of widely differing theology, the baptismal controversy reveals how comprehensiveness was also detrimental to the life of the Church.

The Gorham controversy brought out the very worst of these opposing parties. Deep and bitter internal divisions, prompted by conflicting theological ideas and arguments undoubtedly hampered much of the Church's evangelical work. For some this comprehensiveness and lack of theological precision was seen as a serious threat to the Church's catholicity. In the final analysis, the Judgement resolved nothing and only time was to abate the turbulence it had caused, though the results of the controversy were not all negative and harmful. Some constructive and beneficial changes in the life of the Church of England did eventually evolve out of the conflict. It also prompted the publication of numerous, if not always edifying, theological works.

Both spoken and written word played a vital part in this unique baptismal controversy. Commitment to a particular theological interpretation inevitably influenced a man's ecclesiastical position and the 'party' to which he aligned himself. Attempts to clarify the confused and controversial situation caused by baptism were often far from successful and, in some cases, led to further misunderstanding, as in the case of Pusey's attempts. Very few churchmen saw synthesis as the answer to the dilemma and a possible way to overcome the bitter conflict. The prophetic F. D. Maurice attempted such a synthesis, but with little success, largely due to the general indifference of most of his fellow churchmen. During this period controversy was by no means confined to baptismal regeneration, or indeed to baptismal theology; baptism and burial, lay baptism, the registration of births, the problems of sponsorship, Church education and Prayer Book revision, all provoked considerable literature and debate. Throughout the period many of the Broad Churchmen, and those akin to them, stood on the edge of the baptismal controversy. On some points they were indistinguishable from their fellow churchmen.

Maurice's approach to baptism threw new light on the subject and his views influenced a number of other independent churchmen. Kingsley and Robertson were but two who shared his idea of a common humanity, stressing the theory of the sanctification of the human race through the Incarnation and seeing baptism as the individual's personal recognition of his sonship and call to be a child of God.

For at least some of the Broad Churchmen evangelistic activity and social reform were the practical and logical outworking of their baptismal theology. There were those who emphasized the need for care in teaching and practice, in order to avoid the impression that baptism was some kind of magic. Men like J. W. Colenso, Benjamin Jowett and Rowland Williams helped to show how the findings of biblical criticism could not and must not be divorced from other aspects of the Christian faith. For them theology was an integrated subject and the findings in one area must be applied to the wider field of theology and the Church's teaching and practice, and so they tried to show how some of the insights of biblical criticism affected the sacrament of baptism.

Emphasis upon the ecumenical significance of baptism was by no means confined to one party, but it was Maurice who became the chief exponent of this theological principle, which few of his contemporaries had either seen or grasped.

During the period 1850-1875 a number of issues connected with baptism either underwent change or were in the process of change, but one issue which remained unchanged was the practice of infant baptism. During the Gorham controversy the issue was never whether or not children ought to be baptized, but rather what baptism conferred in the case of infants. For the majority of mid-Victorian churchmen infant baptism created no problem. While a few felt it ought to be confined to the children of believing parents, outright opposition to the practice was neither loud nor heeded.

Before the publication of the Religious Census, churchmen had believed England to be a Christian country and the majority of the population members of the Established Church. The findings of the Census destroyed this illusion, but at the same time stimulated greater evangelistic activity for the remainder of the century. The Church of England had a duty to educate and baptize the children of the nation, but despite this conviction, and all her evangelistic activities, the mid-Victorian Church suffered a steady decline in the percentage of the population receiving baptism.

The gradual, but increasing, estrangement of the masses from the Church and the accompanying decline in baptism were due to many factors. Within the life of the Church each of the following contributed towards the total situation: theological controversy and party division and the unrest they caused; clerical negligence due to theological confusion concerning the official doctrine of baptism; Evangelical neglect of the Sacraments; plurality and non-residence; the unequal distribution of the clergy in relation to the population, especially in the new urban areas; the remoteness of the church's life, buildings and clergy from the urban masses, and the inability to obtain the required number of sponsors. While many churchmen were aware of these problems and worked for their solution, attempts at reform were generally fruitless and very limited.

There were other factors which were completely beyond the Church's control which influenced this increasing neglect of baptism. These included population increase and movement; the growth of secularism and the inevitable erosion of the link between the parish church and the people; increasing ignorance about the true meaning and purpose of baptism; the implementation of the Registration Act; the phenomenal increase of Nonconformity. Despite all this churchmen were not over-despondent, and the zeal and energy expended on confirmation clearly demonstrates that the Established Church was far from admitting that the cause was lost.

Unlike baptism, confirmation during the mid-Victorian period caused no great theological controversy, nor did the relation between the fragmented parts of the initiatory rite create any fundamental problems. Confirmation did, however, encourage new methods of preparation and stimulated a greater pastoral concern for both confirmands and communicants. The minimum age for confirmation was a subject occasionally touched upon in Episcopal Charges, but there was no common policy. The majority looked upon confirmation as the Confirmation of baptismal vows and a public profession of faith and obedience; it was felt to mark the candidates' entrance into a new stage of life. Unfortunately, the social conditions of the period militated against the Church's educational work, which included confirmation preparation. Among these factors were the early school-leaving age; the low level of education; child labor; long working hours; home conditions; poor clothing; ill-health; population movement; the distance to the nearest church; lack of rapport with the clergy and the infrequency of confirmations. All these factors created very real problems for those clergy who were concerned about the confirmation preparation of their young parishioners.

The mid-Victorian period marks an interim stage in the history of catechizing. On the one hand there were bishops and clergy who were distressed at the general neglect of the practice and strongly advocated its re-introduction; others, while appreciating what the method had achieved in the past, nevertheless now questioned its value and felt that new forms of confirmation preparation were needed. Confirmation classes were introduced, but were still in their infancy and by no means widespread. Various new methods of confirmation preparation were being recommended and tried, including lectures, sermons, books and manuals, although some clergy continued to use the Catechism. By the end of the period, even the most fervent and convinced advocates of traditional catechizing were beginning to admit that the Church needed to discover new and more appropriate methods for gathering the young together and instructing them in the Faith. Many believed that there was need for greater flexibility, not only in the method employed, but also in the place used; not only in the length of the course, but in the content and depth of the teaching. During this period there was no lack of enthusiasm or experimentation. Not all were conscientious however; human fallibility and the independence of the Anglican clergy made some negligence of duties and responsibilities inevitable.

Post-confirmation groups also became a feature of church life during this period and, like many other changes, this was partly due to episcopal encouragement. More frequent celebrations of the Holy Communion were undoubtedly influenced by episcopal exhortations, this widespread increase being by no means confined to any one party. A factor which encouraged this increase was the Bishops' observation of the discrepancy between the vast numbers being confirmed and the rather static communicant figures. It was genuinely felt that more frequent celebrations, at more suitable times, would help to improve this situation.

Reception of the Holy Communion was the immediate responsibility or privilege of the newly confirmed and yet for some candidates confirmation and Holy Communion remained two unconnected events. Nevertheless, in this period there was an increasing emphasis upon confirmation as admission to communicant membership, which implied regular reception. While this view was rapidly gaining ground, it cannot be said that it was a common or established practice. Evidence suggests that old ways and attitudes die hard and so for vast numbers of church-people during this period confirmation remained quite unrelated to Holy Communion. Only time and teaching were to change the picture radically.

Most bishops of the period came to feel the need for reform in the administration of confirmation, and a gradual change in this respect is one of the notable features of the mid-Victorian period. Smaller and more frequent confirmations, the improvement in preparation for confirmation and for the actual service, the encouragement of a fuller participation by parents and sponsors--all contributed towards a much-needed reform in the Church's life. Bishops were beginning to look upon the quality and number of candidates presented for confirmation as an indication of the state of a parish and the conscientiousness of the priest. Most churchmen of the period attempted to increase the number of confirmands, but very few seem to have given much constructive thought to the relation between confirmation figures and the vast numbers baptized, or the increasing and moving population, or the problems of child labor, illiteracy and working class mentality, or to the reason for the predominance of female candidates. A later age could well interpret the small number of those confirmed who became regular communicants as an indication of neglect or failure at parish level, but the evidence contradicts such a conclusion.

Churchmen of the period may have been over-concerned with ecclesiastical statistics and at the same time guilty of a failure accurately to analyze and interpret the meaning of the figures they had obtained. Nevertheless, their understanding of the available information did result in a great deal of impressive activity, even if some of this was wrongly conceived and misdirected. While much of their attention was given to 'religion' and 'religious activities' it cannot be said that they neglected the individual or the needs of society, but it must be admitted that some times, having failed to detect the real problem, they implemented unsatisfactory solutions.

Comprehension of Dissenters and the accommodation of a particular theological outlook were the prime motivations behind suggested liturgical revision. Baptismal regeneration was a problem for most Dissenters and for many churchmen, and suggested revisions of the Baptismal Office were all centered upon this one theological point. Despite arguments to the contrary, if such changes had been implemented they would have fundamentally altered the Church's baptismal theology. At the same time, there is no evidence to support the view that such changes would have drawn a large number of Dissenters back into the Church of England. Strictly speaking, none of the suggested changes can be described as liturgical revision; they were aimed at doctrinal change, the re-phrasing of statements and the omission of offending words, in an attempt to make the rites more acceptable to those for whom they created difficulties. Official liturgical revision of the initiatory rites in this period was in fact non-existent.

Theological controversy, evangelistic activity, successful and abortive attempts at reform, all contributed towards the changes which took place in the life of the Church of England between 1850 and 1875. And yet, in spite of the many changes and reforms, in 1875 many of the old difficulties, problems and conflicts still remained.

Facts disclosed by the Religious Census of 1851 had had a dual effect upon many churchmen. On the one hand, the accuracy of the Census was challenged but, at the same time, its disclosures spurred the Church on to even greater evangelistic enterprise. Some members of the Established Church were confident that her years of effort had been fruitful and, in 1871, began campaigning for a second religious census. It was believed that such a census would offer a truer and more favorable picture of the Church's strength, but the census never took place.

Not all churchmen were so confident about the Church's strength and vitality. In 1872 Convocation set up a committee to examine 'Deficiencies of Spiritual Ministration'. The discoveries and conclusions of the committee were published in 1875; for many churchmen the disclosures of the report were as devastating as those of the 1851 Religious Census. It revealed that, in spite of years of strenuous evangelistic activity and reform, the Established Church of the late Victorian period would have to face substantially the same problems as their predecessors at the outset of the mid-Victorian period.

Party conflict, aggravated by the Gorham Judgement, which had hampered much of the Church's work throughout the period, was to continue. Although some of the points of conflict had subsided, a new phase was to begin for, in 1874, the Public Worship Regulation Act was passed and in its train came new conflicts and controversies. In January 1876 F. W. Puller, vicar of Roath, read a Paper before the Chapter of the South-Eastern Division of the Upper Llandaff Rural Deanery, entitled, "What is the Distinctive Grace of Confirmation?" This was to be the germ of a new conflict in the history of Christian initiation in the Church of England, a conflict concerning the relation between baptism and confirmation. It was realized, by some, that the fragmentation of the initiatory rite created fundamental theological and liturgical problems. This latter conflict passed into the twentieth century and still remains unresolved, as do many other problems and conflicts related to Initiation in the Church of England, which had occupied so much of the Church's time and energy between 1850 and 1875.

A century has now passed since the close of the mid-Victorian period and yet Christian initiation in the Church of England continues to be a thorny issue. Theological and liturgical debates, reports and publications, even during the last decade, serve to remind the Church today that many of the theological, liturgical, pastoral and social problems surrounding initiation during the 1850-1875 period remain unresolved. Among the issues which still create problems for the Church of England we can include infant baptism; sponsorship; vicarious faith; indiscriminate baptism of infants; the relation between baptism and confirmation; confirmation training; retaining the newly confirmed; the disparity between male and female confirmation candidates; participation in the eucharistic life of the church; public baptism; the liturgical setting of the initiatory rites; the integration of the initiatory rites into acts of public worship.

Some of the insights of the mid-Victorian church waiting to be examined in depth are: The ecumenical significance of baptism; the place of parents and the local church in the Christian education and upbringing of the baptized infant; the sacramental or non-sacramental nature of confirmation; admission to Communion before confirmation; non-episcopal confirmation; confirmation as an act of commitment independent of the initiatory process; restricting infant baptism to the children of believing parents; the insights of biblical theology and biblical criticism and their implications for Christian initiation.

This study of initiation during the period 1850-1875 reveals how much of what has been said and written on the subject within the Church of England in recent years, and at the present time, raises little, if anything, which is really new. If truth be known and accepted, the Church today is simply taking a new look at old and unresolved problems which have exercised the minds of dedicated and able churchmen for at least one hundred and twenty-five years.

SELECT BIBLIOGRAPHY

The footnotes include many other items, especially Charges and Sermons, not listed in this very select bibliography.

The place of publication is London, except where otherwise stated.

1. MANUSCRIPT SOURCES

Bolton cum Redmire Parochial Records: North Riding Record Office, Northallerton.

Longley Notebooks of Parochial Returns: Brotherton Library, Leeds University, Leeds.

Longley Papers: Lambeth Palace Library.

2. OFFICIAL RECORDS AND DOCUMENTS

Chronicle of Convocation, being a record of the Proceedings of the Convocation of Canterbury.
Church Congress Reports.
Hansard's Parliamentary Debates.
Parliamentary Papers.
York Journal of Convocation, containing the Acts and Debates of the Convocation of the Province of York.

3. JOURNALS, MAGAZINES AND NEWSPAPERS

British Journal of Sociology, The
Christian Observer, The
Christian Remembrancer, The
Church Quarterly Review
Church Times, The
Ecclesiastical Gazette
Ecclesiologist, The
Edinburgh Review
English Churchman

Guardian, The
Journal of Ecclesiastical History
Journal of the Statistical Society
National Church, The
Record, The
Theology

4. CONTEMPORARY AND NINETEENTH CENTURY PAMPHLETS AND TREATISES

Acts of the Diocesan Synod held in the Cathedral Church of Exeter by Henry, Lord Bishop of Exeter, on Wednesday, Thursday and Friday, June 25, 26, 27, of the year of our Lord, 1851, 1851.

Arnold, Thomas, **Principles of Church Reform** 1833.

Badeley, Edward, Substance of a Speech delivered before the Judicial Committee of the Privy Council, on Monday the 17th and Tuesday the 18th December A.D. 1849, Upon an appeal in a cause of duplex Querela, between the Rev. George Cornelius Gorham, Clerk, Appellant, and the Right Reverend Henry, Lord Bishop of Exeter, Respondent, with an Introduction 1850.

Barrow, Isaac. **The Doctrine of the Sacraments,** 6th ed. 1814.

Bather, Edward, **Hints on Scriptural Education and on instruction by Catechising intended for use of the Superintendents of Parochial Schools,** 2nd ed. 1832.

Bethell, Christopher, **A General View of the Doctrine of Regeneration in Baptism,** 3rd ed. 1839.

Bickersteth, E., **A Treatise on Baptism; designed as a help to the due Improvement of that Holy Sacrament, as administered in the Church of England,** 2nd ed. 1844.

Blunt, Henry, **Directorium Pastorale: The Principles and Practices of Pastoral Work in the Church of England,** 1st ed. 1864, revised ed. 1888.

Blunt, Walter, **Dissenters' Baptism and Church Burial,** Exeter 1840.

Bricknell, W. Simcox, **The Judgement of the Bishops upon Tractarian Theology: A complete analytical arrangement of the Charges delivered by the prelates of the Anglican Church, from 1837–1842 inclusive; so far as they relate to the Tractarian Movement. With notes and appendices** 1845.

Britton, Thomas Hopkins, **Horae Sacramentales. The Sacramental Articles of the Church of England vindicated from recent misrepresentations, and illustrated by the writings of their compilers and last editor,** and by other documents published under sanction of the Church between the years 1536 and 1571 1851.

Broderick, G. C. and Freemantle, W. H., **A Collection of the Judgements of the Judicial Committee of the Privy Council in Ecclesiastical Cases relating to Doctrine and Discipline** 1865.

Browne, Edward George Kirwan, **Annals of the Tractarian Movement, from 1842 to 1860,** 3rd ed. 1861.

Burrows, Montagu, **Parliament and the Church of England** 1875.

Burton, Charles James, **Considerations on the Ecclesiastical Courts and Clergy Discipline** 1875.

Champneys, W. Weldon, **Spirit in the Word. Facts gathered from a Thirty Years' Ministry** 1862.

Cheshire, Edward, **Results of the Census of Great Britain in 1851; with a discription of the machinery and processes employed to obtain the returns** 1853.

Colenso, John William, **The Pentateuch and Book of Joshua Critically Examined,** Part II 1863.

Convocations of Canterbury and York: **A Code of Canons for use of the Church of England. Agreed upon by the two Committees of the Provincial Convocations of Canterbury and York, submitted to their respective Convocations** 1873.

Conybeare, W. J., **Essays Ecclesiastical and Social, reprinted, with additions from the Edinburgh Review** 1855.

(Coverdale, Miles), **The Exeter Diocesan Synod Reviewed,** Exeter, n.d., c.1851.

Crosthwaite, Charles, **Baptismal Regeneration, as bearing upon Justification by Faith only; with some remarks on Fatalism; on a pamphlet by the Rev. W. H. Ferrar, F.T.C.D., and the Proposed Revision of the Liturgy; A Series of Letters,** Dublin 1865.

Curtois, George Herbert, **Dissent, in its relation to the Church of England, Eight lectures, preached before the University Oxford in the year 1871** 2nd ed. 1873.

Denison, George Anthony, An appeal to the clergy and laity of the Church of England to combine for the defence of the Church and for the recovery of her rights and liberties 1850.

Dodsworth, William, **Confirmation; or, Laying on of hands; Scriptural in its origin and needful to be observed** 1835.

The Gorham Case briefly considered. In reference to the Judgement which has been given, and to the jurisdiction of the Court 1850.

Drummond, Henry, **Remarks on Dr. Wiseman's Sermon on the Gorham Case** 1850

Ede, W. Moore, **The Attitude of the Church to some of the Social Problems of town life** Cambridge, 1896.

Elwin, Warwick, **The Minister of Baptism. A history of Church opinion from the time of the Apostles: expecially with reference to heretical, schismatical and lay administration** 1889.

Frazer, William, **The Constitutional Nature of the Convocations of the Church of England. With an appendix, containing Archbishop Parker's form for holding a Convocation** 1852.

Fust, Sir Herbert Jenner, Gorham, Clerk, against the Bishop of Exeter: The Judgement of Sir Herbert Jenner Fust, Kt., delivered in the Arches Court of Canterbury, on the 2nd day of August, 1849, as taken in shorthand 1849.

Garden, Francis, **The Nature and Benefits of Holy Baptism** 1843.

George, Trevor, **The Convocations of the two Provinces, their origins, constitution and forms of proceeding: with a chapter on their revival** 1852.

Gibson, John, **The Testimony of the Sacred Scriptures, the Church of the first five centuries, and the Reformed Church of England to the Nature and Effects of Holy Baptism, together with a short preliminary treatise, and an appendix of extracts from the Baptismal Services of the Ancient Eastern, Roman and Gallican Churches; and also from the Baptismal Services of the Greek, Syrian, Chaldean, Armenian and Coptic Churches** 1854.

Gladstone, W. E., **Church Principles considered in their results** 1840.

The State in its relations with the Church 4th ed. 1841.

Goode, William, A Letter to the Bishop of Exeter containing an Examination of his letter to the Archbishop of Canterbury 1850.

Reply to the Letter and Declaration respecting the Royal Supremacy, received from Archdeacons Manning and Wilberforce and Professor Mill 1850.

The Doctrines of the Church of England on the two Sacraments of Baptism and the Lord's Supper. With a prefatory letter to the Cen. Archdeacon Dodgson 1864.

    A Reply to Archdeacon Dodgson's statement prefixed to his sermons on the Sacraments; with remarks on the sermons 1864.

    The Effects of Baptism in the case of Infants n.d.

Goodwin, H. Confirmation Day: Being a Book of Instruction for Young Persons how they ought to spend that solemn day, on which they renew the Vows of their Baptism, and are confirmed by the Bishop with prayer and laying on of hands Cambridge 1872.

    The worthy communicant; or, 'Who may come to the Supper of the Lord?' Cambridge 1872.

    Gorham v Bishop of Exeter: The Judgement of the Judicial Committee of the Privy Council, delivered March 8th, 1850, reversing the Decision of Sir H. J. Fust: Second edition with the appellant's prayer and reasons etc. 1850.

Gouldburn, Edward Meyrick, A Manual of Confirmation; comprising a General account of the ordinance, the Order of Confirmation, with short notes and meditations and prayers, with a pastoral letter on first Communion 1860.

Griffith, T., Confirmation: Its Nature, Importance and Benefits 9th ed. 1872.

Grueber, C. S. Holy Baptism. A complete statement of the Church's Doctrine with an explanatory Comment upon fifty passages of Holy Scripture 1850.

Hoare, William Henry, Baptism According to Scripture 1850.

    Present Position of the Church. The Baptismal and Education Questions. Three letters to the Right Hon. Sir George Grey, Bart., H. M. Secretary of State for the Home Department 1850.

Hume, A., Remarks on the Census of Religious Worship for England and Wales, with suggestions for an improved Census in 1861, and map, illustrating the religious conditions of the country 1860.

    Thoughts unspoken at a Sunday School Teachers' Conference 1880.

Jones, J. S., "The Evangelisation of the Masses" and Free and Open Churches. A letter to the Right Rev. The Lord Bishop of Winchester 1873.

Kaye, John, On Confirmation 1841.

Keble, John, The Case of Catholic Subscription to the Thirty-nine Articles considered: With special reference to the duties and difficulties of English Catholics in the Present Crisis: in a Letter to the Hon. Mr. Justice Coleridge (Privately printed 1841, no place given).

    A Pastoral Letter to the Parishioners of Hursley, &c. on the proposed Synod of Exeter 1851.

    Occasional Papers and Reviews 1877.

Langley, John, The Parochial Minister's Letter: To young people in his Charge on Confirmation 1872.

Laurence, Richard, **The Doctrine of the Church of England upon the Efficacy of Baptism vindicated from misrepresentation** 3rd ed. 1838.

Lee, T. L., **A Clergyman's Advice and Counsel to his Parishioners on the subject of Infant Baptism,** Luton, 4th ed. 1869.

Ley, John, **A Series of Documents and Authorities on the duty, advantage and necessity of Public Catechising in the Church** 1840.

Longley, Charles Thomas, A Pastoral Letter to the Clergy of the Diocese of Ripon 1850.

Ludlow, J. M. and Jones, Lloyd, **Progress of the Working Class 1832–1867** 1867.

Mann, Horace, **Census of Great Britain, 1851: Religious Worship, England and Wales, Report and Tables,** 1853.

Maskell, William, **Holy Baptism. A Dissertation** 1848.
    A First Letter on the Present Position of the High Church Party in the Church of England. The Royal Supremacy and the authority of the Judicial Committee of the Privy Council 1850.
    A Second Letter on the Present Position of the High Church Party in the Church of England. The want of dogmatic teaching in the reformed English Church 1850.

Maurice, Frederick Denison, **The Kingdom of Christ; or Hints on the Principles, Ordinances and Constitution of the Catholic Church in Letters to a Member of the Society of Friends** 3 Vols., 1838.

Meyrick, Frederick, **Baptism; Regeneration; Conversion** n.d.

Moberly, George, **The Administration of the Holy Spirit in the Body of Christ. Eight lectures: Preached before the University of Oxford in the year 1868. Bampton Lecture 1868,** Oxford 1883.

Moor, Edmund F., **The case of the Reverend G. C. Gorham against the Bishop of Exeter as heard and determined by the Judicial Committee of the Privy Council on appeal from the Arches Court of Canterbury** 1852.

Mozley, J. B., **The Primitive doctrine of baptismal regeneration** 1856.
        Essays Historical and Theological, 2 Vols., 1878
        A Review of the Baptismal Controversy, 2nd ed. 1883.

Neale, J. M., **A Few Words of Hope on the Present Crisis of the English Church** 1850.

Lectures principally on the Church Difficulties of the present time 1852.

The XXIX Canon, and Reasons for its Abrogation. A Letter to the Lord Bishop of Oxford 1860.

Additional Reasons for the Abrogation of the XXIX Canon. A Second Letter to the Bishop of Oxford, in which the objections of the Rev. W. J. Irons, D.D., the Rev. W. P. Bingham and others, are considered, with some remarks on the legal opinions obtained by the Archbishop of Armagh 1861.

Newman, John Henry, The Via Media of the Anglican Church: Illustrated Lectures, Letters and Tracts written between 1830 and 1841 2 Vols., 1901.

Lectures on the Doctrine of Justification 3rd ed. 1874.

Oxenden, Ashton, Confirmation; or, Are you ready to serve Christ? 1872.

The Earnest Communicant: A Course of Preparation for the Lord's Table new ed. 1872.

Oxenham, Frank Nutcombe, Lay Baptism. An inquiry into the Spiritual Values and Validity of that Ceremony 1888.

Phillimore, Sir Robert, The principal Ecclesiastical Judgements delivered in the Court of Arches 1867-1875 1876.

Phillpotts, Henry, An apology for the Plain Sense of the Doctrine of the Prayer Book on Holy Baptism, in answer to the Rev. W. Goode's letter to the Bishop of Exeter 1850.

A Letter to the Archbishop of Canterbury from the Bishop of Exeter 1850.

A Pastoral Letter to the Clergy of the Diocese of Exeter on the present state of the Church 3rd ed. 1851.

Pollen, John Hungerford, Narrative of five years at St. Saviour's Leeds: To which is added an extract from the Christian Remembrancer for January, 1850 Oxford 1851.

Puller, F. W., What is the Distinctive Grace of Confirmation? A Paper read before the Chapter of the South Eastern Division of the Upper Llandaff Rural Deanery 1880.

Pusey, E. B., Tracts for the Times. Nos. 67, 68, 69: Scriptural Views of Holy Baptism, with appendix 4th ed. 1836.

Case as to the Legal Force of the Judgement of the Privy Council: In re Fendall v Wilson; with the opinion of the Attorney-General & Sir Hugh Cairns, and a Preface to those who love God and His Truth 1864.

The Church of England: a Portion of Christ's One Holy Catholic Church, and a Means of Restoring Visible Unity. An Eirenicon, In a Letter to the author of "The Christian Year" 1865.

Rawlinson, George, **The Two Sacraments retained in the Church of England, Necessary, and they only Necessary to be retained** Oxford 1842.

Redesdale, Lord, **Observations on the Judgement in the Gorham Case and the way to unity** 1850.

Robertson, James Craigie, The bearing of the Gorham Case: A Letter to a Friend 1850.

Roundell, Earl of Selbourne, **A Defence of the Church of England against Disestablishment, with an introductory letter to the Rt. Hon. W. E. Gladstone, M.P.** 3rd ed. 1887.

Sadler, M. F., **The Sacrament of Responsibility or Testimony of Scripture to the Teaching of the Church on Holy Baptism, with special reference to the case of infants and answers to objections** new ed. 1870.

Sandby, George, To the laity, A Practical Address upon recent and coming events within the Church 1851.

Shipley, Orby (ed.) **The Church and the World: Essays on the Questions of the Day** in 1866, 3rd. ed. 1867.
    (ed.) **Tracts for the Day: Essays on Theological Subjects No. 3. The Seven Sacraments** 1867.

Thorn, William, **Infant Baptism. A divine obligation: Defended from every known objection hitherto brought against it** n.d., c.1850.

Townsend, George (ed. by George Fryler Townsend) Baptismal Regeneration. A reprint of a note on St. John iii.3-6, from The Arrangement of the New Testament 1850.

Tyler, J. Endell, A Father's Letter to His Son on the apostolic rite of Confirmation as administered by the Church of England 1843.

Venn, John, **The Office of Sponsors briefly and practically considered** 1844.

Watson, Alexander, A Letter to All members of the Church of England especially those who are fathers or mothers, or godfathers or godmothers, or have been confirmed, containing words of common sense for common people on the "one baptism for the remission of sins" 1850.

Weir, Archibald and Maclagan, William Dalrymple (eds.) **The Church and the Age; Essays on the Principles and Present Position of the Anglican Church** 1870.

Wilberforce, Robert Isaac, A Letter to the Gentry, Yeomen and Farmers of the Archdeaconry of the East Riding Bridlington 1842.

Church Courts and Church Discipline 1843.

The Doctrine of Holy Baptism: with remarks on the Rev. W. Goode's "Effects of Infant Baptism" 1849.

The Doctrine of the Incarnation of our Lord Jesus Christ: In its relation to mankind and to the Church 1849.

Wilberforce, Samuel, Eucharistica: Meditations and Prayers on the Most Holy Eucharist from old English Divines: with an introduction by Samuel, Lord Bishop of Oxford, Revised by Horace E. Clayton 1877. New and revised ed. 1899.

Woodroffe, John N., The advantages of Public Baptism and the Origins, nature and duties of Sponsors; briefly set forth in a dialogue between a clergyman and his parishioners, Cork 1841.

Wordsworth, Charles, A Report of the Proceedings of the Synod and Visitation, including the Bishop's Visitation Sermon on 2 Tim. iv. 5. The Twofold Ministry of Clergy and Laity (Baptism by immersion). With appendix of diocesan statistics 1855.

Sermon on Confirmation 1869.

Catechesis; or Christian instruction preparatory to Confirmation and First Communion 1872.

5. CHARGES AND SERMONS

Charges referred to are too numerous to list, but details are given in the footnotes.

6. LITURGICAL WORKS

Davis, C. H., Liturgical Revision: Illustrated and Vindicated on Orthodox Principles 1859.

Davys, George, Village Conversations on the Liturgy and Offices of the Church of England 1849.

Ebury, Lord, On the Revision of the Liturgy. The Speech of Lord Ebury, in the House of Lords, May 6th, 1858. Together with an abstract of the Debate, and Lord Ebury's reply 3rd ed. 1859

Everard, E. I., Beware of dogs, beware of evil workers, beware of concision. A Rural Pastor's Address to His Flock on Lord Ebury's Petition for a Revision of the Prayer Book Oxford 1860.

Gell, Phillip, **Thoughts on the Liturgy. The Difficulties of an honest conscientious use of the Book of Common Prayer, considered as a loud and reasonable call for the only remedy, Revision: With closing remarks on the correspondence of Lord Lyttleton with Lord Ebury respecting the Petition for Revision from four hundred and sixty of the clergy** 1860.

Hall, Francis Russell, Liturgical Reform Defended. A Reply to the editor of the "Quarterly Review" Cambridge 1834.

Hildyard, James, **A Revision of the Rubrics and Liturgy urged with a view chiefly to the Abridgement of Morning Prayer** Grantham 1856.
The People's call for a Revision of the Liturgy, in A Letter to Lord Palmerston 1857.

Jasper, R. C. D., **Prayer Book Revision in England 1800-1900** 1954.

Keeling, William, **Liturgiae Britannicae, or The Several Editions of the Book of Common Prayer of the Church of England from its Compilation to the Last Revision; together with the Liturgy set forth for the use of the Church of Scotland arranged to show their respective variations** 1842.

Lee, Frederick George, **The Directorium Anglicanum: Being a Manual of Direction for the Right Celebration of the Holy Communion, for the saying of Matins and Evensong, and for the Performance of other Rites and Ceremonies of the Church, according to the Ancient Use of the Church of England** 3rd ed. 1866.

Littledale, R. F., Catholic Ritual in the Church of England 1865.
Catholic Revision: A Letter to Charles Thomas, Lord Archbishop of Canterbury 1867.

McNeile, Hugh, **Notes on the Declaration Against a Revision of the Prayer Book. With the opinions of the Bishop of Carlisle and the Rev. Dr. Hugh McNeile** 1860.

Minton, Samuel, A Letter to the Lord Bishop of London in favour of Liturgical Revision for the purposes of relief and comprehension, and thereby for the restoration of "Peace and Unity" 1863.

Peace, William, The Dilemma. A Letter addressed to His Grace the Archbishop of Canterbury touching Liturgical Perplexities 1859.
Cogent Reasons for Entertaining the Question of Revising the Prayer Book. Respectfully submitted to the consideration of those who are attached to the Protestant Reformed Religion and Church in this country 1859.

Proby, J. C., A Letter to the Right Rev. The Lord Bishop of Winchester, on the Revision and Re-arrangement of the Liturgy Winchester 1859.

Purchas, John, **Directorium Anglicanum: Being a Manual of Directions for the Right Celebration of the Holy Communion, for the saying of Matins and Evensong, and for the Performance of other Rites and Ceremonies of the Church, according to the Ancient Use of the Church of England** 1858.

Robinson, C., **Church Questions: Practical Methods for the Arrangement of An abridged Morning Service, A New Occasional or Third Service, A Revision of the Liturgy. The Restoration of Dissenters, Church Rates, a Royal Commission, Convocation, National Council, &c.** 1859.

Ryland, William Deane, A Letter to the Lord Archbishop of Canterbury on certain alterations which are required in the Liturgy and Offices of the Church of England 1856.

Sadler, M. F., **Doctrinal Revision of the Liturgy considered. An examination of the subject with special reference to the suggestions of the Bishop of Gloucester and Bristol, Rev. P. Gell and others** 1861.

Stephens, Archibald John, **The Book of Common Prayer: and Administration of the Sacraments and other Rites and Ceremonies of the Church, According to the use of the United Church of England and Ireland... with notes Legal and Historical** 3 Vols. 1849.

Taylor, Isaac, **The Liturgy and the Dissenters** 2nd ed. 1860.

Woodward, F. B., Remarks on a Petition Presented to Her Majesty for a Revision of the Liturgy 1860.

7. BIOGRAPHICAL AND AUTOBIOGRAPHICAL WORKS

Armstrong, Herbert B. J. (ed.) **A Norfolk Diary: Passages from the Diary of the Rev. Benjamin John Armstrong M.A. (Cantab.) Vicar of East Dereham 1850–1888** 1949.

Ashwell A. R. and Wilberforce R. G., **Life of the Right Reverend Samuel Wilberforce, D.D., Lord Bishop of Oxford and afterwards of Winchester, with selections from his diaries and correspondence** 3 Vols. 1880–1882.

Atkinson, J. C., **Forty Years in a Moorland Parish. Reminiscences and re-search in Danby in Cleveland** 1891.

Battiscombe, Georgina, **John Keble: A Study in Limitations** 1963.

Bellasis, Edward, **Memorials of Mr. Serjeant Bellasis 1800–1873** 1895.

Benson, Arthur Christopher, **The Life of Edward White Benson: sometime Archbishop of Canterbury** 2 Vols. 1899.

Biber, George Edward, **Bishop Blomfield and His Times. An historical sketch** 1857.

Bickersteth, Montagu Cyril, **A Sketch of the life and episcopate of the Right Reverend Robert Bickersteth, D.D., Bishop of Ripon, 1857–1884** 1887.

Blomfield, Alfred, **A Memoir of Charles James Blomfield, D.D., Bishop of London, with selections from his correspondence** 2 Vols. 2nd ed. 1864.

Burgon, John William, **Lives of Twelve Good Men** 1891.

Carus, E. (ed.) **Memoirs of the Life of the Reverend Charles Simeon** 1847.

Clayton, Joseph, **Father Dolling: A Memoir** 1902.

Coleridge, Sir J. T., **A Memoir of the Rev. John Keble, M.A., late Vicar of Hursley** 3rd ed. 1870.

Cox, Sir George W., **The Life of John William Colenso, D.D., Bishop of Natal** 2 Vols. 1888.

Davidson, Randall Thomas and Benham, William, **Life of Archibald Campbell Tait: Archbishop of Canterbury** 2 Vols. 1891.

Davies, G. C. B., **Henry Phillpotts, Bishop of Exeter 1778–1869** 1954.

Denison, George Anthony, **Notes on my Life 1805–1878** 1879.

Denison, Louisa Evelyn, **Fifty Years at East Brent. The Letters of George Anthony Denison 1845–1896** 1902.

Dolling, George R., **Ten Years in a Portsmouth Slum** 1897.

Gill, J. C., **The Ten Hours Parson: Christian Social Action in the Eighteen Thirties** 1959.

Hennell, Michael, **John Venn and the Clapham Sect** 1958.

Hinchliff, Peter, **John William Colenso: Bishop of Natal** 1964.

Hort, Arthur Fenton, **Life and Letters of Fenton John Anthony Hort** 2 Vols. 1896.

How, F. D., **Archbishop Maclagan. Being a Memoir of the Most Reverend the Right Hon. William Dalrymple Maclagan, D.D., Archbishop of York and Primate of England** 1911.
　　　　　　Bishop Walsham How, A Memoir 1899.

Hughes, Thomas, **James Fraser, Second Bishop of Manchester: A Memoir 1818–1885** 1887.

Kidd, B. J., **Selected Letters of William Bright, D.D.** 1903.

Kingsley, F., **Charles Kingsley: His letters and memories of his life** 1908.

Kirk-Smith, H., **William Thomson: Archbishop of York, His Life and Times 1819-1890** 1958.

Lawson, May S., **Letters of John Mason Neale, D.D.** 1910.

Liddon, Henry Parry, **Life of Edward Bouverie Pusey, Doctor of Divinity, Canon of Christ Church; Regius Professor of Hebrew in the University of Oxford** 4 Vols. 4th ed. 1894-1898.

Lockhart, J. G., **Charles Lindley, Viscount Halifax** 2 Vols. 1935.

Lowder, C. F., **Twenty years in S. George's Mission. An account of its origin, progress and works of charity, with an appendix** 1877.

Macdonnell, John Cotter, **The Life and Correspondence of William Conner Magee, Archbishop of York** 2 Vols. 1896.

Mason, Arthur James, **Memoir of George Howard Wilkinson** 2 Vols. 1909.

Maurice, Frederick, **The Life of Frederick Denison Maurice: Chiefly told in his own letters** 2 Vols. 1884.

Meacham, Standish, **Lord Bishop: The Life of Samuel Wilberforce 1805-1873** Cambridge, Massachusetts 1970.

Moberly, C. A. E., **George Moberly (D.C.L. Headmaster of Winchester College 1835-1866: Bishop of Salisbury 1869-1885) His family and friends** 1911.

Morley, John, **The Life of William Ewart Gladstone** 2 Vols. 1905.

Mozley, Ann, **Letters and Correspondence of John Henry Newman during his life in the English Church** 2 Vols. 1891.

Newman, John Henry, **Apologia Pro Vita Sua: Being a history of Religious Opinion** 1890.

Newsome, David, **The Parting of Friends. A study of the Wilberforces and Henry Manning** 1966.

Nias, J. C. S., **Gorham and the Bishop of Exeter** 1951.

Osborne, Charles E., **The Life of Father Dolling** 1903.

Overton, J. H. and Wordsworth, Elizabeth, **Christopher Wordsworth, Bishop of Lincoln (1807-1885)** 1888.

Perowne, J. J. Stewart, and Stokes, L., **Letters Literary and Theological of Connop Thirlwall (late Lord Bishop of St. David's) with annotations and preliminary Memoir by the Rev. Louis Stokes** 1881.

Prothero, Rowland E. and Bradley, G. C., **The Life and Correspondence of Arthur Penrhyn Stanley, D.D., Late Dean of Westminster** 2 Vols. 1893.

Pugh, R. K. (ed.) **The Letter-books of Samuel Wilberforce 1843-68** 1970.

Sandford, E. G. (ed.) **Memoirs of Archbishop Temple** 2 Vols. 1906.

Shutte, Reginald N., **The Life, Times and Writings of the Right Rev. Dr. Henry Phillpotts, Lord Bishop of Exeter** 2 Vols. 1863.

Stanley, Arthur Penrhyn, **Life and Correspondence of Thomas Arnold, D.D., sometime Headteacher of Rugby School and Regius Professor of Modern History in the University of Oxford** 2 Vols. 1844.

Stephens, W. R. W., **The Life and Letters of Walter Farquhar Hook, D.D. F.R.S.** 2 Vols. 1879.

Sumner, G. H., **The Life of Bishop C. R. Sumner** 1876.

Thomson, Ethel H., **The Life and Letters of William Thomson, Archbishop of York** 1919.

(Towle, E. A.) **Alexander Heriot MacKonochie. A Memoir** (ed. E. F. Russell) 1890.
> **John Mason Neale, D.D.,** A Memoir 1906.

Trench, Maria, **Charles Lowder: A Biography** 1882.

Trevor, Meriol, **John Henry Newman** 2 Vols. 1962.

Ward, Wilfrid, **The Life of John Henry Cardinal Newman: Based on his private journals and correspondence** 2 Vols. 1912.

8. GENERAL HISTORIES AND OTHER SECONDARY WORKS

Abbey, Charles J. and Overton, John H., **The English Church in the Eighteenth Century** new ed. 1887.

Balleine, G. R., **A History of the Evangelical Party in the Church of England** 1951.

Best, Geoffrey, **Mid-Victorian Britain 1851-1875** 1971.

Bowden, Desmond, **The Idea of the Victorian Church. A study of the Church of England 1833-1889** Montreal 1968.

Briggs, Asa **1851** 1972.
The Age of Improvement 1783-1867 1970.
Victorian People: A re-assessment of Persons and Themes 1850-1867 1954.
Victorian Cities 1963.

Brose, Olive J., **Church and Parliament: The re-shaping of the Church of England 1828-1860** 1959.

Burgess, Henry James, **Enterprise in Education. The story of the Established Church in the education of the people prior to 1870** 1958.

Carpenter, S. C., **Church and People 1789-1889: A History of the Church of England from William Wilberforce to "Lux Mundi"** 3 Vols. 1959.

Chadwick, Owen, **The Victorian Church** 2 Vols. 1970.
The Secularisation of the European Mind in the Nineteenth Century 1975.

Checkland, S. G., **The Rise of Industrial Society in England 1815-1885** 1966.

Church, R. W., **The Oxford Movement: Twelve Years 1833-1845** 3rd ed. 1909.

Clark, G. Kitson, **The Making of Victorian England** 1962.
Churchmen and the Condition of England 1832-1885. A study in the development of social ideas and practice from the Old Regime to the Modern State 1973.

Cole, G. D. H. and Postgate, Raymond, **The Common People 1746-1938** 1938.

Coleman, B. I., (ed.) **The Idea of the City in Nineteenth Century Britain** 1973.

Cornish, Francis Warre, **The English Church in the Nineteenth Century** 2 Vols. 1910.

Crowther, M. A., **Church Embattled. Religious Controversy in mid-Victorian England** Newton Abbot, 1970.

Elliott-Binns, L. E., **The Evangelical Movement in the English Church** 1928.
Religion in the Victorian Era 1936.
The Development of English Theology in the Later Nineteenth Century 1952.
The Early Evangelicals: A religious and social study 1953.

English Thought 1860–1900: Theological Aspects 1956.

Engels, Frederick (tr. Florence Kelly Wischnewetzky) **The Condition of the Working–Class in England in 1844, with a Preface written 1892** 1952.

Fairweather, Eugene R., (ed.) **The Oxford Movement** New York 1964.

Halevy, Elie, (tr. E. I. Watkin) **A History of the English People in the Nineteenth Century** 6 Vols. 1961.

Hammond, J. L. and Hammond, Barbara, **The Town Labourer 1760–1832. The New Civilisation** 1917.
The Skilled Labourer 1760–1832 1919.
The Village Labourer 1760–1832. A Study in the Government of England before the Reform Bill 1919.

Harrison, J. F. C., **The Early Victorians 1832–51** 1971.

Heeney, Brian, **Mission to the Middle Classes: The Woodard Schools 1848–1891** 1969.

Henriques, Ursula R. Q., **The Early Factory Acts and their Enforcement** 1971.

Inglis, Brian, **Poverty and the Industrial Revolution** 1971.

Inglis, K. S., **Churches and the Working Classes in Victorian England** 1964.

Lathbury, D. C., **Correspondence on Church and Religion of William Ewart Gladstone** 2 Vols. 1910.

Marsh, P. T., **The Victorian Church in Decline. Archbishop Tait and the Church of England 1868–1882** 1969.

Newsome, David, **Godliness and Good Learning: Four Studies of a Victorian Ideal** 1961.

Overton, John H., **The English Church in the Nineteenth Century (1800–1833)** 1894.

Perkin, Harold, **The Origins of Modern English Society 1780–1880** 1969.
The Age of the Railway 1970.

Reardon, Bernard M. G., **From Coleridge to Gore: A Century of Religious Thought in Britain** 1971.

Reeve, Robin M., **The Industrial Revolution 1750–1850** 1971.

Reynolds, J. S., **The Evangelicals at Oxford 1735–1871. A record of an unchronicled movement** Oxford 1953.

Roberts, G. Bayfield, **The History of the English Church Union 1859–1894: Compiled from published documents, together with a sketch of the Origins of the Church Unions, and a vindication of the position of the English Church Union** 1895.

Roebuck, Janet, **The Making of Modern English Society from 1850** 1973.

Sanders, Charles Richard, **Coleridge and the Broad Church Movement. Studies on S. T. Coleridge, Dr. Arnold of Rugby, J. C. Hare, Thomas Carlyle and F. D. Maurice** North Carolina 1942.

Storr, Vernon F., **The Development of English Theology in the Nineteenth Century 1800–1860** 1913.

Taine, H. (tr. with introduction by Edward Hyams) **Taine's Notes on England** 1957.

Thompson, David M., (ed.) **Nonconformity in the Nineteenth Century** 1972.

Thompson, E. P., **The Making of the English Working Class** 1963.

Thompson, F. M. L., **English Landed Society in the Nineteenth Century** 1963.

Thomson, David, **England in the Nineteenth Century** 1950.

Ward, W. R., **Religion and Society in England 1790–1850** 1972.

Young, G. M., (ed.) **Early Victorian England 1830–1865** 2 Vols. 1963.

INDEX

60, 112, 139, 141.

Mackonochie, A. H., 46-47, 92.
Maclagan, Archbishop William D., 58, 74, 170-171, 172.
Manchester, Diocese of, 108, 157, 160, 163.
Mann, Horace, 129, 177.
Manning, Henry Edward, 15, 59, 96, 102, 124.
Mant, Dr. Richard, 10.
Marlborough, School, 145.
Martin, Chancellor, 107.
Maskell, William, 104.
Mastin & Escott, 67-68.
Maurice, Frederick Denison, 28-32, 33-34, 37, 38-39, 44-45, 49-50, 76, 102, 190.
Melbourne, Viscount, 123.
Melville, Henry, 18.
Methodists, 52, 178.
Meyrick, Frederick, 23.
Minton, Samuel, 178.
Moberly, Bishop George, 44, 53, 81, 90, 102, 104, 124, 172.
Moreton, Julian, 116.
Morning Prayer, 88-90. 113-114, 171.
Morris, Dr. John, 10.
Mozley, J. B., 9-10.
Mozley, Mrs. John, 101.

National Schools, 126.
National Society, 131.
Neale, John Mason, 82, 102, 110, 117, 138.
Nevile, Christopher, 79.
New Birth, see Baptism, 12-14, 17, 20, 23, 30, 76.
New Testament, see Scripture.
Newman, John Henry, 10-13, 21, 101.
Nicholl, Sir John, 67.
Noel, Gerard, 22-23.
Non-Conformists, see Dissenters.

Norwich, Diocese of, 157, 160, 163.

Ollivant, Bishop Alfred, 89, 176, 178.
Oxenham, H. W., 96.
Oxford, Diocese of, 115, 157, 160-161, 163.
Oxford Movement, see High Churchmen.

Parents, 37, 43-44, 47, 56, 58, 59, 60, 62, 70, 73-75, 79-84, 98, 121-122, 126, 128, 130, 138, 139, 145, 168, 176, 181, 191, 193, 195.
Parliament, 122, 161.
Patristics, 14, 44.
Paul, St., 12.
Peace, William, 179.
Peel, Sir Robert, 99.
Pelham, Bishop John Thomas, 109-110, 153, 160.
Pentateuch, 37-39.
Peterborough, Diocese of, 157, 161, 163.
Phillpotts, Bishop Henry, 2-4, 8, 17, 45, 63, 68, 127-128, 130-131, 172.
Polygamy, 39.
Population Increase, 1, 52, 56, 60, 82, 84, 106-107, 121, 135, 141, 155, 159, 164, 175-176, 191, 193.
Post Confirmation Groups, 140-142, 192.
Potter, Canon, 70.
Prayer, 75-76, 90, 99, 101, 135, 138, 141, 144, 146, 149.
Prayer Book, 18, 28, 30, 38-39, 49, 67, 70, 71, 83, 91, 95, 98, 109, 126-127, 130, 135, 139, 175-184, 190.
Prayer Book Revision Society, 180.
Prentice Houses, 123, 129.
Presbyterians, 52.

Peter John Jagger, was born in Yorkshire England in 1938, and is married. The Jaggers have two teenage children.

Mr. Jagger read Theology at Wesley College, Leeds, from 1962 to 1966 and at the College of the Resurrection, Mirfield, Yorkshire, from 1967 to 1968. In 1971 the then Archbishop of Canterbury, Dr. A. Michael Ramsay, conferred upon him the degree of Master of Arts for his published work in, and contibution to, the study of Christian Initiation in the Anglican Communion. From 1971 to 1976 he was a part-time post-graduate research student at the University of Leeds and received his Master of Philosophy Degree in 1976. Two years later he was made a Fellow of the Royal Historical Society.

Mr. Jagger was ordained deacon in the Church of England in 1968 and priest in 1969. His first curacy was served at All Saints Church, an Inner City Parish in Leeds, from 1968 to 1971, after which he was appointed Vicar of Bolton-cum-Redmire, a rural parish in Wensleydale, Yorkshire, where he continued his research and writing from 1971 to 1977.

In 1977 he was appointed Warden and Chief Librarian of St Deiniol's Residential Library, Hawarden, North Wales, which is the William Ewart Gladstone National Memorial Library.

By the same author

CHRISTIAN INITIATION 1552-1969
Rites of Baptism and Confirmation since the Reformation Period.
Alcuin Club Collections. No. 52 (S.P.C.K. 1970).

BEING THE CHURCH TODAY
A Collection of Sermons and Addresses by Bishop Henry de Candole.
(Faith Press 1974).

THE ALCUIN CLUB AND ITS PUBLICATIONS
An Annotated Bibliography 1897-1974.
(The Alcuin Club 1975).

BISHOP HENRY de CANDOLE
His Life and Times 1895-1971.
(Faith Press 1975).

THE HISTORY OF THE PARISH AND PEOPLE MOVEMENT
(Faith Press 1978).

THE FORMATION OF THE DIOCESE OF NEWCASTLE
(In A Social History of the Diocese of Newcastle).
(Oriol Press/Routledge Kegan and Paul 1981).